.NET Core 2.0 By Example

Learn to program in C# and .NET Core by building a series of practical, cross-platform projects

Rishabh Verma
Neha Shrivastava

BIRMINGHAM - MUMBAI

.NET Core 2.0 By Example

Commissioning Editor: Aaron Lazar
Acquisition Editor: Chaitanya Nair
Content Development Editor: Rohit Kumar Singh
Technical Editor: Romy Dias
Copy Editor: Safis Editing
Project Coordinator: Vaidehi Sawant
Proofreader: Safis Editing
Indexer: Pratik Shirodkar
Graphics: Jason Monteiro, Tom Scaria
Production Coordinator: Deepika Naik

First published: March 2018

Production reference: 1160318

Published by Packt Publishing Ltd.
Livery Place
35 Livery Street
Birmingham
B3 2PB, UK.

ISBN 978-1-78839-509-0

www.packtpub.com

`mapt.io`

Mapt is an online digital library that gives you full access to over 5,000 books and videos, as well as industry leading tools to help you plan your personal development and advance your career. For more information, please visit our website.

Why subscribe?

- Spend less time learning and more time coding with practical eBooks and Videos from over 4,000 industry professionals

- Improve your learning with Skill Plans built especially for you

- Get a free eBook or video every month

- Mapt is fully searchable

- Copy and paste, print, and bookmark content

PacktPub.com

Did you know that Packt offers eBook versions of every book published, with PDF and ePub files available? You can upgrade to the eBook version at `www.PacktPub.com` and as a print book customer, you are entitled to a discount on the eBook copy. Get in touch with us at `service@packtpub.com` for more details.

At `www.PacktPub.com`, you can also read a collection of free technical articles, sign up for a range of free newsletters, and receive exclusive discounts and offers on Packt books and eBooks.

Contributors

About the authors

Rishabh Verma is a Microsoft certified professional and works at Microsoft as a development consultant, helping to design, develop, and deploy enterprise-level applications. He has 10 years' hardcore development experience on the .NET technology stack. He is passionate about creating tools, Visual Studio extensions, and utilities to increase developer productivity. His interests are .NET Compiler Platform (Roslyn), Visual Studio Extensibility, and code generation.

No words can describe my gratitude to my parents, Shri Rakesh Chandra Verma and Smt. Pratibha Verma, who supported me during the writing of this book. Their hard work over the years has been the inspiration behind me taking up this challenging work. I would also like to offer special thanks to my brother, Shri Rishi Verma, who kept motivating me day in and day out. I also want to thank my colleagues, managers, and team at Microsoft for their support.

Neha Shrivastava is a Microsoft certified professional and works as a software engineer for the Windows Devices Group at Microsoft India Development Center. She has 7 years' development experience and has expertise in the financial, healthcare, and e-commerce domains. Neha did a BE in electronics engineering. Her interests are the ASP.NET stack, Azure, and cross-platform development. She is passionate about learning new technologies and keeps herself up to date with the latest advancements.

I would like to thank my parents, Shri O. P. Shrivastava and Smt. Archana Shrivastava, for their continuous support and motivation. Their "Never Say Die" mantra keeps me up and running. Heartfelt thanks to my brother, Dr. Utkarsh Shrivastava, my sister-in-law, Dr. Samvartika Shrivastava, and my little angel Sarvagya, for their continuous support and words of encouragement. This book wouldn't have been possible without the blessings of my beloved Dadi!

About the reviewer

Pavol Rovensky is a software developer living in the UK. Originally from Slovakia, he earned a degree in radio electronics from Czech Technical University and studied medicine from the Charles University in Prague.

He has worked in the Czech Republic, Iceland, Switzerland, and the UK, mostly developing software for the biotech/pharma sector and contracting in various software companies, he has professional experience spanning 25 years.

He has worked with various technologies, including C++, Java, PowerBuilder, C#, WiX Toolset, .NET Framework, ORMs.

His interest in accounting and business management led him to develop ProudNumbers, which is a reporting tool for management accountants.

I would like to thank my wife, Jana, and daughter, Emma, for their patience and encouragement.

Packt is searching for authors like you

If you're interested in becoming an author for Packt, please visit authors.packtpub.com and apply today. We have worked with thousands of developers and tech professionals, just like you, to help them share their insight with the global tech community. You can make a general application, apply for a specific hot topic that we are recruiting an author for, or submit your own idea.

Table of Contents

Preface

In this ever growing world of IT, we have numerous different platforms, frameworks, and languages on which applications are built based on the business needs, requirements, and the developer's interest. To remove this barrier of different platforms, Microsoft came up with the fastest, latest, and greatest version of .NET, the .NET Core cross-platform open source framework. Using this framework, beginner-level developers can work on different platforms, and experienced developers and architects can consume their APIs and libraries across different platforms. This book covers simple examples of using .NET Core to build modern, internet-connected, and cloud-based applications. The book will help us develop simple yet interesting applications to provide the readers with working code examples. We will develop a Tic-Tac-Toe game to begin with, then build a real-time chat application, Lets Chat (for chatting with our online Facebook buddies), a sample chat bot, and a dummy movie booking application.

Who this book is for

This book is for developers and architects who want to learn how to build cross-platform solutions using Microsoft .NET Core. It is assumed that you have some knowledge of the .NET Framework, OOP, and C# (or a similar programming language). This book is also useful for developers who want to develop a cross-platform application that supports already existing libraries or libraries that they have created on different platforms. The book covers a wide breadth of topics and attempts to explain all the fundamentals needed to build a .NET Core app. The book also introduces you to SignalR Core, Entity Framework Core, containers, F# functional programming, and tips and tricks for developing on .NET Core.

What this book covers

Chapter 1, *Getting Started*, discusses all the prerequisites required for all the examples in this book, for example, setting up an Ubuntu VM using VirtualBox and through Hyper-V on Windows, and installing .NET Core 2.0 and tools. We will also be introduced to F# and its features in brief, see how F# is different from other object-oriented programming languages, and look at the differences between C# and F#. We will also create a simple sample application using F#, in order to get familiar with the F# syntax.

Chapter 2, *Native Libraries in .NET Core*, demonstrates what the ncurses library is and how to extend the console capabilities of .NET Core by implementing the ncurses native library on Linux, and also how to interoperate with existing native and Mono libraries. We will build a sample native library and application that implements this new sample library.

Chapter 3, *Building Our First .NET Core Game – Tic-Tac-Toe*, illustrates .NET Core using an example game app, Tic-Tac-Toe. We will be introduced to SignalR Core and learn how it can be used to develop a real-time web application. Instead of using a monochromatic X and O, players can use their images to play the game. With this example game app, we will get an overview of the code (classes, interfaces, models, and so on) and will learn about compiling, building, and testing the application, which applies to .NET Core in general.

Chapter 4, *Let's Chat Web Application*, introduces web development with ASP.NET Core. This is done through a simple chat application, Let's Chat, on Windows. We also cover project setup, application architecture and its description, SignalR Core, Dependency Injection, configuration, logging, and more. We will also get familiar with the fundamentals of the features of ASP.NET Core, which are introduced while developing the components of the application.

Chapter 5, *Developing the Let's Chat Web Application*, demonstrates numerous examples and code snippets in order to fundamentals and features of ASP.NET Core. By the end of this chapter, the Let's Chat application will be ready for use. We will also get acquainted with testing, hosting, security, and the performance aspects of web development.

Chapter 6, *Testing and Deploying – The Let's Chat Web Application*, explains the .NET Core deployment model. We will deploy the Let's Chat application. We will be introduced to Docker containers. We will also develop and deploy a ASP.NET Core-based chat bot and integrate it with the Let's Chat application.

Chapter 7, *To the Cloud*, teaches you what the cloud is and why the modern-day developer should be conversant with cloud technologies. We will get started with Azure, and make ourselves aware of the Azure management portal. We will learn to create a VM from the portal and see that it is automated using PowerShell or other languages using the Azure SDK. We will then manage the VM using PowerShell and see how to start and stop it. We will also learn how to create a web app in Azure from Visual Studio 2017 itself and learn how to publish profiles. Finally, we will have an overview of App Services, and take a quick look at Azure storage.

Chapter 8, *Movie Booking Web App*, discusses **Entity Framework (EF)** and Entity Framework Core. We will learn about the features of and differences between the two. We will also learn that we should use EF Core only if EF cannot be used or there is a pressing cross-platform requirement to use EF Core. We will learn how to perform CRUD operations using EF Core by creating a simple app. We will then develop a simple movie booking app and learn how to deploy it using Visual Studio. We will also see how we can monitor our web app by enabling Application Insights.

Chapter 9, *Microservices with .NET Core*, gives an overview of the microservice architecture and how it is an extension of SOA and overcomes the limitations of traditional monolithic apps. We will learn about the important architectural differences between ASP.NET and ASP.NET Core. We will look at tips to keep in mind while developing ASP.NET Core 2.0 applications, due to the architectural differences. We will then discuss handy information, steps, and tips to improve the performance of ASP.NET Core apps, a few tips on Azure as well, and then a new experimental project of the ASP.NET Core team, which is called Blazor. We'll wrap up the chapter with a discussion on the .NET Core 2.1 roadmap and the features expected in this new version.

Chapter 10, *Functional Programming with F#*, discusses functional programming and its features, such as higher-order functions, purity, lazy evaluation, and currying. We will learn about F# basics, such as classes, `let` and `do` bindings, generic type parameters, properties in F#, how to write functions and lambda expressions in F#, and exception handling. Also, we'll look at different types of data providers in F# and how different types of data parser work. We will also learn about querying SQL Server vNext with F#.

To get the most out of this book

This book is aimed at experienced developers who use different platforms—Windows, Linux, Ubuntu, macOS—and want to try Microsoft .NET Core 2.0 cross platform. Developers using C#, C, or C++ for development who are interested in extending their knowledge of functional programming, beginners who want to understand F# and functional programming, we assume that you have a basic understanding of C# and are aware of the .NET framework and Windows.

Download the example code files

You can download the example code files for this book from your account at `www.packtpub.com`. If you purchased this book elsewhere, you can visit `www.packtpub.com/support` and register to have the files emailed directly to you.

You can download the code files by following these steps:

1. Log in or register at `www.packtpub.com`.
2. Select the **SUPPORT** tab.
3. Click on **Code Downloads & Errata**.
4. Enter the name of the book in the **Search** box and follow the onscreen instructions.

Once the file is downloaded, please make sure that you unzip or extract the folder using the latest version of:

- WinRAR/7-Zip for Windows
- Zipeg/iZip/UnRarX for Mac
- 7-Zip/PeaZip for Linux

The code bundle for the book is also hosted on GitHub at `https://github.com/PacktPublishing/.NET-Core-2.0-By-Example`. We also have other code bundles from our rich catalog of books and videos available at `https://github.com/PacktPublishing/`. Check them out!

Download the color images

We also provide a PDF file that has color images of the screenshots/diagrams used in this book. You can download it here: `https://www.packtpub.com/sites/default/files/downloads/.NETCore2.0ByExample_ColorImages.pdf`.

Conventions used

There are a number of text conventions used throughout this book.

`CodeInText`: Indicates code words in text, database table names, folder names, filenames, file extensions, pathnames, dummy URLs, user input, and Twitter handles. Here is an example: "By doing this in `_Layout.cshtml`, we ensure that this functionality is common across all the pages."

A block of code is set as follows:

```
# include<stdio.h>

int hello()
{
   return 15;
}
```

When we wish to draw your attention to a particular part of a code block, the relevant lines or items are set in bold:

```
else
       {
            app.UseExceptionHandler("/Home/Error");
       }
       app.UseStaticFiles();
       app.UseMvc(routes =>
       {
```

Any command-line input or output is written as follows:

```
mcs -out:helloNative.exe InteropWithNativeSO.cs
```

Bold: Indicates a new term, an important word, or words that you see onscreen. For example, words in menus or dialog boxes appear in the text like this. Here is an example: "Enter **Display Name** and **Contact Email**, and click on the **Create App ID** button."

Warnings or important notes appear like this.

Tips and tricks appear like this.

Get in touch

Feedback from our readers is always welcome.

General feedback: Email `feedback@packtpub.com` and mention the book title in the subject of your message. If you have questions about any aspect of this book, please email us at `questions@packtpub.com`.

Errata: Although we have taken every care to ensure the accuracy of our content, mistakes do happen. If you have found a mistake in this book, we would be grateful if you would report this to us. Please visit `www.packtpub.com/submit-errata`, selecting your book, clicking on the Errata Submission Form link, and entering the details.

Piracy: If you come across any illegal copies of our works in any form on the Internet, we would be grateful if you would provide us with the location address or website name. Please contact us at `copyright@packtpub.com` with a link to the material.

If you are interested in becoming an author: If there is a topic that you have expertise in and you are interested in either writing or contributing to a book, please visit `authors.packtpub.com`.

Reviews

Please leave a review. Once you have read and used this book, why not leave a review on the site that you purchased it from? Potential readers can then see and use your unbiased opinion to make purchase decisions, we at Packt can understand what you think about our products, and our authors can see your feedback on their book. Thank you!

For more information about Packt, please visit `packtpub.com`.

1
Getting Started

In this chapter, we are going to learn about tools used to perform development tasks for .NET Core 2.0 on Windows and Linux operating systems. Also, we will learn how to set up Linux and virtualization using VirtualBox and Hyper-V. This chapter will cover how to install .NET Core 2.0 and tools for Windows and Linux (Ubuntu). We will learn about the **virtual machine** (**VM**) setup for Ubuntu and create your first simple .NET Core 2.0 running application code. We will configure the VM to manage your first application. The purpose of this chapter is to get a general idea of the required tools and how to install .NET core 2.0 SDK for Windows and Linux, and give you basic F# understanding.

This chapter will cover the following:

- Downloading the required tools for Windows and Linux
- Installing .NET Core 2.0 and tools (Windows)
- Setting up an Ubuntu Linux VM
- Installing .NET Core 2.0 and tools (Linux)
- Creating simple running code
- F# primer

Downloading required tools for Windows and Linux

In this section, we will discuss the prerequisites to be downloaded for both Windows and Linux operating systems to start development with .NET Core 2.0. We will start with Windows and then move to Linux.

Downloads for Windows

Microsoft offers the Visual Studio **integrated development environment** (IDE) for developers to develop computer programs for Microsoft Windows, as well as websites, web applications, web services, and mobile applications. Microsoft gives us the choice to pick from four Visual Studio adaptations—Community, Professional, Enterprise, and Code. You can download one of these, depending on your individual prerequisite. How these versions differ from each other is explained next.

Navigate to `https://www.visualstudio.com/downloads` in the browser of your choice. You will see four choices. Select the Visual Studio product based on your requirements.

All versions of Visual Studio 2017 are available for Windows and Macintosh operating systems:

- **Visual Studio Community**: This is a free, open source version of Visual Studio with limited features. This is for the individual developer.
- **Visual Studio Professional**: This version has professional developer tools, services, and subscription benefits for small teams (five members).
- **Visual Studio Enterprise**: This version supports all Visual Studio features and is meant for end-to-end solution development to meet the demanding quality and scaling needs of teams of all sizes. It is great for enterprise organizations. Some of the key features that come with this version are testing tools, architectural layer diagrams, live dependency validation, architecture validation, code clone detection, IntelliTrace, .NET memory dump analysis, and so on.
- **Visual Studio Code**: This is a free, open source version and cross-platform (Linux, macOS, Windows) editor that can be extended with plugins to meet your needs. It includes support for debugging, embedded Git control, syntax highlighting, extension support, intelligent code completion, snippets, and code refactoring.

Make a note that Visual Studio is an IDE, while Visual Studio Code is an editor, just like Notepad is an editor. So Visual Studio Code is much more lightweight, fast, and fluid with great support for debugging and has embedded Git control. It is a cross-platform editor and supports Windows, Linux, and Macintosh. Debugging support is good and has rich IntelliSense and refactoring. Like most editors, it is keyboard-centric. It is a file and folders-based editor and doesn't need to know the project context, unlike an IDE. There is no **File** | **New Project** support in Visual Studio Code as you would be used to in Visual Studio IDE. Instead, Visual Studio Code offers a terminal, through which we can run dotnet command lines to create new projects.

So, for development in Windows, we can use either of these:

- Visual Studio 2017 IDE
- Visual Studio Code editor

If we choose Visual Studio 2017, all we need to do is download Visual Studio 2017 version 15.3 from `https://www.visualstudio.com/downloads`. It comes bundled with the .NET Core 2.0 SDK and its templates and so we will be ready for development immediately after installing it. Also with Visual Studio 2017, F# tools automatically get installed once we create an F# project or open an F# project for the very first time. So, the F# development setup is taken care of as well. We will see the installation of Visual Studio 2017 in the *Installing .NET Core 2.0 and tools (Windows)* section of this chapter.

If we choose Visual Studio Code for development, we need to download Visual Studio Code from `https://code.visualstudio.com/download` and the .NET Core 2.0.0 SDK from `https://www.microsoft.com/net/core#windowscmd`. We will look at the installation of Visual Studio Code in the *Installing .NET Core 2.0 and tools (Windows)* section of this chapter.

Downloads for Linux

As mentioned in the preceding section, Microsoft Visual Studio Code is a cross-platform editor, and it supports Linux operating systems. So, we are going to use Visual Studio Code to create all the example applications on Linux in this book.

Let's start downloading the tools required to stop our development of .NET Core 2.0 applications on the Linux operating system:

1. Download Visual Studio Code from `https://code.visualstudio.com/`. We are going to install the Ubuntu 32-bit version, so we will download the Visual Studio Code 32-bit version. Select the **Linux x86 .deb** stable package for download, as shown in the following image:

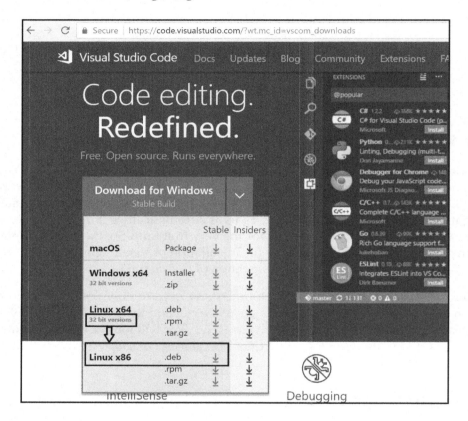

If you have a Linux machine handy, you can skip the next download step. If you wish to try development on the Linux platform and have a Windows machine to work with, then the next two steps are for you.

2. Download VirtualBox from `https://www.virtualbox.org/`. It is Oracle's open source general-purpose full virtualizer. At the time of writing this chapter, the latest version of VirtualBox is 5.1. The version 5.1.26 was released on July 27, 2017. Using this, we will set up a Linux (Ubuntu) virtual machine on the Windows host machine. Click on **Download VirtualBox** 5.1. It will open a page that has options on **VirtualBox binaries**. We can select an option based on the machine on which we are installing it. We are installing it on a Windows machine, so we will click on **Windows hosts**. In a similar way, we can select different platforms. On clicking **Windows hosts**, it will download the VirtualBox executable `VirtualBox-5.1.26-117224-Win.exe`:

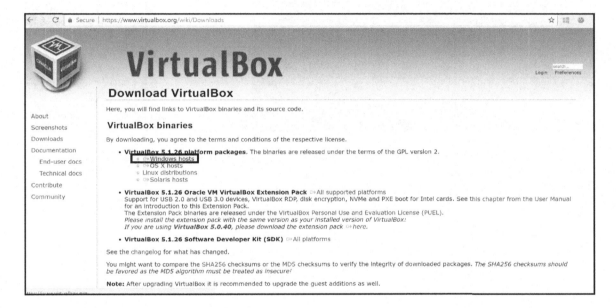

VirtualBox needs the Ubuntu **International Standards Organization (ISO)** image to create the Ubuntu VM, so next we need to download the ISO image of Ubuntu.

3. Download the ISO image of Ubuntu by navigating to `https://www.ubuntu.com`. By default, the virtual machine software uses 32-bit Linux, so we will select 32-bit. Hover over the **Downloads** menu and click on the highlighted **Desktop** link:

It will take us to the downloads page for the desktop. Click **Download** on Ubuntu for the desktop. It will start the download of Ubuntu 17.04 ISO. An ISO image of approximately 1.5 GB will be downloaded.

4. Download .NET Core 2.0 SDK from `https://www.microsoft.com/net/download/ linux`:

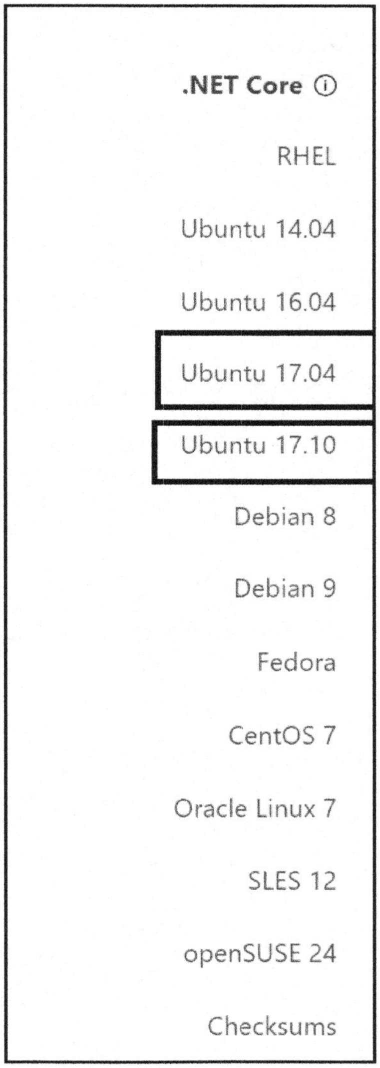

```
                    .NET Core ⓘ

                       RHEL

                  Ubuntu 14.04

                  Ubuntu 16.04

               ┌──────────────┐
               │ Ubuntu 17.04 │
               ├──────────────┤
               │ Ubuntu 17.10 │
               └──────────────┘

                    Debian 8

                    Debian 9

                    Fedora

                   CentOS 7

                Oracle Linux 7

                    SLES 12

                 openSUSE 24

                   Checksums
```

With this, we are done with the downloads for our setup in Linux. In the next section, we will learn how to install and set up these tools.

 Ubuntu 17.04: As of writing this chapter, this is the latest version, and its code name is **Zesty Zapus**, released on April 13, 2017. Ubuntu releases carry a version number in the form of XX.YY, with XX representing the year and YY representing the month of the official release. For example, the latest version released in April 2017 is represented by 17 (year) and 04 (month). Ubuntu code names use an adjective animal combination, that is an adjective word followed by the name of an animal, typically one that's unique. At the time of writing, Ubuntu 17.10 is due to be released in October 2017; examples covered here used the Ubuntu 17.04 version.

Installing .NET Core 2.0 and tools (Windows)

Now that we are done with the downloads, it's time to install. As seen in the last section on Windows, we have two options for development in Windows:

- Visual Studio 2017 version 15.3
- Visual Studio Code

Based on your choice, you can follow the appropriate installation steps.

Installing Visual Studio 2017 version 15.3

Double-click on the executable file downloaded for Visual Studio 2017 version 15.3 in the earlier section. This will start the installation. C# comes by default in every Visual Studio installation, so there is nothing to do for C#. Visual Studio 2017 also comes with F# support in all its editions: Community, Professional, and Enterprise. F# is an optional component though. The installer includes it as a selectable workload, or you can select it manually in the **Individual components** tab, under the **Development activities** category. Select **F# language support**:

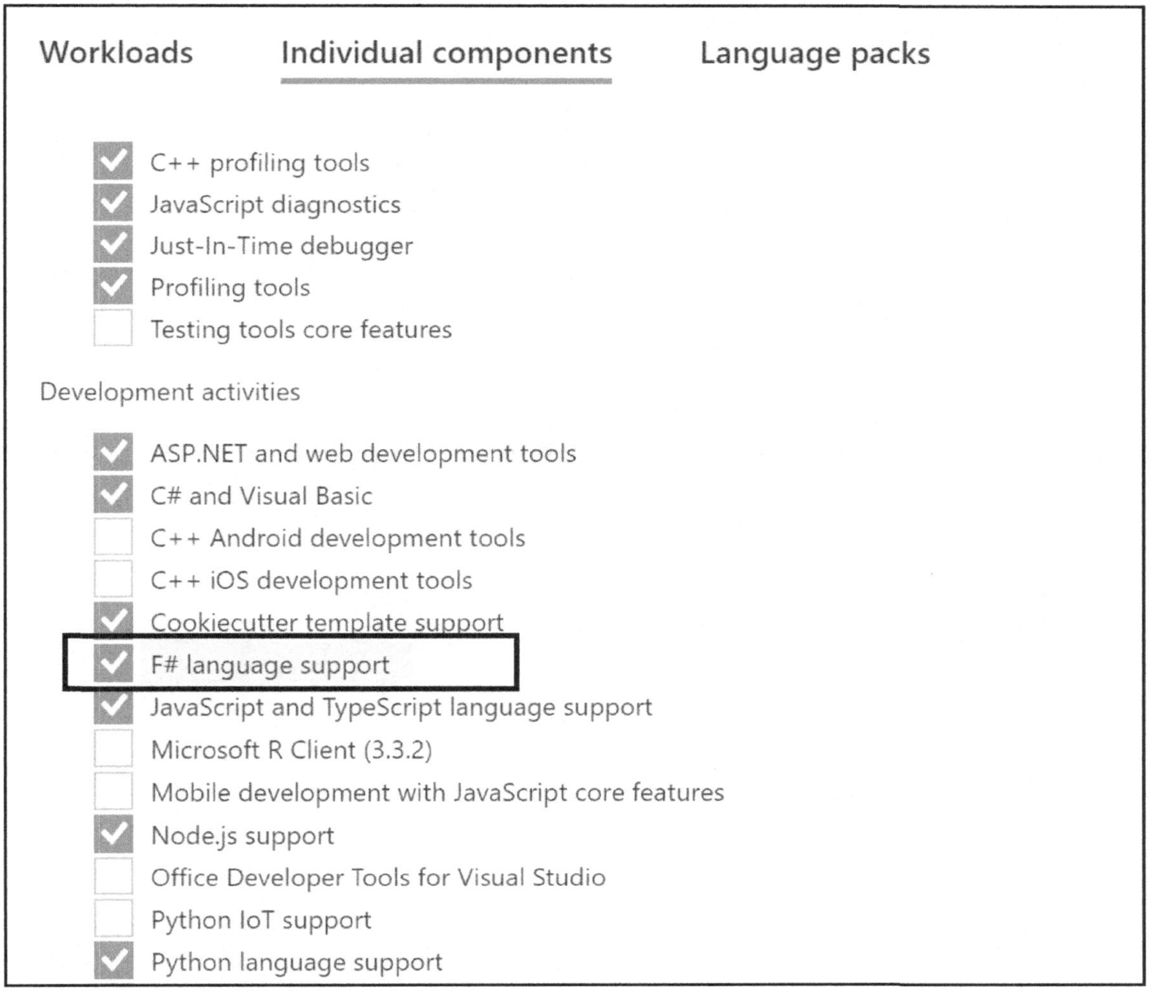

Workloads	Individual components	Language packs

☑ C++ profiling tools
☑ JavaScript diagnostics
☑ Just-In-Time debugger
☑ Profiling tools
☐ Testing tools core features

Development activities

☑ ASP.NET and web development tools
☑ C# and Visual Basic
☐ C++ Android development tools
☐ C++ iOS development tools
☑ Cookiecutter template support
☑ F# language support
☑ JavaScript and TypeScript language support
☐ Microsoft R Client (3.3.2)
☐ Mobile development with JavaScript core features
☑ Node.js support
☐ Office Developer Tools for Visual Studio
☐ Python IoT support
☑ Python language support

Visual Studio 2017 version 15.3 comes with the .NET Core SDK. Select **.NET Core cross-platform development** under **Workloads** during the Visual Studio 2017 version 15.3 installation:

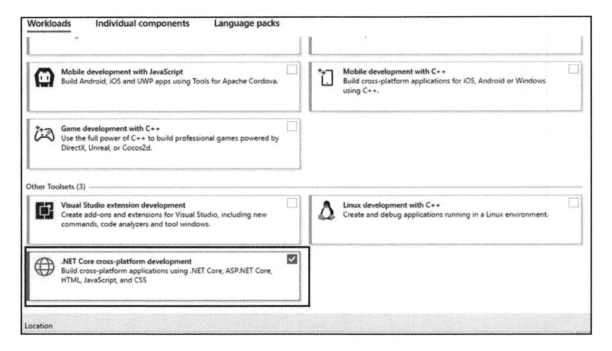

For other versions of Visual Studio, download the .NET Core 2.0 SDK from `https://www.microsoft.com/net/download/core`, or update Visual Studio to 2017 15.3 and select **.NET Core cross-platform development** under **Workloads**.

Installing Visual Studio Code

Install Visual Studio Code by double-clicking the Visual Studio Code setup executable from its download location. It's a simple installation for Windows. Once Visual Studio Code is installed, launch it. The following screenshot shows the user interface layout of Visual Studio Code. It follows the conventional editor style and displays files and folders you have access to on the left side and the code content in the editor on the right side. It can be roughly divided into seven sections, as shown in the following screenshot:

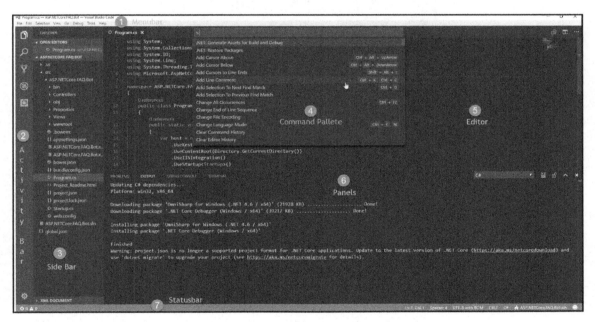

Let's discuss them:

1. **Menu bar**: The standard menu bar for doing various operations in the editor, such as opening a file/folder, editing, viewing and installing extensions, changing themes, debugging, running and configuring tasks, and getting help.

2. **Activity bar**: Groups the most commonly performed activities on the leftmost side of the editor. It lets the user switch between the views. It is customizable and lets the user choose the views to be displayed in the bar, by right-clicking on the bar and selecting/unselecting the views. The bar itself can be hidden in the same way. By default, it has five views, as shown in the following screenshot:

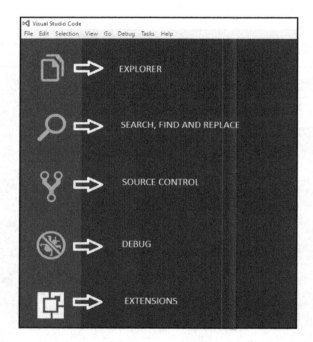

- **EXPLORER**: This view lets your browse, open, and manage all the files and folders in your project. You can create, delete, and rename files and folders, as well as move files and folders from here. You can also open the files/folders in Terminal (Command Prompt in Windows) from here by right-clicking and selecting **Open in Command Prompt**. You can find the file/folder location as well from here.

- **SEARCH**: This view lets you search and replace globally across your open folder.

- **SOURCE CONTROL**: This lets you work with Git source control by default.

- **DEBUG**: This view displays the breakpoints, variables, and call stack for debugging.

- **EXTENSIONS**: This is used to install and manage extensions in Visual Studio Code.

3. **Side bar**: This contains the view selected from the activity bar.
4. **Command Palette**: As stated earlier, Visual Studio Code is keyboard-centric, so anyone who loves using a keyboard is going to have a great time working on Visual Studio Code. The *Ctrl + Shift + P* key combination brings up what is called a Command Palette. We can access all the functionality of Visual Studio Code from here. To make effective use of Visual Studio Code, it is highly recommended that the reader makes himself/herself well versed with the commands from the help menu item links:

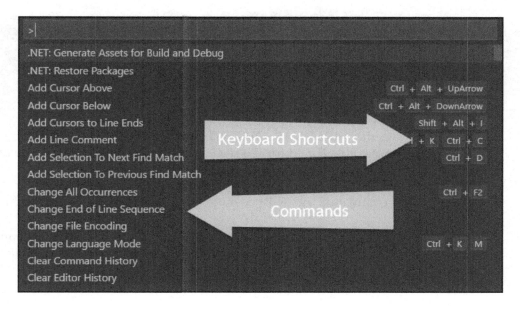

5. **Editor**: The editor is where the content of the file is displayed and the user can edit it. Visual Studio Code provides a feature called Split Editor (open to the side in Linux). Go to the **View** menu in the menu bar and select **Split Editor** (alternatively you can type the command *Ctrl +*). This will create a new editor region, where you can edit a group of files. These regions are called editor groups. The open editors can also be seen in the Explorer view in the sidebar. Visual Studio Code allows up to three editor groups, designated as **LEFT**, **CENTER**, and **RIGHT,** as shown in the following screenshot:

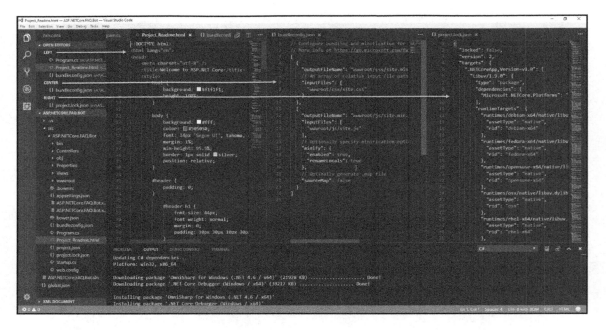

6. **Panels**: Displays the **TERMINAL, OUTPUT, PROBLEMS,** and **DEBUG CONSOLE** panes below the editor. To see it in action, go to the **View** menu and click any of the menu items from **PROBLEMS, OUTPUT, DEBUG CONSOLE,** and TERMINAL. Alternatively, you can also press their corresponding commands. We will see more on panels when we write our first application.

7. **Status Bar**: Displays information about the opened project and files being edited, such as errors, warnings, current line and column number, encoding, and file type.

Now we are familiar with Visual Studio Code, its layout, and basic functionality.

 Go to the **Help** menu and explore in detail the features that Visual Studio Code offers. The **Interactive Playground** highlights a number of features in Visual Studio Code and also lets you interactively try them out. The **Help** menu also has **Documentation**, **Introductory Videos**, **Tips and Tricks**, which are very handy.

Remember, Visual Studio Code is an editor and therefore we need to add support for the language we want to work with through extensions. Visual Studio Code is very rich in extensions. For our example and for the purpose of learning .NET Core 2.0, we will install extensions for C# and F#, as we will be working with them.

Let's start with C#, as after a fresh install we do not have support for C# and hence there would be no IntelliSense to work with on the editor. To install C#, let's switch to **Extension View** and search for C#. We will choose **C# for Visual Studio Code (powered by OmniSharp),** as shown in the following screenshot:

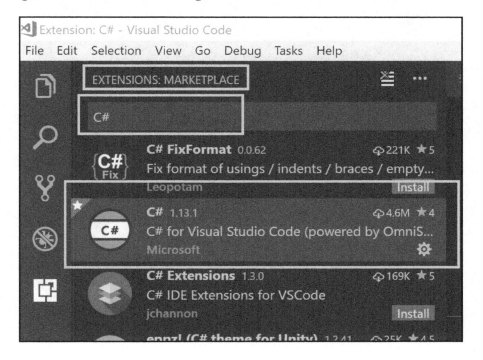

Click **Install** and then click on **Reload** and Visual Studio Code will start supporting C# along with its IntelliSense.

Similarly, search F# and **Install** it. We will be using the **Ionide-fsharp** extension, as shown in the following screenshot:

With Visual Studio Code, we need to install **.NET Core SDK - 2.0.0 (x64)** also, as Visual Studio Code doesn't install it. Double-click on the executable of .NET Core 2.0 SDK to install it, as shown in the following screenshot:

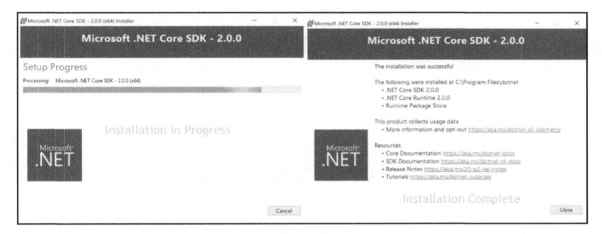

And with this, we are done with the installation of our prerequisites for development on the Windows platform. Next, we will set up a Linux (Ubuntu) VM and perform the installation of prerequisites there. If you are using a Windows platform and do not wish to set up a Linux VM, the next section can be skipped.

 The Visual Studio Code user interface was developed on the Electron framework, which is an open source framework used to build cross-platform desktop applications with JavaScript, HTML, and CSS. The editor is powered by Microsoft's Monaco Editor and gets its intelligence from OmniSharp/Roslyn and TypeScript. As all of these are open source, you can search them and see the source code in GitHub.

Setting up an Ubuntu Linux VM

In this section, we will see how to set up Linux (Ubuntu) on a virtual machine, so that a Windows user can also develop and test their .NET Core 2.0 applications in Linux. To do so, let's start with the VirtualBox setup. Oracle provides an open source VirtualBox executable, which we downloaded in the previous section. The following are the steps we need to follow to set up VirtualBox:

1. Double-click on the VirtualBox executable. It will open a wizard. Before installation, click on **Disk usage** and check **Disk Space Requirement**. It is recommended that the virtual machine for Ubuntu Linux is set up with at least 2 GB RAM and 25 GB free hard drive space. So, instead of choosing the default drive (the C drive in our case, where Windows is installed), select another drive if it exists (for example, the D drive) so that you can easily allocate more space, and it also prevents any impact on the host operating system.
2. The VirtualBox setup needs approximately 241 MB of disk space to install. It's recommended to create a new folder (for example, VirtualBox) to easily identify and track the VM.

3. Keep clicking the **Next** button until the last page. At the end, a warning will be displayed that the installation of VirtualBox will reset the network connection and temporarily disconnect the machine from the network. This is alright if you are working on the same physical machine. So, click on the **Yes** button and continue, and then click on the **Install** button and finish the installation:

4. Once the preceding installation is done, open the VirtualBox manager to create a new virtual machine. Click on **New** and give the **Name** of the machine (for example, Ubuntu, as shown), and select the **Type** as **Linux** and the **Version** as **Ubuntu (32 bit)**:

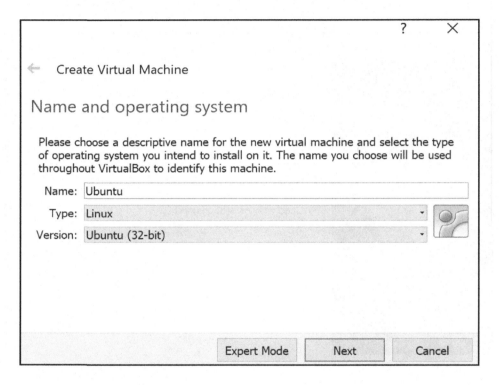

5. We need to specify the memory size. More memory is good, but we should consider our disk space before selecting it. A minimum of 2 GB system memory is required for Ubuntu 17.04. Select **Create** and then select **VDI (VirtualBox Disk Image)** as **Hard disk file type**. Select a **Dynamically allocated** hard disk. It will use space on your physical hard disk as it fills up (up to the maximum fixed size). Set the disk space maximum size to 25 GB and click on **Create**. It will create a virtual machine with the Ubuntu operating system (32-bit) and 4 GB RAM, and the full details will be displayed on the final page:

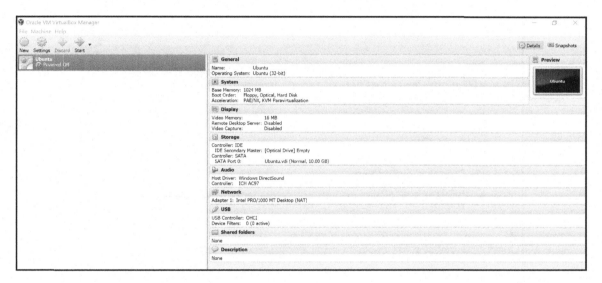

Ubuntu setup using Hyper-V

For Windows machines, we can use Hyper-V to create a Linux virtual machine. Let's start with the basic settings and important configuration changes:

1. First, enable **Hyper-V Management Tools** and **Hyper-V Platform** from **Windows Features**:

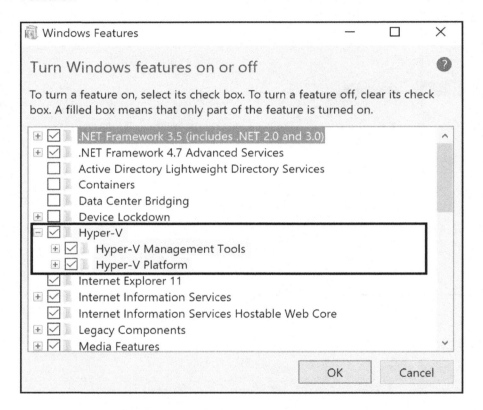

2. Change the default virtual directory. By default, Hyper-V uses the same drive as that on which the OS is installed but this is not a good practice. We should change the default drive the drive on which the operating system is not installed, such as the D drive in our case. It's a good practice to keep Windows and system files separate from other files. To make configuration changes, open **Hyper-V Manager** and then **Hyper-V Settings**. Instead of the default selection, change it to some other drive (D in our case). Create a new folder named `Virtual Machine` on this new drive location:

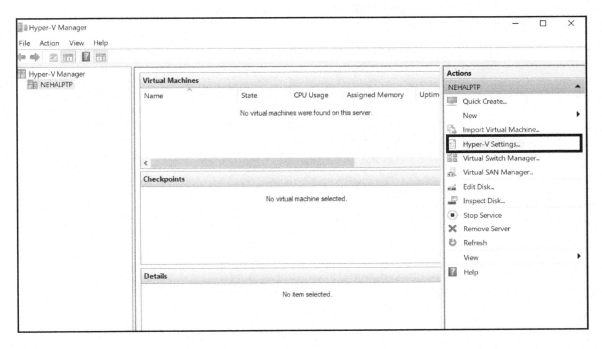

3. Create a virtual switch. A virtual switch is used to join computers and to create networks. We can create three types for virtual switches:
    - **External**: An accessible network where the virtual machines are hosted on the same physical computer and all external servers from which the host machine can connect.
    - **Internal**: Creates a virtual switch that can be used only by the virtual machines that run on the same physical computer, and between virtual machines and the physical computer. An internal virtual switch doesn't provide connectivity to a physical network connection.
    - **Private**: Creates a virtual switch that can be used only by the virtual machines that run on the same physical computer.

Create a **Private** or **External** type of virtual switch. This will be used for the virtual machine:

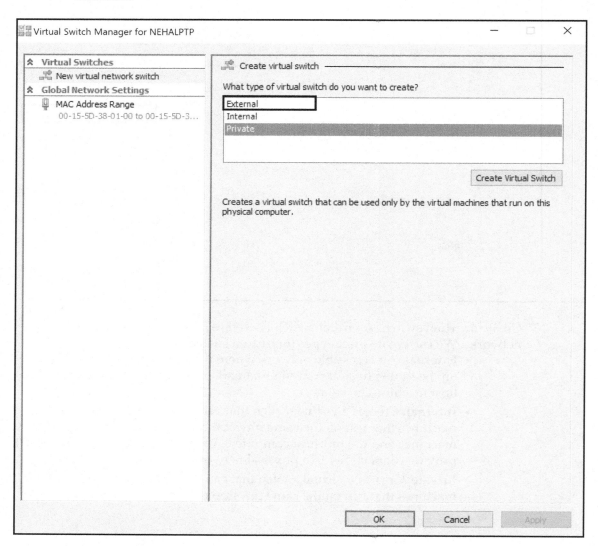

Open **Network and Sharing Center** on your host machine and then open the external virtual switch properties. You will find **Hyper-V Extensible Virtual Switch.** This provides network connectivity to the virtual machine. Enable this or the virtual machine won't be able to connect to the host machine network:

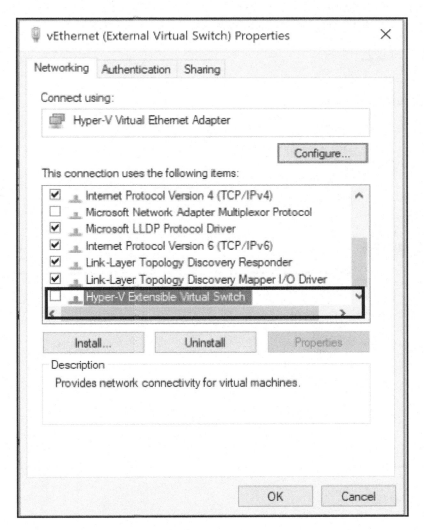

4. Create a new virtual machine, and choose the name and location for the virtual machine. Select **Generation 1** on the next page and select **External Virtual Switch**. Select the **Install an operating system from a bootable CD/DVD-ROM** option and select **Image file (.iso),** which we downloaded earlier for Ubuntu. Continue clicking the **Next** button in the wizard and the Ubuntu virtual machine will be created. Click on **Start** and connect to it:

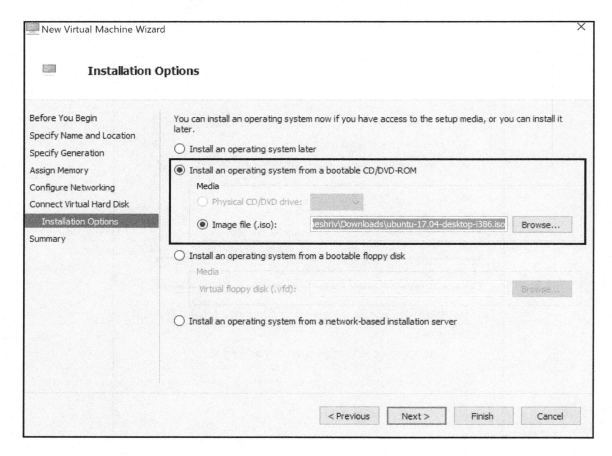

5. After connection, we will be able to see the following screen. Select **Install Ubuntu** and set the language as **English**. Choose the **Erase disk and install Ubuntu** option and then click **Continue**:

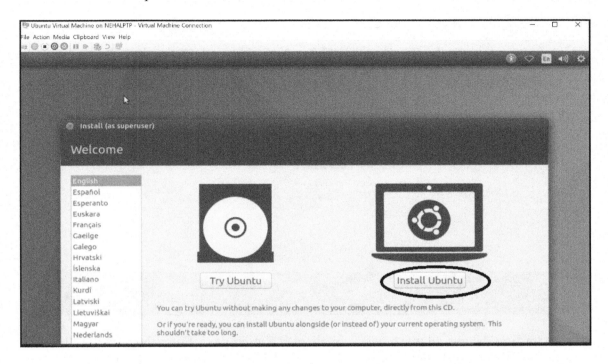

6. Provide the username and password that you want and click **Continue**. Restart the system once the installation is done:

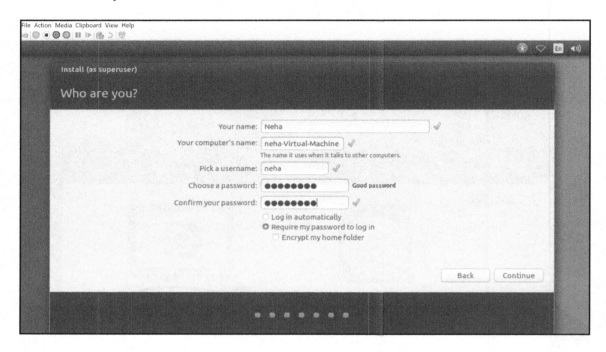

After restarting the virtual machine, it will display a login page. Enter the password that you provided while installing Ubuntu. On successful login, it will open the homepage, from where we can start Visual Studio Code and .NET Core 2.0 SDK installation on this Ubuntu machine.

Installing .NET Core 2.0 and tools (Linux)

To install Visual Studio Code in Linux, download the **.deb (32 bit)** file from `http://code.visualstudio.com/download`, as shown in the following screenshot:

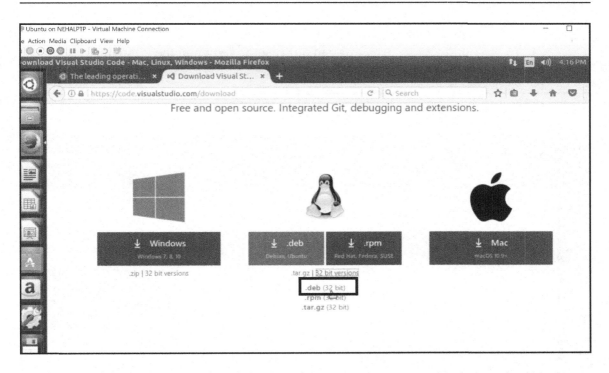

Open the folder location the `.deb` file has been downloaded to. Right-click and select **Open in Terminal.** This will open Terminal from this location. Run the following command:

```
sudo dpkg -i <fileName>.deb
```

`<fileName>`: Enter the filename that was downloaded, which is `code_1.15.1-1502903950_i386.deb` in our case, as shown in the following screenshot:

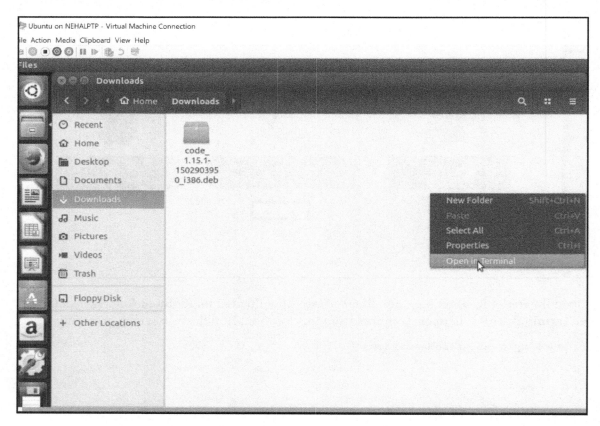

Right-click on the `Downloads` folder, and select **Open in Terminal**. It will display the following terminal window:

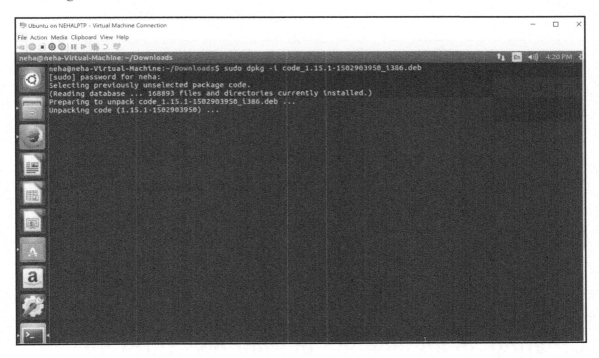

It may show error messages stating that dependencies have not been installed. Run the following command to install the dependencies:

```
sudo apt-get install -f
```

This will complete the installation of Visual Studio Code in this Ubuntu machine.

Now, let's install the .NET Core 2.0 SDK. Open the folder location where the `dotnet-sdk-2.0.0` file is downloaded. Right-click and select **Open in Terminal**. It will open Terminal from this location. Run the following command:

```
sudo apt-get install dotnet-sdk-2.0.0
```

Congratulations! We are all set to run Visual Studio Code! Please refer to the *Installing Visual Studio Code* section of this chapter to get an overview of Visual Studio Code.

Open **Extensions View** from the Visual Studio Code activity bar. Search F# and install the **Ionide-fsharp** extension for F# language support, as we discussed in the *Installing Visual Studio Code* section under the *Install .NET Core 2.0 and tools (Windows)* section.

Now, search C# and install the **C# for Visual Studio Code (powered by OmniSharp)** extension for C# language support.

Creating simple running code

Let's create our very first .NET Core 2.0 application. We will create it using Visual Studio Code as well as Visual Studio 2017 in Windows, and with Visual Studio Code in Ubuntu.

The .NET Core 2.0 SDK installs the templates for creating the class library, console, web, MVC, razor, web API, and so on, for applications based on .NET Core 2.0. As our first application, we will create a simple MVC application on .NET Core 2.0, and get familiar with the application code and the .NET Core 2.0 command-line integration.

Let's start by creating this application in Windows using Visual Studio 2017, and then we will create the same application from Visual Studio Code, first in Windows and then in Linux.

Creating an application in Windows through Visual Studio 2017 version 15.3

For this, we need to perform the following steps:

1. Open Visual Studio 2017.
2. Go to **File** | **New** | **Project**. In the **New Project** dialog, you should see the **.NET Core** template inside Visual C#:

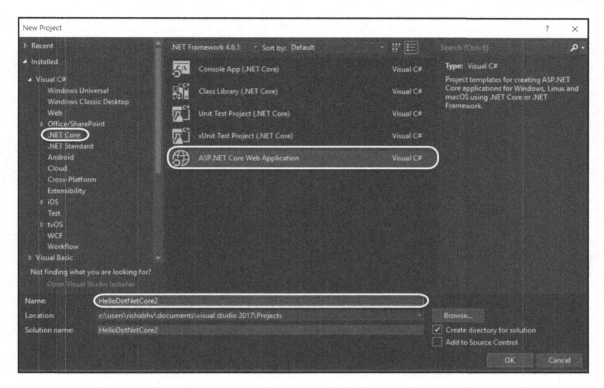

3. Click on **.NET Core** and select **ASP.NET Core Web Application**.
4. Name the project `HelloDotNetCore2` and click **OK**.

5. It will show a **New ASP.NET Core Web Application** dialog. Ensure **.NET Core** and **ASP.NET Core 2.0** are selected in the two dropdowns displayed in this dialog, as we are discussing .NET Core 2.0 here. The first dropdown signifies the target framework of the application and the second dropdown is the version of ASP.NET Core that we are using. You have the option to choose **.NET Framework** as the target framework in the first dropdown, but then the resulting application would not be cross-platform. If the application has to be cross-platform, it should target .NET Core. The second dropdown has the different versions of ASP.NET Core that have been released so far, such as 1.0, 1.1, and 2.0. We will keep it as **ASP.NET Core 2.0**. You will also notice that with ASP.NET Core 2.0, the number of templates has increased from the previous version. Apart from **Empty**, **Web API**, and **Web Application**, which were present in ASP.NET 1.1, we also have templates for **Web Application (Model-View-Controller)**, **Angular**, **React.js**, and **React.js and Redux**. We will choose **Web Application (Model-View-Controller)** as our template. There is support for a Docker container but let's keep it unchecked for the time being. We will discuss Docker in detail in a later chapter. Also, keep the **Authentication** as **No Authentication**. We will explore authentication options in detail in a later chapter. Click **OK:**

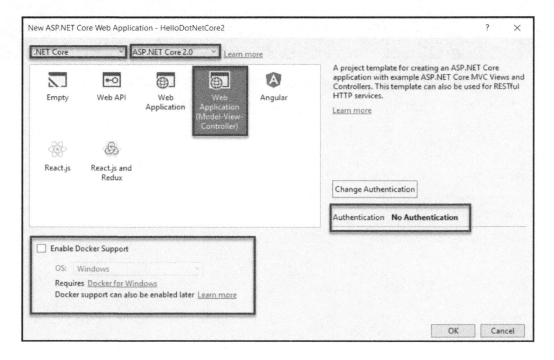

6. And *voila*! Visual Studio creates the `HelloDotNetCore2` project for us and restores the required packages to build in the background. You can check this by inspecting the **Package Manager Console** output. Your very first ASP.NET Core 2.0 is ready to be run:

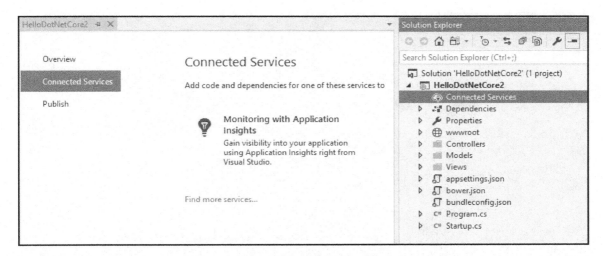

7. Click **Debug** or press *F5* to run the application. We will see a detailed walk-through of all the project artifacts in the next chapter.

Creating application in Windows through Visual Studio Code

Visual Studio is the IDE and is aware of projects and templates. As stated earlier, Visual Studio Code is a file and folder-based editor and hence it is not aware of projects and templates. So to create the same application through Visual Studio Code, we will make use of the .NET command line. Let's get going!

Open Visual Studio Code, go to **View**, and click on **TERMINAL**. It will open Command Prompt/the PowerShell terminal in the bottom section of Visual Studio Code. If you see the PowerShell terminal, type `cmd` so that it turns into Command Prompt. This is an optional step if you are comfortable with PowerShell.

Let's try and explore the commands available to create a new project, so let's type `dotnet --help`. This is the help command for dotnet and will let us know about the options that we have available for creating a .NET Core 2.0 MVC application as shown in the following screenshot:

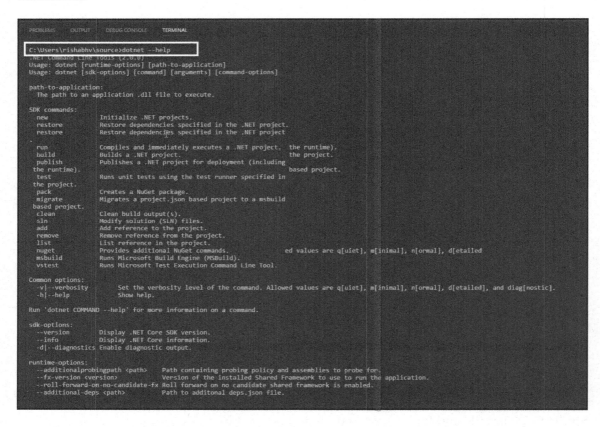

The SDK lists all the possible commands and options that can be used with explanations. So keep in mind, any time you need any help with .NET commands, SDK is there to help us. Just ask for help by typing `dotnet --help` in the terminal.

From the command list, it looks like the command of interest to us is the `new` command, as its description reads that this command initializes .NET projects.

So, let's ask SDK how to use the new command by typing `dotnet new --help`. This will let us know the command that we need to run to create a new MVC application:

```
PROBLEMS    OUTPUT    DEBUG CONSOLE    TERMINAL

  --version          Display .NET Core SDK version.
  --info             Display .NET Core information.
  -d|--diagnostics   Enable diagnostic output.

runtime-options:
  --additionalprobingpath <path>      Path containing probing policy and assemblies to probe for.
  --fx-version <version>              Version of the installed Shared Framework to use to run the application.
  --roll-forward-on-no-candidate-fx  Roll forward on no candidate shared framework is enabled.
  --additional-deps <path>           Path to additonal deps.json file.


C:\Users\rishabhv\source>dotnet new --help
Usage: new [options]

Options:
  -h, --help          Displays help for this command.
  -l, --list          Lists templates containing the specified name. If no name is specified, lists all templates.
  -n, --name          The name for the output being created. If no name is specified, the name of the current directory is used.
  -o, --output        Location to place the generated output.
  -i, --install       Installs a source or a template pack.
  -u, --uninstall     Uninstalls a source or a template pack.
  --type              Filters templates based on available types. Predefined values are "project", "item" or "other".
  --force             Forces content to be generated even if it would change existing files.
  -lang, --language   Specifies the language of the template to create.


Templates                                          Short Name      Language        Tags
--------------------------------------------------------------------------------------------------
Console Application                                console         [C#], F#, VB    Common/Console
Class library                                      classlib        [C#], F#, VB    Common/Library
Unit Test Project                                  mstest          [C#], F#, VB    Test/MSTest
xUnit Test Project                                 xunit           [C#], F#, VB    Test/xUnit
ASP.NET Core Empty                                 web             [C#], F#        Web/Empty
ASP.NET Core Web App (Model-View-Controller)       mvc             [C#], F#        Web/MVC
ASP.NET Core Web App                               razor           [C#]            Web/MVC/Razor Pages
ASP.NET Core with Angular                          angular         [C#]            Web/MVC/SPA
ASP.NET Core with React.js                         react           [C#]            Web/MVC/SPA
ASP.NET Core with React.js and Redux               reactredux      [C#]            Web/MVC/SPA
ASP.NET Core Web API                               webapi          [C#], F#        Web/WebAPI
global.json file                                   globaljson                      Config
Nuget Config                                       nugetconfig                     Config
Web Config                                         webconfig                       Config
Solution File                                      sln                             Solution
Razor Page                                         page                            Web/ASP.NET
MVC ViewImports                                    viewimports                     Web/ASP.NET
MVC ViewStart                                      viewstart                       Web/ASP.NET


Examples:
    dotnet new mvc --auth Individual
    dotnet new xunit
    dotnet new --help
```

Based on the preceding help text, let's enter the following command:

```
dotnet new mvc -lang C# -n HelloDotNETCore2
```

This will create a new MVC project named `HelloDotNetCore2` in the C# language, in the folder named `HelloDotNetCore2` at the location of the terminal. Now let's build and run the application by typing the following commands:

```
cd HelloDotNetCore2
dotnet build
dotnet run
```

The first command navigates to the newly created folder, `HelloDotNetCore2`. Then, we build the application with the second command and run it through the third command. The `dotnet build` command is just to show that we have a build command as well. The `dotnet run` command actually builds and runs the application. Now, go to the browser of your choice and navigate to `http://localhost:5000` to see the application running in your browser:

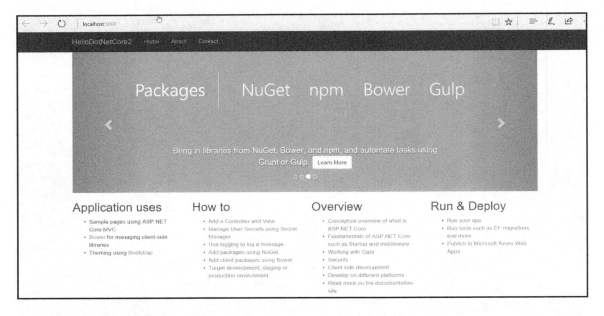

Alternatively, you can go to the **Explorer** view in the activity bar, open the `HelloDotNetCore2` folder, and press *F5*. This will also build the application and launch it in the browser.

 Steps for creating the application in Ubuntu through Visual Studio Code are the same as in Windows, but instead of Command Prompt, we have Bash.

F# primer

F# is a functional programming language. Functional programming treats programs as mathematical expressions. It focuses on functions and constants that don't change, rather than variables and states. F# is a Microsoft programming language for concise and declarative syntax. Let's begin with a brief history of how this language came into existence. The first attempt at functional programming was **Haskell .NET**. F# development began in 2005 and after that, various versions came along. At the time of writing this chapter, F# 4.1 is the latest version; it was released in March 2017. This comes with Visual Studio 2017 and supports .NET Core.

The F# language can be used for the following tasks:

- To solve mathematical problems
- For graphic design
- For financial modeling
- For compiler programming
- For CPU design

It is also used for CRUD applications, web pages GUI games, and other programs.

F# keywords

Keywords and their use in the F# language are outlined in the following table:

Keyword	Description
abstract	Indicates that either it has no implementation or is a virtual and has default implementation.
begin	In verbose syntax, indicates the start of a code block.
default	Indicates an implementation of an abstract method; used together with an abstract method declaration to create a virtual method.
elif	Used in conditional branching. A short form of else-if.
end	Used in type definitions and type extensions, indicates the end of a section of member definitions. In verbose syntax, used to specify the end of a code block that starts with the begin keyword.
exception	Used to declare an exception type.
finally	Used together with try to introduce a block of code that executes regardless of whether an exception occurs.
fun	Used in lambda expressions, and is also known as anonymous functions.
function	Used as a shorter alternative to the fun keyword and a match expression in a lambda expression that has pattern matching on a single argument.

inherit	Used to specify a base class or base interface.
interface	Used to declare and implement interfaces.
let	Used to associate or bind a name to a value or function.
member	Used to declare a property or method in an object type.
mutable	Used to declare a variable; that is, a value that can be changed.
override	Used to implement a version of an abstract or virtual method that differs from the base version.
rec	Used to indicate that a function is recursive.
select	Used in query expressions to specify what fields or columns to extract. Note that this is a contextual keyword, which means that it is not actually a reserved word and it only acts like a keyword in an appropriate context.
static	Used to indicate a method or property that can be called without an instance of a type, or a value member that is shared among all instances of a type.
struct	Used to declare a structure type. Also used in generic parameter constraints. Used for OCaml compatibility in module definitions.
type	Used to declare a class, record, structure, discriminated union, enumeration type, unit of measure, or type abbreviation.
val	Used in a signature to indicate a value, or in a type to declare a member, in limited situations.
yield	Used in a sequence expression to produce a value for a sequence.

This reference is taken from the Microsoft official website, and a detailed explanation and description can be found at `https://docs.microsoft.com/en-us/dotnet/fsharp/language-reference/keyword-reference`.

Comments

In the F# language, we have two types of comments for a single line and for multiple lines. This is the same as C#. The following are the two types of comments:

- A single-line comment which starts with the `//` symbol.

Example: `// returns an integer exit code`

- A multi-line comment which starts with (* and ends with *).

Example: `(*Learn more about F# at http://fsharp.org *)`

Data types

F# has a rich data type system. We can broadly classify them as:

- **Integral types**: sbyte, byte, int16, uint16, int32, uint32, int64, and bigint
- **Floating point types**: float32, float, and decimal
- **Text types**: char and string
- **Other types**: bool

These types are also referred to as fundamental primitive types in F#. Apart from these, F# has an exhaustive list of predefined types as well, such as lists, arrays, records, enumerations, tuples, units, sequences, and so on. It is recommended that a person learning F# goes through the official Microsoft documentation on F# at https://docs.microsoft. com/en-us/dotnet/fsharp/.

Variable declaration

F# uses the let keyword for the declaration of a variable, for example:

```
let square x = x*x
```

The compiler automatically detects this as a value type. If we pass a float value, the compiler will be able to understand that without declaring a data type. Variables in F# are immutable, so once a value is assigned to a variable, it can't be changed. They are compiled as static read-only properties.

The following example demonstrates this:

```
let x:int32 = 50
let y:int32 = 30
let z:int32 = x + y
```

Variables x, y, and z are all of type int32 and are immutable, meaning their value cannot be changed.

Let's print their values. The syntax is as follows:

```
printfn "x: %i" x
printfn "y: %i" y
printfn "z: %i" z
```

After the preceding code executes, the result is as follows:

```
x:  50
y:  30
z:  80
```

Now, suppose we want to modify the value of x from 50 to 60 and check that z reflects the updated sum; we will write the code as:

```
let x = 60
let y = 30
let z = x + y
```

On executing this code, we get the following errors, and rightly so because x and z are immutable:

```
Duplicate definition of value 'x'
Duplicate definition of value 'z'
```

The correct way of doing it would be to use mutable variables for the declaration, as shown here:

```
let mutable x = 60
let y = 30 //It's optional to make y mutable.
let mutable z = x + y
x <- 70
z <-  x + y
```

On printing the values again, we will see:

```
x:  70
y:  30
z:  100
```

Operators

F# has the following operators:

- Arithmetic operators
- Comparison operators
- Boolean operators
- Bitwise operators

Let's discuss these operators in detail.

Arithmetic operators

Arithmetic operators supported by the F# language are outlined in the following table. Assuming variable X = 10 and variable Y = 40 , we have the following expressions:

Operator	Description	Example
+	Adds two values	X + Y = 50
−	Subtracts the second value from the first	X − Y = −30
*	Multiplies both values	X * Y = 400
/	Divides two values	Y / X = 4
%	Modulus operator and gives the value of the remainder after an integer division	Y % X = 0
**	Exponentiation operator; raises one variable to the power of another	Y**X = 40^{10}

Comparison operators

The following table shows all the comparison operators supported by F# . These operators return true or false.

Let's take X = 20 and Y = 30:

Operator	Description	Example
==	Verifies the values of two variables are equal; if not, then the condition becomes false.	(X == Y) returns false
<>	Verifies the values of two variables are equal; if values are not equal then the condition becomes true.	(X <> Y) returns true
>	Verifies the value of the left variable is greater than the value of the right variable; if not, then the condition becomes false.	(X > Y) returns false
<	Verifies the value of the left variable is less than the value of the right variable; if yes, then the condition becomes true.	(X < Y) returns true

>=	Verifies the value of the left variable is greater than or equal to the value of the right variable; if not, then condition becomes `false`.	`(X >= Y)` returns `false`
<=	Verifies the value of the left variable is less than or equal to the value of the right variable; if yes, then the condition becomes `true`.	`(X <= Y)` returns `true`

Boolean operators

The following table shows all the Boolean operators supported by the F# language. Let's take variable X as `true` and Y as `false`:

Operator	Description	Example
`&&`	Boolean AND operator. If both the bool values are `true` means 1, then the condition is `true`.	`(X && Y)` is `false`
`||`	Boolean OR operator. If either of the two bool values is `true` means 1, then the condition is `true`.	`(X || Y)` is `true`
`not`	Boolean NOT operator. If the condition is `true`, then the logical NOT operator will become `false` and vice versa.	`not (X && Y)` is `true`

Bitwise operators

Bitwise operators work on bits and perform bit-by-bit operations. The truth tables for `&&&` (bitwise AND), `|||` (bitwise OR), and `^^^` (bitwise exclusive OR) are shown as follows. In the following table, the first variable is X and the second variable is Y:

X	Y	X &&& Y	X ||| Y	X ^^^ Y
0	0	0	0	0
0	1	0	1	1
1	1	1	1	0
1	0	0	1	1

It also supports ~~~(Unary, effect of flipping bits) , <<< (left shift operator), and >>>(right shift operator).

Decision-making statements

The F# language has the following (if...else and loop) types of decision-making statements.

if statements

The following table shows all the ways of implementing if statements:

Statement	Description
if/then statement	An if/then statement consists of a Boolean expression followed by one or more statements.
if/then/else statement	An if/then statement can be followed by an optional else statement, which executes when the Boolean expression is false.
if/then/elif/else statement	An if/then/elif/else statement allows you to have multiple else statements.
Nested if statements	You can use one if or else if statement inside another if or else if statements.

Loop statements

F# provides the following types of loop:

Loop type	Description
for...to and for...downto expressions	The for...to expression is used to iterate in a loop over a range of values of a loop variable. The for...downto expression reduces the value of a loop variable.
for...in expression	This form of for loop is used to iterate over collections of items; that is, loops over collections and sequences.
while...do loop	Repeats a statement or group of statements while the given condition is true. It tests the condition before executing the loop body.
nested loops	We can use one or more loop inside any other for or while loop.

F# functions

F# functions act like variables. We can declare and use them in the same way as we use variables in C#. A function definition starts with the `let` keyword, followed by the function name and parameters, a colon, its type, and the right-side expression, showing what the function does. The syntax is follows:

```
Let functionName parameters [ : returnType] = functionbody
```

In the preceding syntax:

- `functionName` is an identifier of the function.
- `parameters` gives the list of parameters separated by spaces. We can also specify an explicit type for each parameter and if not specified, the compiler tends to presume it from the function body as variables.
- `functionbody` comprises an expression, or a compound expression, which has number of expressions. The final expression in the function body is the return value.
- `returnType` is a colon followed by a type and it is optional. If the `returnType` is not specified, then the compiler determines it from the final expression in the function body.

Have a look at the following example for our syntax:

```
let addValue (x : int) = 5 + x
```

Calling a function

A function can be called by passing the function name followed, by a space, and then arguments (if any) separated by spaces, as shown here:

```
let sum = addValue 3
```

We can perform many tasks using F# functions, some of which are as follows:

- We can create a new function and link that function with a type as it acts as a variable type:
  ```
  let square x = x*x
  ```
- We can perform some calculations as well, such as:
  ```
  let square x = x*x
  ```

- We can assign a value. Taking the same example:
  ```
  let square x = x*x
  ```

- We can pass a function as a parameter to another function like this:
  ```
  let squareValue = List.map square[1;2;3] // using square
  function
  ```

- We can return a function as a result of another function example:
  ```
  let squareValue = List.map square[1;2;3]
  ```

File sequence

The order of files in a project matters in an F# solution. The file used in any function should be placed above the file where the function is used, because F# has a forward-only model of compilation.

Unlike C#, where the file sequence doesn't matter, the sequencing of files does matter in F#. For example, consider that `Program.fs` is using `DotNetCorePrint.fs`. So, `DotNetCorePrint.fs` should be placed above `Program.fs` in the solution; otherwise, it will throw a compilation error. To move a file up or down, we can right-click on the file and select **Move Up** or the keys *Alt* + the up arrow to move the file. The ordering of the files in **Solution Explorer** can be seen in the following screenshot:

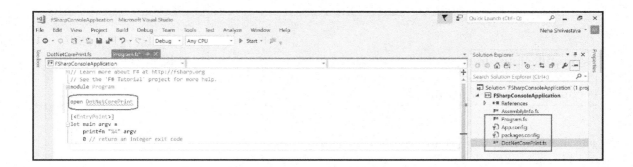

Basic input/output syntax

We are now going to see how to write and read in F#. To read and write into the console, we can use the following commands:

- To write: `System.Console.Write("Welcome!")`
- To read: `System.Console.Read()`

- To print: `printfn "Hello"`

Let's compare F# with C#:

F#	C#

The F# user is free from the obligation of defining types; for example: `let square x = x* x` The compiler can identify (`integer * integer`) or (`float * float`) when we pass a value.	The C# user is bound to provide a type:
	`Public int`
	`square(int x){`
	`return x = x*x ; }`

F# has immutable data, and the value never changes; for example: `let number = [3;2;1]`
`let moreNumber = 4:: number`
In the preceding example, to add one more number, (4), we need to create a new list of items using `number`, and add the new record, 4 in this case. The same list doesn't get modified for safer asynchronous execution and a simplified understanding of a function.
	C# has mutable as well as immutable data. Strings are immutable, the rest are all mutable, for example:
	`var number = new`
	`List<int> {1,2,3};`
	`number.Add(4);`
	In the preceding example, we created a list and added a new item to the same list. The list gets modified.

F# compiles code in an order. It is favoured for data processing and algorithmic computation. It doesn't work on visibility; it works sequentially.	C# code works on visibility. The sequence doesn't matter.
The order of files in a project matters in the F# solution. A file used in any method should be placed above the file where the method has been used.	The order doesn't matter in C#.

F# has precise syntax; it focuses on *what not* and *how*; for example: ``` let square x = x*x let squared = List.map square[1;2;3] // using square function ``` **Right-click execute | result** 1;4;9 F# uses declarative syntax, not imperative syntax as in C#. F# helps us to minimize accidental complexity, meaning complexity that is not a part of the problem, but which we introduced as part of the solution, for example: ``` let rec quicksort = function | [] -> [] | x :: xs -> let smaller = List.filter((>)x) xs let larger = List.filter ((<=)x) xs ``` Quicksort smaller @ [x] @ quicksort larger: ``` Let sorted = quicksort [4;5;4;7;9;1;6;1;0;-99;10000;3;2] ``` rec is used for a recursive function. It is assigned in the sorted result. Run it and you will get a sorted result. It is a very simple sorting function with less complexity than C#, which has a high chance of errors.	C# code implementation is more about how to implement. It sometimes increases unnecessary complexity as part of the solution to a problem. Quick sort has a very complex algorithm and a high chance of increasing accidental complexity.

Summary

In this chapter, we discussed downloading Visual Studio Code, .NET Core 2.0, an Ubuntu 17.04 ISO image, and the tools required to start .NET Core application creation, as well as how to install them on Windows and Linux machines. We also discussed how to set up a Ubuntu Linux virtual machine and introduced the F# language.

In the following chapter, you'll be introduced to native libraries in .NET Core, used to extend console capabilities. We will discuss Interop with existing libraries and ncurses.

2
Native Libraries in .NET Core

In this chapter, we are going to learn about ncurses native libraries and how to extend console capabilities in .NET Core on Linux. We will also learn how to Interop with existing native code. This chapter will introduce the ncurses native library and Interop with existing native and Mono libraries. We will build a sample native library in C++ and we will also learn how to create an application that implements the new library and ncurses. The purpose of this chapter is to get an understanding of Interop with existing libraries, and the ability to extend console capabilities through implementing ncurses.

This chapter will cover the following topics:

- Introduction to ncurses
- Interop with existing native and Mono libraries
- Building a sample native library (C++)
- A sample application to implement the new library and ncurses

Introduction to ncurses

New curses (ncurses) is an openly distributable library of functions that deals with an application's **user interface (UI)** in text mode. It creates a wrapper over terminal abilities. ncurses is a free software, it is not an open source. It provides functions to make imaginary screen windows for logical calculations, print windows, and so on. Libraries for panels, menus, and forms use the ncurses library and extend the basic functionality of ncurses as required. We can make applications that contain numerous windows, menus, panels, and forms; windows can be overseen autonomously, can give scrollability, and can even be covered up.

Menus give the client a simple order determination choice, forms permit the formation of easy–to–use information sections and show windows, and panels stretch out the abilities of ncurses to manage covering and stacked windows. These are a portion of the essential things we can do with ncurses. As we progress, we will see how to build a native library using C++.

ncurses comes with the Visual Studio Code installation and we can download `ncurses-6.0.tar.gz`, from `http://ftp.gnu.org/pub/gnu/ncurses/`. After downloading, unzip and install ncurses 6.0 (the latest version at the time of writing this book):

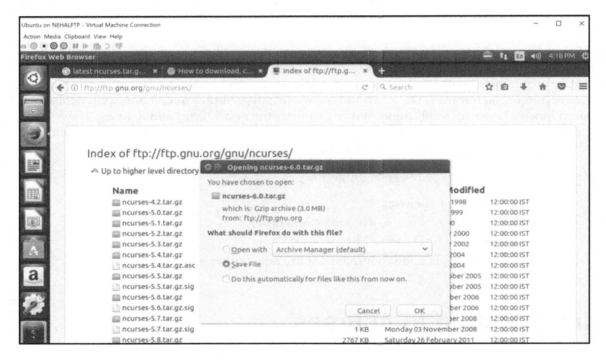

Open the Terminal from the folder, `ncurses-6.0`, and run the following commands to install ncurses:

- `./configure`: Configure the build according to your environment
- `make`: Make it
- `su root`: Become root
- `make install`: Install it

Let's start with a simple application, `"Welcome to .NET Core 2.0"`, to understand how to start, use, alter, and close ncurses:

```
#include <ncurses.h>

Void WelcomeMessage()
{
    initscr(); /* Start ncurses mode */
    printw("Welcome to .NET Core 2.0"); /* Print welcome message */
    Move(3, 2); /* moves the cursor to 3rd row and 2nd column */
    Addch('a' | A_Bold | A_UNDERLINE); /* Move() and addch() functions
    can be replaced by mvaddch(row,col,ch); */
    refresh(); /* Print it on to the real screen */
    getch(); /* Wait for user input */
    endwin(); /* End curses mode */
}
int main()
{
    WelcomeMessage();
    return 0;
}
```

Write a function called `WelcomeMessage()` which returns void, and call it from `main`, as shown in the example. Let's try to understand each function that we called inside the `WelcomeMessage` function:

- `Initscr()`: This function initiates the Terminal in curses mode. It is typically the main curses method to call while introducing a program. A couple of uncommon methods, once in a while, should be called before it; these are `slk_init()`, `channel()`, `ripoffline()`, and `use_env()`. For different Terminal applications, `newterm()` might be called before `initscr()`. The `initscr()` code decides the Terminal sort and instates all curses data structures. `initscr()` likewise makes the main call, `refresh()`, to clear the screen. On the off chance that errors arise, `initscr()` composes an error message to standard error and exits; otherwise, a pointer comes back to stdscr. A program that yields to more than one Terminal should utilize the `newterm()` routine for every Terminal, rather than `initscr()`. The method `newterm()` ought to be called once for every Terminal.

- `printw("Welcome to .NET Core 2.0")`: This prints " Welcome to .NET Core 2.0" on the screen. `printw()` is a class of functions:
  - `printw()`: This function works similar to `printf()` with the exception that it prints the information on a window called stdscr and with the added capability of printing at any position on the screen at the current (y, x) coordinates. If the cursor is at coordinates (0,0), the string is printed at the left corner of the window.
  - `mvprintw()`: This function can be used to move the cursor to a position and then print. If you want to move the cursor first and then print using the `printw()` function, use `move()` first and then use `printw()`. I think instead of using `move()` and `printw()`, using `mvprintw()` is better, because you get the flexibility to manipulate.
  - `wprintw()` and `mvwprintw()`: These two functions are similar to the preceding two functions, except that they print in the corresponding window given as an argument.
  - `vwprintw()`: This function is similar to `vprintf()`. This can be used when a variable number of arguments are to be printed.

The earlier program demonstrates how easy it is to use `printw`. You just feed the message to be shown on the screen, then it does what you want. When we call `printw`, the information is really composed for an imaginary window, which isn't refreshed on the screen yet. The activity of `printw` is to refresh a couple of banners and information structures and compose the information to a support as compare to `stdscr()`. With a specific end goal of demonstrating it on the screen, we have to call `refresh()`, and advise the curses framework to dump the substance on the screen. The logic behind this is to enable the software engineer to do different updates on the imaginary screen or windows, and do a revive once all his/her screen refresh is finished.

 All these functions take the y coordinate first and after that, x in their arguments. A typical slip up by beginners is to pass x,y in a specific order. In the event that you are doing an excess amount of manipulations of (y, x) coordinates, consider isolating the screen into windows and control every one independently.

- `Move(row, col)`: The function `move()` moves the cursor to the desired position by passing row and column values.

- `Addch(ch | A_attribute)`: This function is utilized to print a character at the current cursor position on the stdscr window. We can pass attributes to print characters based on the attribute, for instance, `addch(ch |A_Bold |A_underline)` will print characters in bold and underlined. The following specified attributes characterized in `<ncurses.h>` can be passed to functions `attron()`, `attroff()`, and the `attrset()`, `attron()` functions turn on the attribute, and correspondingly `attoff()` turns off the attribute. To set the quality for a window, we should utilize `attrset()`, for instance, in the event that we compose `attrset(A_NORMAL)`, it sets a typical show with no feature for a window, and it turns off all attributes.

We can use multiple attributes at the same time using OR (|) with the characters passed to `addch()`. They are as shown in the following table:

Sr. No.	Attribute name	Attribute use
1	A_NORMAL	Normal display (no highlight)
2	A_UNDERLINE	Underlining
3	A_BOLD	Extra bright or bold
4	A_PROTECT	Protected mode
5	A_INVIS	Invisible or blank mode
6	A_ALTCHARSET	Alternate character set
7	A_CHARTEXT	Bit-mask to extract a character
8	A_DIM	Half bright
9	A_BLINK	Blinking
10	A_REVERSE	Reverse video
11	A_STANDOUT	Best highlighting mode of the Terminal
12	COLOR_PAIR(n)	Color-pair number n

If we want to print a character in a specific location or cursor position, we can use the following functions, instead of using the `move()` and `addch()` functions:

- `mvaddch()`: This function is used to print characters at the desired location by passing the cursor location, for example, `mvaddch(row,col,ch)`

- `waddch()`: This function is useful for printing characters at the present cursor location in a specified window
- `mvwaddch()`: This function is used to print characters at a definite cursor location in a specific window by passing row, column, character, and window
- `refresh()`: This function checks the window and updates only the bit which has been changed. This improves execution and offers more significant flexibility. A beginners' common error is to not call `refresh()` after they did some refreshing through the `printw()` class of functions.
- `getch()`: This function sits tight for the client to press a key, unless you stipulated a timeout, and when the client presses a key, the matching integer number gets returned. At that point, we can check that the value came back with the constants characterized in `curses.h`, to compare against the keys you need. On the off chance that it is a normal character, the integer number value will be equal to the character, otherwise it restores a number which can be coordinated with the constants characterized in `curses.h`. For instance, if the client presses *F1*, the number returned is `265`. This can be checked utilizing the full scale `KEY_F()`, characterized in `curses.h`. This makes reading keys convenient and simple to oversee.
- `endwin()`: This function ends the curses mode, else our Terminal may behave unusually after the program stops. `endwin()` frees up the memory taken by the curses subsystem and its data structures, and puts the Terminal in normal mode. This function must be called when we are finished with the curses mode. A program should reliably call `endwin()` before quickly leaving or closing curses mode. This function restores `tty` modes, moves the cursor to the lower left-hand corner of the screen, and resets the Terminal into the best non-visual mode. Calling `revive()` or `doupdate()` after a short escape, makes the program go to visual mode. The `isendwin()` routine returns `TRUE` if `endwin()` has been called with no subsequent calls to `wrefresh()`.

To run this program in Ubuntu, ncurses should be installed on the system, otherwise during compilation, we will get an error stating `ncurses.h:no such file or directory` and compilation will terminate. Use the following command to install ncurses:

```
sudo apt-get install libncurses5-dev libncursesw5-dev
```

The preceding command installs the latest version of the ncurses library onto the system. Once installation is done, open Visual Studio Code, go to **File**, and click on **New File**—it opens up a new untitled page. Write code as in the earlier example and save it at your desired location. Rename the file and give it an extension of .c or whatever suits your requirements. In this example, we created a file called IntoToNcurses.c. Run the following command to execute this program.

To compile a program, we use the following command syntax:

```
gcc  <Program_name_with_Extension> -o <Out_FileName> -lncurses
```

Here is an example:

```
gcc IntroToNcurses.c -o ExampleOfNcurses -lncurses
```

The output for the preceding command can be seen in the following screenshot:

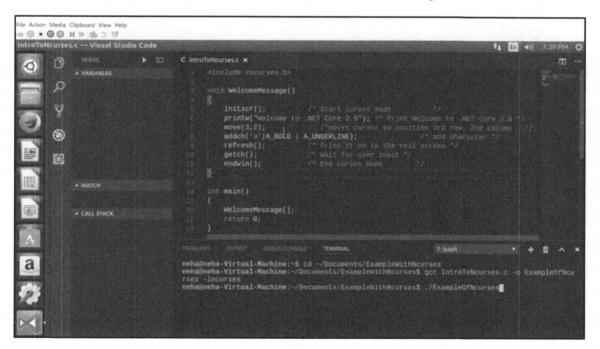

In the preceding example, we are passing our C program with the extension .c. After the -o command, we pass the output, or rather the compiled filename. Here, we can give it any name we want, as we did with ExampleOfNcurses in this example. To include the ncurses library, we have to link it during compilation using -lncurses, otherwise the compilation will fail with the error undefined reference to functions, as those functions are ncurses functions.

Once compilation is successful, it creates an output file, as shown in the following screenshot:

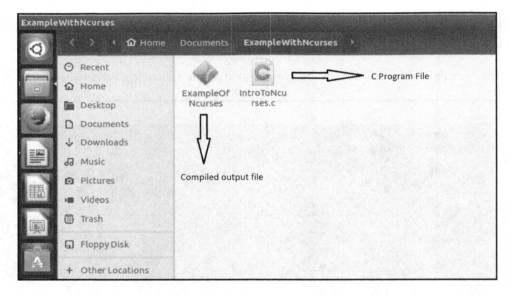

We can run our program after the compilation is successful and the output file is created in the same folder. On the Terminal, pass the output filename as ./hello to execute the program, as shown in the following screenshot:

Interop with existing native and Mono libraries

Code reusability is one of the key principles in programming. For example, in an application we may use a certain functionality multiple times, so we keep it in a useful place and refer it from that place, whenever we need it in our application. Now, suppose our application implemented some common functionality which we can use in other applications, in this case, instead of writing the same logic again, we can create a library. It is easily distributable and reusable.

Asp.NET Core supports cross-platform programming, so any Linux user who has built many reusable libraries, API-like console support, and filesystem access, and wants to use them while writing code in ASP.NET Core, can access them. In this section, we will see how to access these native libraries (.dll) and Mono libraries (.so) in the program.

Common Language Infrastructure (**CLI**) helps to interoperate with existing code. We need to handle three basic problems to get things to work. First, where and how to specify the library, second, determining which function we want to invoke, and third, passing parameters. **Common Language Runtime** (**CLR**) provides Platform Invocation services—we call it P/Invoke. It enables managed code to call C, C++ functions in native libraries (DLLs). Let's discuss what Platform Invoke is and how to use it.

Platform Invoke (P/Invoke)

P/Invoke allows us to access structures and functions of unmanaged libraries from our managed code ASP.NET Core 2.0. To use P/Invoke API, we use the `System.Runtime.InteropServices` namespace. This namespace allows us to access attributes the way we want, to use them with native components. The `DllImport` attribute is used for the declaration.

If you want to dig more into the details, online resources are available at: `http://www.pinvoke.net` . It has all the functions which are widely used.

For example: `AllowSetForegroundWindow (user32)`—this enables the mentioned process to set the foreground window by utilizing the `SetForegroundWindow` method; the only condition is that the calling process should be able to set the foreground window. In C# code, we will write it as:

```
[DllImport("user32.dll")]
static extern bool AllowSetForegroundWindow(int dwProcessId);
```

The following diagram demonstrates where Interop stands between native and managed code:

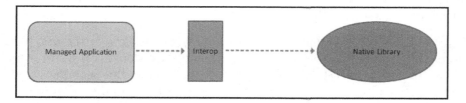

For example, if we want to use the `AnyPopup()` method of `user32.dll`, we use it as follows:

```
using System.Runtime.InteropServices;
public class Demo
{
    // Import user32.dll (contains the method we need) and define
    // the method corresponding to the native method
    [DllImport("user32.dll")]
    static extern bool AnyPopup();

    public static void Main(string[] args)
    {
        // Invoke the method as a regular managed method.
        AnyPopup();
    }
}
```

In this program, we used the `DllImport` attribute which calls the **dynamic-link library (DLL)**, and we can use all these methods inside this DLL which is decorated with the `_declspec(dllexport)` keyword or `extern "c"`. We will discuss more about the import and export of methods from the library in the following section.

DLLImport attribute

The attribute, `[DllImport()]`, falls under the `DllImportAttribute` class. It provides the information required to call a function exported from an unmanaged DLL. The minimum prerequisite is that we should pass the name of the DLL which contains the entry point. We can apply this attribute straightforwardly to C# and C++ function definitions. Let's check what the `DllImport` attribute has inside it. In the code window, click on `DllImport` and press the *F12* key (referred to as the go-to definition). This key is bound to the de-compile command in Visual Studio and will de-compile the selected type, if it can. Upon de-compilation, Visual Studio will display the de-compiled code in a new window. In the de-compiled code of `DllImport`, we can see each and every parameter. The code is very well commented and self-explanatory, as can be seen here:

```
namespace System.Runtime.InteropServices
{
    //
    // Summary:
    // Indicates that the attributed method is exposed by an unmanaged
        dynamic-link
    // library (DLL) as a static entry point.
    [AttributeUsage(AttributeTargets.Method, Inherited = false)]
```

```csharp
public sealed class DllImportAttribute : Attribute
{
    //
    // Summary:
    // Enables or disables best-fit mapping behavior when
       converting Unicode characters
    // to ANSI characters.
    public bool BestFitMapping;
    //
    // Summary:
    // Indicates the calling convention of an entry point.
    public CallingConvention CallingConvention;
    //
    // Summary:
    // Indicates how to marshal string parameters to the method and
       controls name mangling.
    public CharSet CharSet;
    //
    // Summary:
    // Indicates the name or ordinal of the DLL entry point to be
       called.
    public string EntryPoint;
    //
    // Summary:
    // Controls whether the
       System.Runtime.InteropServices.DllImportAttribute.CharSet
    // field causes the common language runtime to search an
       unmanaged DLL for entry-point
    // names other than the one specified.
    public bool ExactSpelling;
    //
    // Summary:
    // Indicates whether unmanaged methods that have HRESULT or
       retval return values
    // are directly translated or whether HRESULT or retval return
       values are automatically
    // converted to exceptions.
    public bool PreserveSig;
    //
    // Summary:
    // Indicates whether the callee calls the SetLastError Win32
       API function before
    // returning from the attributed method.
    public bool SetLastError;
    //
    // Summary:
    // Enables or disables the throwing of an exception on an
       unmappable Unicode character
```

```
        // that is converted to an ANSI "?" character.
        public bool ThrowOnUnmappableChar;

        //
        // Summary:
        // Initializes a new instance of the
           System.Runtime.InteropServices.DllImportAttribute
        // class with the name of the DLL containing the method to
           import.
        //
        // Parameters:
        // dllName:
        // The name of the DLL that contains the unmanaged method. This
           can include an assembly
        // display name, if the DLL is included in an assembly.
        public DllImportAttribute(string dllName);

        //
        // Summary:
        // Gets the name of the DLL file that contains the entry point.
        //
        // Returns:
        // The name of the DLL file that contains the entry point.
        public string Value { get; }
    }
}
```

We can characterize the following attributes with the DLL name:

- ThrowOnUnmappableChar: This field is False by default, which means the ThrowOnUnmappableChar field is disabled. Best-fit mapping empowers the Interop marshaler to give a nearby coordinating character when no correct match exists, every time the Interop marshaler changes over an unmappable character. For example, the marshaler changes over the Unicode character into c for unmanaged techniques that acknowledge ANSI characters. A few characters do not have a best-fit portrayal; these are called unmappable characters. These unmappable characters are typically changed over to the default ? ANSI character.

- SetLastError: By default, SetLastError is set to false, but in Visual Basic it is set to true by default. GetLastError is called by runtime marshaler and it caches the return value so it is not overwritten by other API calls. You can recover the error code by calling GetLastWin32Error.

- ExactSpelling: The ExactSpelling field, as the name suggests, impacts the behavior of the CharSet field to figure out the exact entry point name to invoke. If the ExactSpelling field is set to False, Platform Invoke looks for the unmangled alias first; if the unmangled alias is not found, then it will look for the mangled name.
- BestFitMapping: By default, the BestFitMapping field is true. On the off chance that this field is true, it overrides any level settings for System.Runtime.InteropServices.BestFitMappingAttribute. Best-fit mapping empowers the Interop marshaler to give a nearby matching character when no correct match exists. For instance, the marshaler changes over the Unicode copyright character to c for unmanaged functions that acknowledge ANSI characters. A few characters do not have a best-fit representation, and these characters are called unmappable. Unmappable characters are generally changed over to the default ? ANSI character.
- CallingConvention: Specifies the calling convention required to call methods implemented in unmanaged code. It is defined as an enumeration. The values of this enumeration are used to specify the calling conventions. This determines how a function is called, for example, the argument passing order behaviour is set to right to left, or stack maintenance responsibility such as the Calling function pops the arguments from the stack, and so on. There are fundamentally five calling convention fields: Cdecl, StdCall, FastCall, ThisCall, and Winapi. The default is StdCall for unmanaged functions with P/Invoke. More about this can be read at: https://msdn.microsoft.com/en-us/library/system.runtime.interopservices.callingconvention(v=vs.110).aspx.
- StdCall: The callee cleans the stack. To call unmanaged functions with Platform Invoke, this is the default convention.
- Cdecl: This empowers calling functions with variable args, which means it is good to use for functions that use a variable number of parameters, for example, on the Windows platform, the System.Runtime.InteropServices.CallingConvention.Cdecl convention will act as: Argument-passing order | right to left
- Winapi: This part isn't really a calling convention, rather it utilizes the default platform calling convention. For instance, in Windows, the default is StdCall, and on Windows CE .NET, it is Cdecl.
- ThisCall: The primary parameter is the pointer and is put away in register ECX. Other parameters are pushed on the stack. This calling convention is utilized to call functions on classes exported from an unmanaged DLL.

- CharSet: It determines the marshaling conduct of string parameters and is useful for indicating which entry point name to invoke (the correct name given or a name finishing with net or As). The default list part for C# is CharSet.Ansi and the default count part for C++ is CharSet.

- Entrypoint: You can determine the entry point name by providing a string showing the name of the DLL containing the entry point, or you can recognize the entry point by its ordinal. Ordinals are prefixed with the # sign. We can utilize the DllImportAttribute.EntryPoint field to indicate a DLL function by name or ordinal. On the off chance that the name of the function in your function definition is the same as the entry point in the DLL, you don't need to expressly recognize the function with the EntryPoint field. Utilize syntax to demonstrate a name or ordinal:

```
[DllImport("dllname", EntryPoint="MethodName")]
[DllImport("dllname", EntryPoint="#XYZ")]
```

Notice that you should prefix an ordinal with the pound sign (#). To know the entry point of DLL, we can use DUMPBIN.exe also. Just open the Developer Command Prompt and go to the DLL location and type the command, DUMPBIN /EXPORTS ExampleDLL.dll. Running this command returns information about the entry point and functions of DLL, shown as follows:

It gives all the information about DLL such as:

- It has one ordinal base
- It has three functions
- The names of functions and their ordinal value

There are many commands which we can use to get information about DLL. To find out all the commands, enter the following command, `Dumpbin.exe`. It gives us a list of commands that we can use.

Certain Unicode characters are changed over to risky characters, for example, the oblique punctuation line \ character, which can unintentionally change a way. By setting the `ThrowOnUnmappableChar` field to genuine, you can flag the nearness of an unmappable character to the guest by tossing a special case.

You can't change the default values given by the `BestFitMapping` and `ThrowOnUnmappableChar` fields when passing a managed array whose components are ANSI characters or LPSTRs to an unmanaged safe exhibit. Best-fit mapping is constantly empowered and no special case is tossed. Know that this blend can trade-off your security information.

Interop with existing native libraries with example

Let's create DLL and create a header file (`.h`) inside it using C++, and we will see how we can consume it in our .NET Core application. In the following example, we created a DLL project for example, calling it `ExampleDLL`. Create a source `.cpp` file and a header file. Open the header file and write the following code, which returns the sum of two values. To consume public data and functions in class, we have to add the keyword `_declspec(dllexport)` before the public member which we want to consume from outside. While creating a DLL, we usually add the header file which contains the function or class prototype and we can export this using the `__declspec(dllexport)` keyword, while doing a declaration in the header file.

The named header file is `Calculate`, and the method name is `Sum` which takes two variables, integer `a` and integer `b`. Build this solution and open the project location. We can find DLL inside the debug folder:

```
#ifndef Calculate
#define Calculate

extern "C"
{
   __declspec(dllexport)int Sum(int a, int b)
   {
     return a + b;
   }
}

#endif
```

Add the preceding code in the `Calculate.h` file, as shown in the following screenshot:

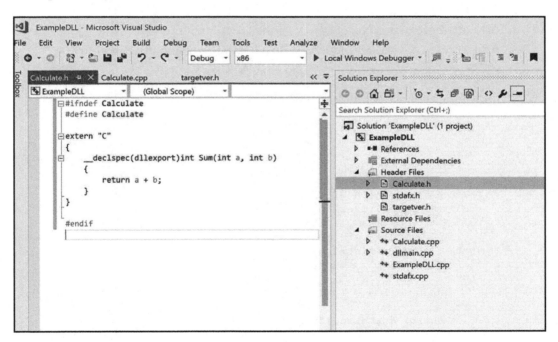

This DLL is created inside the debug folder of the `ExampleDLL` project:

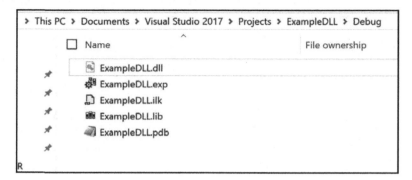

Now we have our C++ DLL ready to be consumed from C# code. For example, I am creating a C# console application and we just need three lines of code to consume C++ DLL:

1. Add namespace using `System.Runtime.InteropServices;`
2. Add attribute using `[DllImport(@"<DLL Location>")]`
3. Add `static extern` functions with a compatible signature in your C# code, `public static extern int Sum(int a, int b);`

The C# script for the same is as follows:

```
using System.Runtime.InteropServices;

class Program

    {
        //Insert file path of dll you want to import
        [DllImport(@"C:\Users\neshriv\Documents\Visual Studio
        2017\Projects\ExampleDLL\Debug\ExampleDLL.dll")]
        public static extern int Sum(int a, int b);
        static void Main(string[] args)
        {

            int sumValue = Sum(3, 4);

            Console.WriteLine("Sum of 3 and 4 is {0}",sumValue);

            Console.ReadKey();

        }

    }
```

The result is as follows:

In the preceding section, we saw how to consume native libraries in a DLL. In this section, let's take the example of a Mono library. We will create a .so file in Ubuntu and will consume it from .NET Core. We will see the backward compatibility of .NET Core.

Mono is an open source development platform in light of the .NET Framework; it enables engineers to fabricate cross-platform applications with enhanced designer efficiency. Mono's .NET execution depends on the **Ecma (Ecma International—European association for standardizing information and communication systems**) norms for C# and the Common Language Infrastructure. Mono incorporates both engineer devices and the foundation expected to run .NET customer and server applications. Mono works cross platform, and runs on Linux, Microsoft Windows, and many others. All Mono dialects take advantage from many highlights of the runtime, similar to programmed memory administration, reflection, generics, and threading. Its highlights enable us to focus on composing your application, as opposed to composing framework foundation code.

In this example, we are creating a simple library which displays an integer value.

The code is as follows:

```
# include<stdio.h>

int hello()
{
   return 15;
}
```

Run the following command in the Terminal to create the .so file:

```
gcc -shared -o libHelloSO.so -fPIC HelloSOLib.c
```

In the preceding command, -shared -o creates an (.o) object file and from the object file creates a .so file. -fPIC is used to declare a flag for the position independent code. -fPIC generates position-independent code which can be loaded from any memory location at runtime, so we can access static or global variables and methods at runtime.

The preceding command can be seen in the following screenshot:

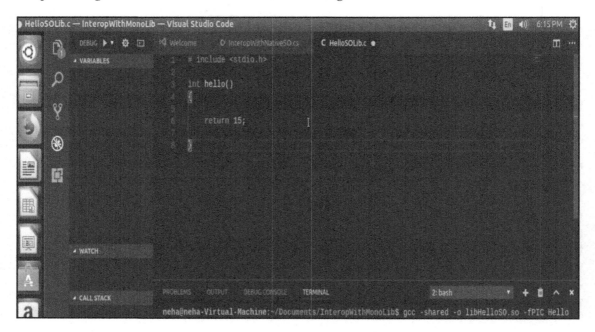

Now we will see how to consume this .so file in C# code. We created a C# file and added the namespace, system.Runtime.InteropServices, and gave the path of the .so file inside the DLLImport attribute.

The code is as follows:

```csharp
Using System;
Using System.Runtime.InteropServices;

Namespace Hello
{
  Class Program
  {
    [DllImport("/home/neha/Documents/InteroWithMonoLib/libHelloSO.so")]
    Private static extern int hello()
    Static void Main(string[] args)
    {
      int a = hello();
      Console.WriteLine(a);
    }
  }
}
```

Now, when we are done with the code and `DLLImport`, let's discuss Mono, which we will use to create our executable and run this application. Mono is an open source tool which is created by the Microsoft subsidiary, Xamarin. It is a tool which makes the Linux developer's life easy if they want to run Microsoft .NET applications on Linux or on any other cross platform. The latest version at the time of writing this book is Mono 5.4.0, which was released in October 2017. This version supports the Core API of .NET Framework and also C# 7.0. Mono provides several command line utilities, a few of the main useful commands are:

- **Mono**: It is a **just-in-time (JIT)** compiler and it supports both 32-bit and 64-bit types of systems. It also supports multiple platforms such as Microsoft Windows, Sun Solaris, Android, Apple iOS, macOS, Linux, Sony PlayStation, and so on. Mono runtime offers Code Execution, Garbage Collection, Code Generation, Exception Handling, OS interface, Thread management, Console access, and Security System, Program isolation using AppDomain. It allows a project to be extended in C# by reusing all existing C, C++ code libraries. As we said earlier, it is a JIT compiler. Since we have `ngen.exe` in Microsoft.NET to generate a pre-compiled code, which reduces the start up time, we use the following command with Mono to compile assemblies:

  ```
  mono -O=all --aot <exe name>
  ```

  In the preceding command, `-O=all` instructs to enable all optimizations, then the Mono command tells Mono to compile the code to native code, `--aot` for a precompiled image

- **MCS:** It's a C# compiler. Though many versions of compiler are available which are specific to the version, for example, `gmcs` compiler targets 2.0 mscorelib, `smcs` targets 2.1 mscorelib and moonlight applications (Silverlight implementation for mainly Linux), while `dmcs` targets 4.0 mscorlib. Now, the new compiler version MCS is present which takes the latest version by default. We can also specify which version we want to use. MCS runs with Mono runtime on a Linux machine, and with both .NET and Mono runtime on a Windows machine.
- **Global Assembly Cache tool (Gacutil)**: This tool is used for maintaining versions of assemblies in a system's global assembly cache.
- **XSP**: The web service and web application server of Mono.
- **mono-config**: The format configuration of Mono runtime.

Install Mono using the following command. When we use `mcs`, it will install the latest version:

```
sudo apt install mono-mcs
```

Compile this C# program in Visual Studio Code using the following command; it creates an `.exe` file at the same location from where we opened the Terminal:

```
mcs -out:helloNative.exe InteropWithNativeSO.cs
```

Now, it's time to run and check if it is displaying the value `15`, which we have passed in our `.so` file, as shown in the following screenshot:

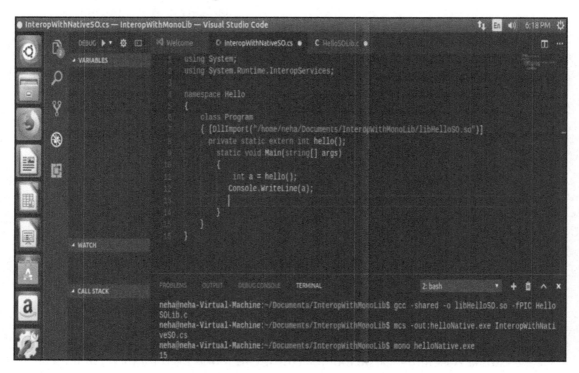

To run `helloNative.exe`, use the following command:

```
mono helloNative.exe
```

When not to use P/Invoke

Utilizing P/Invoke isn't fitting for all C-style methods in DLLs. Let's take an example where we create a string in a C++ program and display it in a C# application:

```
#include "stdafx.h"

const char * HelloMsg()
{
  char * msg = "Hello .NET Core.";
  return msg;
}
int main()
{
  printf(HelloMsg());
}
```

Now, using P/Invoke, pass the library in the `DllImport` attribute:

```
[DllImport("HelloMsgLib.so")]
public static extern char *  HelloMsg();
```

The trouble here is that we can't erase the memory for the unmanaged string returned by `msg`. Different methods called through P/Invoke restore a pointer and do not need to be deallocated by the client. For this situation, utilizing the marsheling is a more suitable approach.

Building a sample native library (C++)

In the previous section, we learned about cross-platform implementation, and how to Interop with existing native and Mono libraries. To demonstrate interoperability, we created small sample applications. Let's start with building our first native library in C++. Follow these steps:

1. Open Visual Studio and select **Windows Desktop** under **Visual C++** and select the project type **Dynamic-Link Library (DLL)**. In this example, we name the project `ExampleDLL` and provide the location where we want to create the project:

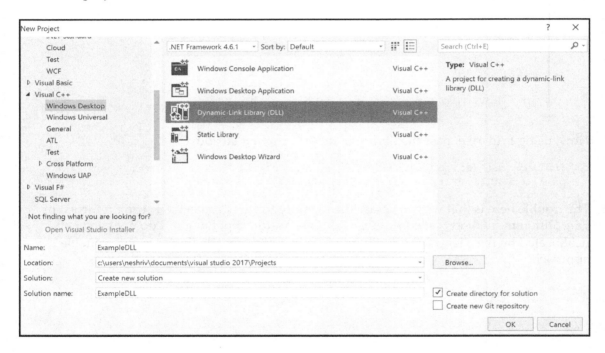

2. Right-click on the header files folder and create a new header file. In this example, we named it `Calculate.h`. The `Calculate` header file contains mathematical operations such as the summation of two integer numbers, multiplication, and division:

```
#ifndef Calculate
#define Calculate

extern "C"
{
  __declspec(dllexport)int Sum(int a,  int b)
  {
    return a + b;
  }
  __declspec(dllexport) int Multiply(int number1, int number2)
  {
    int result = number1 * number2;
    return result;
  }
  __declspec(dllexport) double divide(int number1, int number2)
  {
    double result = 0.0;
    if (number2 != 0)
    result = number1 / number2;
    return result;
  }
}
#endif
```

In the preceding example, we defined a header called `Calculate`.

3. `extern "C"` is used to instruct that the compiler will use the C function naming convention, not C++. Most code uses this directive because C function names are clearer to understand than C++. `__declspec(dllexport)` is utilized for export. In Microsoft's new versions of compiler, we can export data, functions, classes, or class member functions from a DLL utilizing this keyword, `__declspec(dllexport)`, the export directive to the object file, so we don't have to utilize a `.def` record. This accommodation is most obvious when endeavoring to export decorated C++ function names. Since there is no standard specification for name decoration, the name of an exported function may change between compiler versions. To export functions, the `__declspec(dllexport)` keyword must appear to the left side of the calling-convention keyword, if a keyword is indicated, for instance: `__declspec(dllexport)int Sum(int a, int b)`.

To export all public data members and functions in a class, the keyword must appear to the left side of the class name, as shown here:

```
Class __declspec(dllexport)int Calculations : public CPPObj {
Class definition};.
```

When building your DLL, we normally make a header file that contains the function models, as well as classes we are trading, and include `__declspec(dllexport)` to the announcements in the header file. To make our code more intelligible, we can define a macro for `__declspec(dllexport)` and use the macro with each symbol we are sending out:

```
# define DLLExplort __declspec(dllexport):
```

4. In the preceding example, we created a sample native library, and now we will see how we can access it. In the preceding code, we used
__declspec(dllexport); to acccess this DLL, we will use DllImport. Click on **Add | New Project**; under C#, select **.NET Core Console Application**. In this example, we called it InteropWithCS. Open the solution and add the following code:

```
using System;
using System.Runtime.InteropServices;
namespace InteropWithCS
{
    class Program
    {
        [DllImport(@"C:\Users\neshriv\Documents\Visual Studio
        2017\Projects\ExampleDLL\Debug\ExampleDLL.dll")]

        static extern int Multiply(int number1, int number2);

        [DllImport(@"C:\Users\neshriv\Documents\Visual Studio
        2017\Projects\ExampleDLL\Debug\ExampleDLL.dll")]

        static extern double divide(int number1, int number2);

        [DllImport(@"C:\Users\neshriv\Documents\Visual Studio
        2017\Projects\ExampleDLL\Debug\ExampleDLL.dll")]

        static extern int Sum(int a, int b);
        static void Main(string[] args)
        {

            Console.WriteLine("Enter number1");
            int number1 = Convert.ToInt32(Console.ReadLine());
            Console.WriteLine("Enter number2");
            int number2 = Convert.ToInt32(Console.ReadLine());
            Console.WriteLine("Select Operation : 1 for Sum , 2 for
            multiply, 3 for divide");
            int option = Convert.ToInt32(Console.ReadLine());
            int result ;
            switch (option)
            {
                case 1:
                    result = Sum(number1, number2);
                    Console.WriteLine("You have selected Sum
                    operation!
                    Sum is : " + result);
                    Console.ReadLine();
```

```
                            break;
                    case 2:
                        result = Multiply(number1, number2);
                        Console.WriteLine("You have selected Sum
                        operation!
                        multiplication is : " + result);
                        Console.ReadLine();
                        break;
                    case 3:
                        double result1 = divide(number1, number2);
                        Console.WriteLine("You have selected Sum
                        operation!
                        division is : " + result1);
                        Console.ReadLine();
                        break;
                }

            }

        }

    }
```

5. In this example, we are using `ExampleDLL` and doing our calculations, taking input for `number1` and `number2` values. The user can select an operation—sum, multiply, or divide by pressing the corresponding number. On option number input, we check the user option, use switch case, and display the result:

```
Enter number1
6
Enter number2
6
Select Operation : 1 for Sum , 2 for multiply, 3 for divide
1
You have selected Sum operation! Sum is : 12
```

This simple application gives us an understanding of how to create our own native library in C or C++, and how to set functions which can be exported and accessed from other languages, such as C#. The intention of making it simple and using small functions, such as sum, and multiplication, for example, is to make you aware of the functionality, so that the user won't get distracted with the heavy logic of functions.

A sample application to implement new library and ncurses

Now that we know the fundamentals, let's start building a sample application which implements ncurses. We will create a C# application which imports a C library or we can say `.so` file. This library has implemented ncurses functions. P/Invoke allows us to use those ncurses functions in our C# application.

First, we will create a C program which implements ncurses functions using an ncurses header. Let's create an application which takes an input character; this character will be printed in a window, based on the number of rows and columns the user enters from the application where we will import this library. The function `drawCharOnWindow()` prints the character, based on the number of rows and columns present in the window; it takes character, row, and column as input parameters. We get the size of the window using the ncurses function, `getmaxyx()`, and if the user enters q, it quits the printing of the character. Open Visual Studio Code and write the following code:

```c
# include <stdio.h>
# include <ncurses.h>

int row, column, // current row and column (Top left is (0,0))
numberOfRows, // number of rows in current window
numberOfColumns; // number of columns in current window

void drawCharOnWindow(char drawChar, int row, int column)

{
  move(row, column); // ncurses call to move cursor to given row, given
  column

  delch(); //ncurses calls to replace character
  insch(drawChar); //under cursor by drawChar

  refresh(); // ncurses call to update screen
  row++; // go to next row
  // check for need to shift right or wrap around
```

```
    if (row == numberOfRows)
    {
      row = 0;
      column++;
      if (column == numberOfColumns) column = 0;
    }
  }
  void hello(int i, int j, char c)
  {
    initscr(); // ncurses call to initialize window
    refresh(); // curses call to implement all changes since last refresh
    while (1)
    {
      if (c == 'q') break; // quit?
      {
        drawCharOnWindow(c, i, j);
      }
    }
  }
}
```

Create a library using the following command. It will create a .so file at the location from where the Terminal is open, and we run this command:

gcc —shared —o libHelloSO.so —fPIC HelloSOLib.c —lncurses

Now, we will use this library from the C# program using Mono. The following example application takes input from the user for the character we will print and its location, row, and column value. To use the library which implemented ncurses and to use it in C# , we need to use the namespace, System.Runtime.InteropServices and import DLL, using the DllImport attribute:

```
using System;
using System.Runtime.InteropServices;

namespace Hello
{
    class Program
    {
        [DllImport("/home/neha/Documents/
        InteropWithMonoLib/libHelloSO.so")]
        private static extern void hello(int i, int j, int c);

        static void Main(string[] args)
        {
            Console.WriteLine("Enter Character you want to print:\n");
            char c = Convert.ToChar(Console.ReadLine());
            Console.WriteLine("Enter row numbers till where to want to
```

```
see pattern of character:\n");
int i = Convert.ToInt32(Console.ReadLine());
Console.WriteLine("Enter column numbers till where to want
to see pattern of character:\n");
int j = Convert.ToInt32(Console.ReadLine());
for (int a = 0; a < i; a++)
{
    for (int b = 0; b < j; b++)
    {
        hello(i, j, c);
    }
}
        }
    }
}
```

To create the .exe file, use the following Mono command:

```
mcs -out:helloNative.exe InteropWithNativeSO.cs
```

To run the program in Mono, use the following command:

```
mono helloNative.exe
```

We learned how to create an executable using Mono and run it; now, we will see how to create a .NET Core 2.0 console application. Open Visual Studio Code and set the location on the Terminal where we want to create the application, and run the following command for the console application:

```
dotnet new console
```

After the creation of the application, use the preceding code. Run this code using the following command:

```
dotnet run
```

It will take the input parameter, the character to print, row, and column location, and it will print that character in the window at the specified location, as shown here:

After passing this detail, it prints the character at the specified row and column on the screen, as follows:

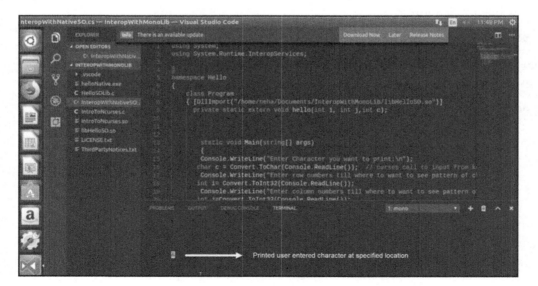

Summary

In this chapter, we learned about the ncurses library and how to use this library in C or C++ programs. Also, we learned about how to reuse libraries created in Ubuntu or on a Linux machine which implemented ncurses in a .NET Core 2.0 application, using P/Invoke. We have seen how Mono works efficiently with a Linux machine and makes programming easy in .NET Core 2.0, using C# for Linux user. The next chapter will be very interesting, and it will be where we will build our first game, Tic-Tac-Toe, using .NET Core and we will learn about its compilation, building, and testing.

3
Building Our First .NET Core Game – Tic-Tac-Toe

Learning is more fun if we do it while playing games. With this thought, let's continue our quest to learn .NET Core 2.0 by writing our very first game in .NET Core 2.0, Tic-Tac-Toe. In this chapter, we will understand the anatomy of the ASP.NET Core 2.0 application that we created in Chapter 1, *Getting Started*, and understand each file and its purpose in the application. Then, we will quickly understand the basics of SignalR Core, which is the technology we will use to write the game in .NET Core 2.0. We will then proceed with the quick setup of SignalR Core, followed by the design and coding of the basic Tic-Tac-Toe game, in which players can specify their own images instead of conventional *X* and *O*.

Here are the topics that we will cover in this chapter:

- Anatomy of ASP.NET Core 2.0 application
- Tic-Tac-Toe
- Game design
- SignalR Core
- Solution

Anatomy of an ASP.NET Core 2.0 application

In this section, we will discuss the *who is who and what is what* of the ASP.NET Core 2.0 application that we created in the *Creating a simple running code* section of Chapter 1, *Getting Started*. The idea is to understand the purpose and use of each file that comes with the MVC template when creating the application, so that we can make the best possible use of them when needed.

The following screenshot shows what our application structure looks like:

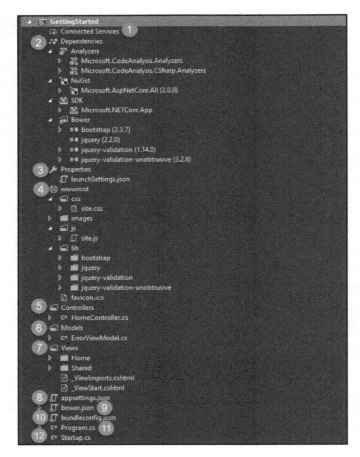

For ease of understanding, the items are numbered from 1 to 12. We will walk through each item and understand what they bring to the table:

1. **Connected Services**: This doesn't present itself as a physical file in the project template created by .NET Core 2.0 tooling, and is only visible when the project is opened from Visual Studio 2017 IDE; that is, it's a Visual Studio 2017 feature. The intent is to make it easier for developers to add connected services to their application. The services may be deployed on-premises or in the cloud. Earlier, this used be available as **Add Connected Service** in the project's, right-click context menu; now it's available as a node in **Solution Explorer** for web and mobile projects. One of the services that every ASP.NET Core web app can leverage is Application Insights. The entire comprehensive list of services can be found at `https://docs.microsoft.com/en-us/azure/#pivot=servicespanel=all`. If we click on the **Connected Services** node in **Solution Explorer**, we will see a new full page window in Visual Studio which has three tabs:

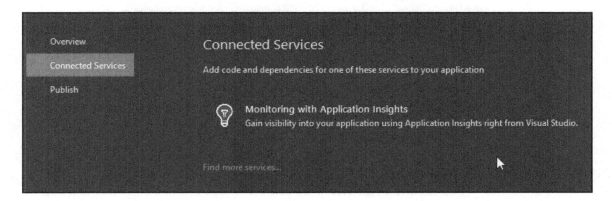

1. **Overview**: This tab is in the `GettingStarted` section of the ASP.NET Core app. It lists Microsoft's official documentation links for ASP.NET Core app development, adding services, and deploying it to the cloud.
2. **Connected Services**: This is the section that enables us to add connected services to the application. Right-click on the **Connected Services** node in **Solution Explorer**; we see a context menu item, **Add Connected Service**. If we click this item, it also navigates to the same place. We will add connected services in subsequent chapters, when we discuss Azure:

3. **Publish**: To publish the web app in the cloud or on-premises. We will discuss this further in a later chapter, when we publish our app in Azure.

- **Dependencies**: This node has been around in Visual Studio for a while now. Again, this isn't present as a physical file in the system. There is a tooling update in Visual Studio 2017, which categorizes the dependencies and groups them into the following:

    1. **Analyzers**: The analyzers are included in the project by default, as shown here:

    2. **NuGet**: The NuGet packages referred by the project are listed here. In the default ASP.NET Core 2.0 MVC template, we will see just one NuGet package called `Microsoft.AspNetCore.All` and that's awesome, as we no longer need to worry about versioning different packages and plumbing them to use in our app. `Microsoft.AspNetCore.All` is a metapackage; that is, it only references other packages. It references all ASP.NET Core packages and their dependencies, and all Entity Framework Core packages and their dependencies. The version of this package represents the ASP.NET Core and Entity Framework Core version. And the best part is that even though it's just one package, you can still go ahead and visualize all the packages that come with it alongside their dependencies:

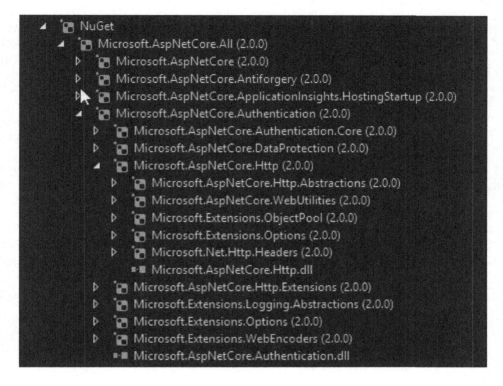

3. **SDK**: Displays the target SDK. For the default ASP.NET Core 2.0 app, it would be **Microsoft.NETCore.App**.

4. **Bower**: This is the package manager for the web. It helps manage all the client-related stuff, such as HTML, CSS, JavaScript, fonts, and images. All the client-side packages are listed here. In the default project template, we can see stuff such as **bootstrap**, **jquery**, and so on.

These are the four types of dependency that come with the default ASP.NET Core 2.0 MVC template. But we are not limited to these dependencies alone. Based on the package manager of choice, we may also have **node package manager** (**npm**) or other package managers as the dependency listed here. In this chapter, we will use npm to install the SignalR client package, as it is available through npm.

 The immediate question that comes to mind is what is Node.js? Node.js is a platform built on Chrome's JavaScript runtime engine for easily building fast and scalable applications. It uses an event-driven, non-blocking, asynchronous I/O model, which makes it lightweight and efficient, perfect for data-intensive (and non-CPU-intensive) real-time applications. So, npm is the package manager for JavaScript. To use npm, we need to install Node.js.

3. **Properties**: Double-clicking on the **Properties** node of the project in **Solution Explorer** takes us to the project properties page and, on expanding this, displays the launchSettings.json file, where all the launch/startup-related configurations are serialized and saved as JSON. The following is the default code:

```
"iisSettings": {
    "windowsAuthentication": false,
    "anonymousAuthentication": true,
    "iisExpress": {
        "applicationUrl": "http://localhost:52845/",
        "sslPort": 0
    }
},
"profiles": {
    "IIS Express": {
    "commandName": "IISExpress",
    "launchBrowser": true,
    "environmentVariables": {
    "ASPNETCORE_ENVIRONMENT": "Development"
    }
},
    "GettingStarted": {
    "commandName": "Project",
    "launchBrowser": true,
    "environmentVariables": {
        "ASPNETCORE_ENVIRONMENT": "Development"
    },
    "applicationUrl": "http://localhost:52846/"
    }
}
```

```
}
```

It's evident that the values in the preceding code match the **Debug** section of the properties page of the project:

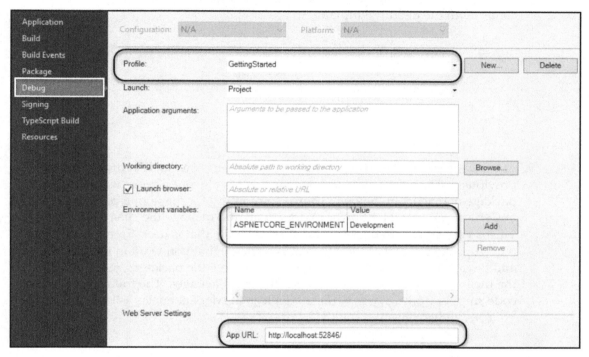

4. **wwwroot**: All client-side packages and images are part of this folder. Files in this folder are served as static content and can be bundled and minified to reduce payloads and page rendering by using `bundleconfig.json`. A few of the common folders are:
   - `css`: Contains cascading style sheets
   - `images`: Contains the image assets that are needed in the app
   - `js`: Contains JavaScript files
   - `lib`: Contains the client-side packages
5. **Controllers**: Contains the controllers as per the Model-View-Controller (MVC) architecture.
6. **Models**: Contains the models as per the MVC architecture.
7. **Views**: Contains the views as per the MVC architecture.

8. `appsettings.json`: The application settings for the application. It contains the key and value-based settings in JSON format. If you are an old school ASP.NET web developer, you can think of it as the `appSettings` section defined inside `web.config`. The following is the sample configuration for `Logging`, which comes with the default template:

```
{
    "Logging": {
    "IncludeScopes": false,
    "LogLevel": {
    "Default": "Warning"
    }
  }
}
```

9. `bower.json`: The Bower package manager is part of Visual Studio, as mentioned previously. This client-side package manager is one of the most widely-used package managers in the open source community for managing packages. `bower.json` is used by Bower to download and manage the client-side packages. This is very similar to the `packages.config` file that is used for managing NuGet packages. Just specify the package name that you want in the JSON file and Bower will do the rest. In case you do not see the packages, just right-click on the file in **Solution Explorer** and click **Restore Packages**. The following is the code snippet from `bower.json`, which lists the dependencies as `bootstrap`, `jquery`, and so on:

```
{
  "name": "asp.net",
  "private": true,
  "dependencies": {
    "bootstrap": "3.3.7",
    "jquery": "2.2.0",
    "jquery-validation": "1.14.0",
    "jquery-validation-unobtrusive": "3.2.6"
    }
}
```

In case you do not like this approach of adding the client-side dependency in the `bower.json` file, right-click on the `bower.json` file and click on **Manage Bower Packages**. This has a very similar user interface to the NuGet package manager and can be used in the same way. Just search the package and click **Install**. The following image shows the installed Bower packages in the project:

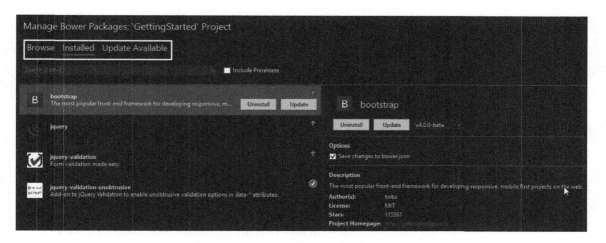

10. `bundleconfig.json`: This JSON file used to store the project bundling and minification configuration for the static content of the site, that is, scripts and styles. The following is what the default MVC project template, `bundleconfig.json`, looks like. The names and comments are intuitive to understand:

```
[
    {
        // The name and relative path of output minified css file.
        "outputFileName": "wwwroot/css/site.min.css",
        // An array of relative input file paths. Globbing
patterns
            supported
        "inputFiles": [
            "wwwroot/css/site.css"
        ]
    },
    {
        // The name and relative path of output minified
JavaScript
            file.
        "outputFileName": "wwwroot/js/site.min.js",
        // The array of relative input file paths.
        "inputFiles": [
            "wwwroot/js/site.js"
        ],
        // Optionally specify minification options
        "minify": {
            "enabled": true,
            "renameLocals": true
```

```
        },
        // Optionally generate .map file
        "sourceMap": false
    }
]
```

Bundling and minification are techniques to improve request load time:

- Bundling improves load time by reducing the number of requests sent to the server by the client to fetch static content; that is, CSS, JavaScript. Most major modern browsers limit the number of simultaneous connections for each hostname to six; that is to say, if six requests are being processed, any additional requests from the client for assets on the same hostname would be queued by the browser. With bundling, this issue is avoided, as all CSS files can be bundled as one file and, likewise, one file for JavaScript. This improves the first-time load performance. For subsequent requests, it's not much of an improvement, as the browser caches the files.
- Minification improves performance by reducing the size of the requested assets, that is, CSS and JavaScript, by removing unnecessary white spaces and comments, and shortening the variable names to one character. We have all seen the `jquery.min.js` file while doing web development. The `min` in the name is to help the user identify that it is the minified version of the file.

11. `Program.cs`: This is the main entry point to the ASP.NET Core 2.0 app. It has the minimum code needed to get the app up and running with the default configurations:

```
public class Program
{
    public static void Main(string[] args)
    {
        BuildWebHost(args).Run();
    }

    public static IWebHost BuildWebHost(string[] args) =>
        WebHost.CreateDefaultBuilder(args)
        .UseStartup<Startup>()
        .Build();
}
```

As we can see, this looks more like a console application and, actually, that is what it is—a console app. In its entry point `Main` method, it creates a web server, hosts the application, and starts listening to HTTP requests. Notice here that `BuildWebHost` is a method which returns an object that implements `IWebHost`, accepting a string array argument. This method is implemented as an expression bodied member, just to make the developers aware that the sole purpose of this method is to build the web host and no other code should be put here. The method follows the builder pattern to build the host. There are several methods that we can hook up, one after another, as needed, and they would be added to the object incrementally, one after the other. The `CreateDefaultBuilder` method builds the web host with the default configuration wired up from various configuration providers (such as JSON and environment variables, to name a few), sets the logging configuration, and sets up a Kestrel web server with IIS integration, which is good enough for the app to run. The `Build` method builds the object and returns. Notice the `UseStartup<Startup>` method call, which actually specifies the `Startup` class for the app. We will discuss this class next.

The **Builder pattern** is an object creation design pattern. It is one of the 23 well-known **Gang of Four (GoF)** design patterns. The intent behind this pattern is to separate the construction of a complex object from its representation, so that the same construction process can create different representations. To do so, this pattern builds a complex object using simple objects in a step-by-step approach.

12. `Startup.cs`: This is the class, where we define the request handling pipeline and configure the services needed by the application. Let's look at the code and then discuss it in depth:

```
public class Startup
{
    public Startup(IConfiguration configuration)
    {
        Configuration = configuration;
    }

    public IConfiguration Configuration { get; }

    // This method gets called by the runtime. Use this method to
        add services to the container.
    public void ConfigureServices(IServiceCollection services)
    {
        services.AddMvc();
    }
```

```
// This method gets called by the runtime. Use this method to
    configure the HTTP request pipeline.
public void Configure(IApplicationBuilder app,
IHostingEnvironment env)
{
    if (env.IsDevelopment())
    {
        app.UseDeveloperExceptionPage();
        app.UseBrowserLink();
    }
    else
    {
        app.UseExceptionHandler("/Home/Error");
    }
    app.UseStaticFiles();
    app.UseMvc(routes =>
    {
        routes.MapRoute(
            name: "default",
            template:
"{controller=Home}/{action=Index}/{id?}");
    });
}
}
```

The key takeaways from the class code are:

1. The class should be `public`.
2. The constructor has a dependency on `IConfiguration`, which is injected as the core service and assigned to the `public` property `Configuration` of type `IConfiguration`.
3. This makes `Configuration` a first class citizen of the ASP.NET Core application and can be easily used to read the `appSettings` value just by using this code: `Configuration["<KeyName>"]`.
4. There are only two public methods in the class:
   - `ConfigureServices`: This method is called by the runtime. This method is the place to add services to the container, such as MVC, antiforgery, application insight telemetry, authentication, authorization, localization, identity, and so on. There is a huge list of services available, which can be seen through IntelliSense. In the preceding code, we are c files, such as css, js, images, HTjust adding the MVC service, so that we can leverage all the MVC goodness in our app.

- `Configure`: As the comment in the code explains, this method is called by the runtime and is used to configure the HTTP request pipeline. In this method, we have access to the application builder and the hosting environment, which is another first class citizen of the .NET Core 2.0 app and is available in the container for injection into the objects that we construct. In the preceding code, which comes with the default MVC template, we can see the following:

  1. First, it checks whether the environment is for development or not. This is determined by the environment variable, `ASPNETCORE_ENVIRONMENT`. If its value is `Development`, it will detect the host environment to be `Development`; otherwise, it will be `Production`. If this environment variable is not available, it defaults the environment to `Production`. The variable can be set in the project properties page in the **Debug** section. The screenshot of the preceding properties section displays the **Environment variable** clearly.

  2. If the environment is `Development`, it tells the app to use the developer exception page by calling the `UseDeveloperExceptionPage()` method. The developer exception page gives a detailed error message with the exception stack trace to help the developer pinpoint the issue and resolve it. This should not be used in `Production`, as the exception information may be used by a hacker to attack your site. Also, your end user may not be a technical person, and may prefer to see a more user-friendly message than a .NET stack trace, so in production we use a custom error page, which is specified by calling the `UseExceptionHandler("/Home/Error");` method.

  3. During the development phase, you may want to test your web app against multiple browsers, and hence may want to open multiple browsers and browse the page to check for compatibility issues and refresh them when you make a fix. The `UseBrowserLink()` method helps you do just that. **Browser Link** is a feature in Visual Studio that creates a communication channel between the `Development` environment and one or more web browsers. We can use Browser Link to refresh the web application in several browsers at once.

2. Static files, such as `css`, `js`, images, HTML, and so on, which are placed in the `wwwroot` folder, are not servable by default. To make them servable, we need to call the `UseStaticFiles()` method.

3. Finally, the last piece of the code configures the MVC service (added in the `Configure` method) by specifying the default route.

4. To sum up, in this method we just configure the HTTP request pipeline using middleware. We will look at middleware in the next chapter, but for the time being, just think of them as HTTP modules in the earlier versions of ASP.NET. We added the services and then configured them as per our requirements using middleware. We will find three types of middleware configuration in the code samples:

   - `app.Run()`: The first `app.Run` delegate terminates the HTTP request pipeline. If you use `Run`, it expects the handler and hence the request is served back to the client. No further middleware will be called in the request path.

   - `app.Map*`: This extension is used as a convention for branching the pipeline. `Map` branches the request pipeline based on matches of the given request path. If the request path starts with the given path, the branch is executed.

   - `app.Use[Middleware]`: `Use` can be used to chain the middleware; that is, we can arrange them to execute one after another. `Use` can also be used to short-circuit the request pipeline as needed.

If this sounds scary, don't worry! We will discuss middleware, dependency injection, and containers in detail in the next chapter while developing our Let's Chat application.

Last but not least, the `.csproj` file has major and long-anticipated enhancements. The `.xproj` from .NET Core 1.0 is now gone and we have our familiar `.csproj` back in business with ASP.NET Core 2.0. It's better than earlier, as it is lightweight and easier to manage. Visual Studio 2017 also has a tooling update, which enables us to edit the `.csproj` file without having to unload the project and edit. This is super awesome. Just right-click on the project in **Solution Explorer** and then click `Edit <Project Name>.csproj`:

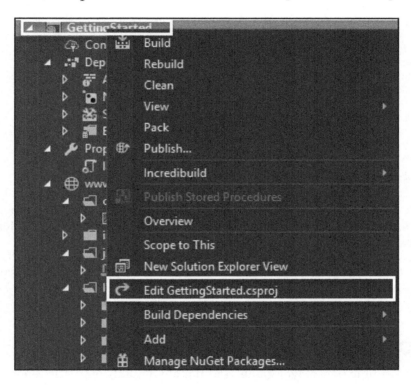

We will have the `.csproj` file opened as an XML file in the code editor, with the entire project still loaded. The following is the `.csproj` file code:

```
<Project Sdk="Microsoft.NET.Sdk.Web">
    <PropertyGroup>
        <TargetFramework>netcoreapp2.0</TargetFramework>
    </PropertyGroup>
    <ItemGroup>
        <PackageReference Include="Microsoft.AspNetCore.All"
        Version="2.0.0" />
    </ItemGroup>
    <ItemGroup>
        <DotNetCliToolReference
        Include="Microsoft.VisualStudio.Web.CodeGeneration.Tools"
        Version="2.0.0"          />
    </ItemGroup>
</Project>
```

It's very lean, with just `TargetFramework`, which is `netcoreapp2.0`; `PackageReference`, which has just one metapackage, `Microsoft.AspNetCore.All`; and `DotNetCliToolReference` included as part of `ItemGroup`. This is much better than the conventional `.csproj` file, where we had different build configurations, property groups, all the projects, DLL, NuGet package references, and all the files and folders that need to be included in the project, making it really hard to manage.

This concludes our basic anatomy of an ASP.NET Core 2.0 app. Let's get started with our game development in ASP.NET Core 2.0.

Tic-Tac-Toe

Tic-Tac-Toe is a simple two-player game, traditionally with its marks as *X* and *O*. Each player places his/her mark in a space and alternate turns in a 3×3 grid. The player who succeeds in placing three of their marks in a horizontal, vertical, or diagonal row wins the game.

This is what the pen and pencil game board looks like. In the following illustration, the player with the **X** marker is the winner:

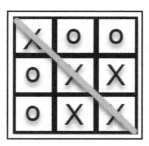

Requirement specifications

In this chapter, we will create a two-player Tic-Tac-Toe game with the following basic requirements:

1. As a player, I should be able to register with my name and display a picture
2. As a player, I should be able to find an opponent, that is, the second player to play against
3. The first two players to find opponents should be paired as opponents in the game
4. The decision as to which player gets the chance to make the first move should be fair
5. As a player, I should be able to use my display picture as my mark, rather than the conventional X and O
6. The decision as to who wins should be made fairly
7. In future, we want multiple players playing online simultaneously

Now that we have the requirement specifications in place, let's see the activity flow of the game and come up with a flowchart. The following is a rough flowchart of the game workflow:

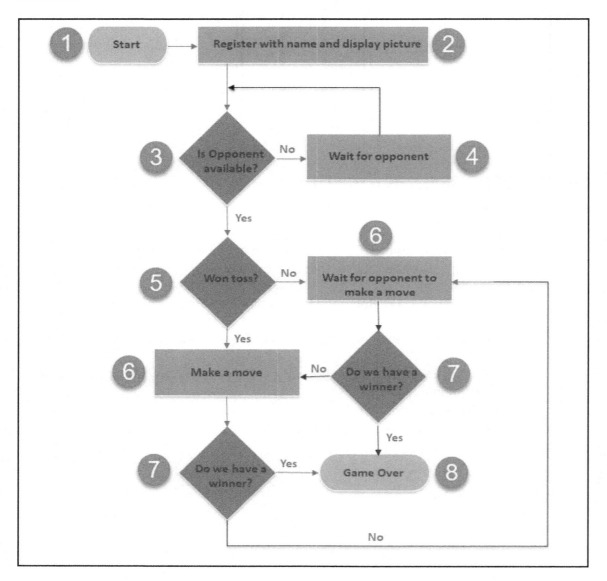

1. **Start**: This is the start of the flow. The player browses the game site URL. It is being conceptualized as a site, since in future we want to allow multiple players to play simultaneously online (requirement *Step 7*).

2. **Register with name and display picture**: The player registers himself/herself with a name and display picture (requirement *Step 1*).

3. **Is Opponent available?:** The player finds an opponent to play against. If an opponent is found, the game can start with a toss; otherwise, the player needs to wait for the opponent (requirement *Steps 2* and *3*).

4. **Wait for opponent**: There may be a scenario where the player is alone and registered with no one to play against, so the player needs to wait until another player registers and looks for an opponent (requirement *Steps 2* and *3*).

5. **Won toss?**: Once the players are paired as opponents, the game starts and one of the players gets the opportunity to make the first move. To keep this fair, we will have a toss. The player may either win the toss or lose the toss (requirement *Step 4*).

6. **Make a move/Wait for opponent to make a move**: The player winning the toss gets the first move, while their opponent would waits for the first player to make their move.

7. **Do we have a winner?**: After every move, we check whether the win/draw criteria have been met and check whether we have a winner. If not, then the game continues with each player moving alternately until the game ends (requirement *Step 6*).

8. **Game Over**: Finally, the players will either run out of moves or a player will win the game.

As we can see, the game will be played only in *Steps 6* and *7* of the flowchart. The other steps are required only for setting up the game. Also, notice that this flow covers all our requirements.

Designing the game

Looking at the preceding flow chart, which meets our requirements, we know we need to develop the following in the ASP.NET Core 2.0 application to constitute a basic two-player Tic-Tac-Toe game:

1. A web page where players can go and register themselves with their name and display a picture

2. A module to find an opponent to play against

3. A module to simulate a coin toss to ensure fairness in giving players the option of making the first move

4. The UI for the Tic-Tac-Toe game board in the web page, that is, a 3×3 grid where players can place their image

5. Logic to indicate to the player whether it's their turn or the opponent's turn

6. A module to show the opponent and player the move that was made

7. A mechanism to ensure that the player and opponent's board are in sync with their moves

8. Logic to check whether the game is over

9. Logic to determine the winner

Sounds simple enough! Let's see how we can design and implement each of the preceding points by using ASP.NET Core 2.0 goodness:

1. **Web page for registration:** We have multiple options available to code this. We can either use a static HTML page, or a regular .cshtml view of MVC, or the new Razor Pages introduced by ASP.NET Core 2.0. Since we will be working extensively with Razor Pages in the next chapter, we will use the .cshtml Razor view to create the UI of the game.

2. **Opponent-finding module:** When a player registers, we can store his details somewhere on the server so the server knows how many players are registered to play. When a player finds an opponent, we can pair them as opponents based on their registration time. The problem with just relying on registered users, though, is when a player registers and closes the browser window knowingly or unknowingly, or decides not to play the game after registering. So, we need to ensure that we pair up only those players who are registered, are actively connected to the server, and are looking for an opponent to play the game with. If a player disconnects in the middle of the game, award the game to the opponent and inform them that the opponent has disconnected. We will need to do additional housekeeping to refresh the registered players in the server as new players join and existing players disconnect. To check whether a user is connected or not, we may need to perform additional housekeeping by writing additional code or making use of sessions.

3. **Simulate coin toss:** There are many ways to simulate a coin toss, such as generating a random number between two numbers and seeing whether it's even or odd. In our case, to keep things simple, we will generate a random number, either 0 or 1. If it's 0, it's heads; otherwise, it's tails.

4. **UI for game board:** As already discussed, we will be using the standard MVC Razor view to create the registration form as well as the Tic-Tac-Toe game board user interface. Designing the game board for Tic-Tac-Toe is rather simple with CSS; we just need to get the correct box style and arrange the boxes in a 3×3 grid. To place the player's image on the board, we pass the player image to each of the players and update the box background style to the image when the user clicks on that grid box. The challenge we can see here is how we will keep the game board of both the players in sync at any given time. Although the individual player and server know which player has a marker placed at which position, the opponent needs to have the same picture of the game board. This is something that the server needs to inform both players of after every turn.

5. **Logic to indicate whose turn it is:** Although the server knows the toss result, it needs to inform one player to make a move and the other to wait for the other player to make a move. And after each turn, the server needs to inform both players (clients) about the turn, so the server has to push data to the clients after every move.

6. **Module to show the players the move that was made:** Like the preceding point, it is again the server's responsibility to update the players about the last move and ensure both players have a game board view after each move.

The last two modules are straightforward. We need to check whether the game is over and we have a winner. The interesting part of our discussion is that in *Steps 2, 4, 5,* and *6*, we came across scenarios where the server needs to push data to the client. This is something that has already been made incredibly easy by the ASP.NET team who developed a library called SignalR. So, we will use SignalR to cover these scenarios. Before we dive into coding, let's understand what SignalR is, how it works, and how it saves us from writing all this stuff ourselves.

SignalR

SignalR is a library for ASP.NET developers for developing real-time web experiences. In traditional web applications, the client makes requests and the server responds. With SignalR, we have the ability to push the content from the server to the connected clients in real time. SignalR provides a simple API for creating server-to-client remote procedure calls that call JavaScript functions in client browsers (and other client platforms) from server-side .NET code. Anywhere in an application, if we need to refresh the browser for fresh data or have polling code wriiten to refresh the data, SignalR may be a good candidate for this. Some real-world applications of SignalR are chat applications where multiple users can chat, dashboards for monitoring, stock ticker applications that update a stock price as and when it changes, and multiplayer games. Basically, for any app that needs to display live data, SignalR makes it incredibly simple to broadcast a message to all clients, a group of clients, or a specific client as needed.

SignalR transport mechanisms

SignalR connects through WebSockets, Server-Sent Events, Forever Frames, and long polling. The following is a short description of each of these transport mechanisms:

- **WebSockets**: WebSockets is an advanced computer communication protocol that enables you to open an interactive communication session between the user's browser and a server with a lower overhead. With the advent of HTML5, WebSockets is supported by the latest version of all major browsers, such as Microsoft Edge, Microsoft Internet Explorer, Google Chrome, Firefox, Safari, and Opera. With WebSockets, we can send messages to a server and receive event-driven responses without having to poll the server for a reply. This is full-duplex communication.

- **Server-Sent Eevents**: Server-Sent Events are a technology that enables web pages to receive automatic updates from the server through a HTTP connection. The server can initiate the data transmission toward a client after an initial connection has been established. This is not supported by the current version of Microsoft Edge and Microsoft Internet Explorer, but is available in Google Chrome, Mozilla Firefox, Safari, Opera, and others. This is simplex communication, as the server pushes the data to the client. This is part of the HTML5 specification.

- **Forever Frame**: Forever Frame is a Microsoft Internet Explorer concept and is not supported by any other browser. When a connection is established between a client web page and a server through Forever Frame, it creates a hidden IFrame in the client page. This IFrame makes a request to the server endpoint, which never completes; that is, it keeps the connection alive forever (hence the name, Forever Frame). Since the connection remains open, the server can use this connection to push scripts to the client, which are loaded and executed immediately in the client page, thus providing a real-time one-way communication from the server to the client. This is supported in old SignalR but removed from SignalR Core.
- **Long polling**: Long polling is something that most web developers do in their regular web development without realizing it is actually long polling. Long polling does not create a persistent connection, but instead polls the server with a request that stays open until the server responds. This may introduce some latency while the connection resets. Long polling is basically an approach used for backward compatibility with old browsers and is definitely not a preferred method for client-server communication for the modern web.

SignalR Core

SignalR Core is the complete rewrite of SignalR for ASP.NET Core 2.0 and, at the time of writing this chapter, is available as an alpha release for ASP.NET Core 2.0. As per the road-map, it is scheduled to be released in the fourth quarter of 2017 and will be shipped with ASP.NET Core 2.1. The current alpha release consists of a server component, .NET client, and JavaScript/TypeScript client.

We will be using SignalR Core for our game development as it will take care of all the heavy duty stuff needed to push the content from the server to the client and let us concentrate on the problem at hand. With the ASP.NET Core 2.0 and SignalR Core basics in place, and the design and approach finalized, let's get started with our implementation.

Solution

In this section, we will develop the Tic-Tac-Toe game in the ASP.NET Core 2.0 web app, using SignalR Core. We will follow a step-by-step approach and use Visual Studio 2017 as the primary IDE, but will list the steps needed while using the Visual Studio Code editor as well. Let's do the project setup first and then we will dive into the coding.

Project setup

Create a new ASP.NET Core 2.0 MVC app named `TicTacToeGame`, like we did in the *Creating a simple running code* section in `Chapter 1`, *Getting Started*.

With this, we will have a basic working ASP.NET Core 2.0 MVC app in place. However, to leverage SignalR Core in our app, we need to install SignalR Core NuGet and the client packages.

To install the SignalR Core NuGet package, we can perform one of the following two approaches in the Visual Studio IDE:

- In the context menu of the `TicTacToeGame` project, click on **Manage NuGet Packages**. It will open the **NuGet Package Manager** for the project. In the **Browse** section, search for the `Microsoft.AspNetCore.SignalR` package and click **Install**. This will install SignalR Core in the app. Please note that currently the package is in the preview stage and hence the pre-release checkbox has to be ticked:

```
.NET   Microsoft.AspNetCore.SignalR

Installed:   1.0.0-alpha1-final                                    Uninstall

Version:     1.0.0-alpha1-final                              ▼      Update


⌄ Options


Description
Components for providing real-time bi-directional communication across the Web.

Version:           1.0.0-alpha1-final
Author(s):         Microsoft
License:           http://www.microsoft.com/web/webpi/eula/net_library_eula_enu.htm
Date published:    Thursday, September 14, 2017 (9/14/2017)
Project URL:       http://www.asp.net/
Report Abuse:      https://www.nuget.org/packages/Microsoft.AspNetCore.SignalR/1.0.0-alpha1-final/
                   ReportAbuse
Tags:              aspnetcore, signalr


Dependencies
.NETStandard,Version=v2.0
Microsoft.AspNetCore.SignalR.Core (>= 1.0.0-alpha1-final)
Microsoft.AspNetCore.Sockets.Http (>= 1.0.0-alpha1-final)
```

- Edit the `TicTacToeGame.csproj` file, add the following code snippet in the `ItemGroup` code containing package references, and click **Save**. As soon as the file is saved, the tooling will take care of restoring the packages and in a while, the SignalR package will be installed. This approach can be used with Visual Studio Code as well. Although Visual Studio Code detects the unresolved dependencies and may prompt you to restore the package, it is recommended that immediately after editing and saving the file, you run the `dotnet restore` command in the terminal window at the location of the project:

```
<ItemGroup>
    <PackageReference Include="Microsoft.AspNetCore.All"
    Version="2.0.0" />
```

```
        <PackageReference Include="Microsoft.AspNetCore.SignalR"
        Version="1.0.0-alpha1-final" />
    </ItemGroup>
```

Now we have server-side packages installed. We still need to install the client-side package of SignalR, which is available through npm. To do so, we need to first ascertain whether we have npm installed on the machine or not. If not, we need to install it. npm is distributed with Node.js, so we need to download and install Node.js from `https://nodejs.org/en/`. The installation is quite straightforward.

Once this installation is done, open a Command Prompt at the project location and run the following command:

```
npm install @aspnet/signalr-client
```

This will install the SignalR client package. Just go to the package location (npm creates a `node_modules` folder in the project directory). The relative path from the project directory would be `\node_modules\@aspnet\signalr-client\dist\browser`.

From this location, copy the `signalr-client-1.0.0-alpha1-final.js` file into the `wwwroot\js` folder. In the current version, the name is `signalr-client-1.0.0-alpha1-final.js`.

With this, we are done with the project setup and we are ready to use SignalR goodness as well. So let's dive into the coding.

Coding the game

In this section, we will implement our gaming solution. The end output will be the working two-player Tic-Tac-Toe game. We will do the coding in steps for ease of understanding:

1. In the `Startup` class, we modify the `ConfigureServices` method to add SignalR to the container, by writing the following code:

   ```
   //// Adds SignalR to the services container.
   services.AddSignalR();
   ```

2. In the `Configure` method of the same class, we configure the pipeline to use SignalR and intercept and wire up the request containing `gameHub` to our SignalR hub that we will be creating with the following code:

   ```
   //// Use - SignalR & let it know to intercept and map any
   request having gameHub.
   ```

```
app.UseSignalR(routes =>
{
        routes.MapHub<GameHub>("gameHub");
});
```

The following is the code for both methods, for the sake of clarity and completion. Other methods and properties are removed for brevity:

```
// This method gets called by the run-time. Use this method to add
    services to the container.
public void ConfigureServices(IServiceCollection services)
{
    services.AddMvc();
    //// Adds SignalR to the services container.
    services.AddSignalR();
}

// This method gets called by the runtime. Use this method to
    configure the HTTP request pipeline.
public void Configure(IApplicationBuilder app, IHostingEnvironment
env)
{
        if (env.IsDevelopment())
        {
            app.UseDeveloperExceptionPage();
            app.UseBrowserLink();
        }
        else
        {
            app.UseExceptionHandler("/Home/Error");
        }

    app.UseStaticFiles();
    app.UseMvc(routes =>
    {
        routes.MapRoute(
            name: "default",
            template: "{controller=Home}/{action=Index}/{id?}");
    });

    //// Use - SignalR & let it know to intercept and map any
request
        having gameHub.
    app.UseSignalR(routes =>
    {
        routes.MapHub<GameHub>("gameHub");
    });
```

3. The previous two steps set up SignalR for us. Now, let's start with the coding of the player registration form. We want the player to be registered with a name and display the picture. Later, the server will also need to know whether the player is playing, waiting for a move, searching for an opponent, and so on. Let's create the `Player` model in the `Models` folder in the app. The code comments are self-explanatory:

```
/// <summary>
/// The player class. Each player of Tic-Tac-Toe game would
    be an instance of this class.
/// </summary>
internal class Player
{
    /// <summary>
    /// Gets or sets the name of the player. This would be
        set at the time user registers.
    /// </summary>
    public string Name { get; set; }

    /// <summary>
    /// Gets or sets the opponent player. The player
        against whom the player would be playing.
    /// This is determined/ set when the players click Find
        Opponent Button in the UI.
    /// </summary>
    public Player Opponent { get; set; }

    /// <summary>
    /// Gets or sets a value indicating whether the player
        is playing.
    /// This is set when the player starts a game.
    /// </summary>
    public bool IsPlaying { get; set; }

    /// <summary>
    /// Gets or sets a value indicating whether the player
        is waiting for opponent to make a move.
    /// </summary>
    public bool WaitingForMove { get; set; }

    /// <summary>
    /// Gets or sets a value indicating whether the player
        is searching for opponent.
    /// </summary>
    public bool IsSearchingOpponent { get; set; }
```

```
/// <summary>
/// Gets or sets the time when the player registered.
/// </summary>
public DateTime RegisterTime { get; set; }

/// <summary>
/// Gets or sets the image of the player.
/// This would be set at the time of registration, if
    the user selects the image.
/// </summary>
public string Image { get; set; }

/// <summary>
/// Gets or sets the connection id of the player
    connection with the gameHub.
/// </summary>
public string ConnectionId { get; set; }
}
```

4. Now, we need to have a UI in place so that the player can fill in the form and register. We also need to show the image preview to the player when he/she browses the image. To do so, we will use the Index.cshtml view of the HomeController class that comes with the default MVC template. We will refer to the following two .js files in the _Layout.cshtml partial view so that they are available to all the views. Alternatively, you could add these in the Index.cshtml view as well, but its highly recommended that common scripts should be added in _Layout.cshtml. The version of the script file may be different in your case. These are the currently available latest versions. Although jQuery is not required to be the library of choice for us, we will use jQuery to keep the code clean, simple, and compact. With these references, we have jQuery and SignalR available to us on the client side:

```
<script src="~/lib/jquery/dist/jquery.js"></script> <!-- jQuery-->
<script src="~/js/signalr-client-1.0.0-alpha1-final.js"></script>
<!-- SignalR-->
```

After adding these references, create the simple HTML UI for the image preview and registration, as follows:

```
<div id="divPreviewImage"> <!-- To display the browsed image-->
    <fieldset>
        <div class="form-group">
            <div class="col-lg-2">
                <image src="" id="previewImage"
```

```
                        style="height:100px;width:100px;border:solid
                        2px dotted; float:left" />
                    </div>
                    <div class="col-lg-10" id="divOpponentPlayer"> <!--
                    To display image of opponent player-->
                        <image src="" id="opponentImage"
                        style="height:100px;width:100px;border:solid
                        2px dotted; float:right;" />
                    </div>
                </div>
            </fieldset>
        </div>

    <div id="divRegister"> <!-- Our Registration form-->
        <fieldset>
            <legend>Register</legend>
            <div class="form-group">
                <label for="name" class="col-lg-2 control-
                label">Name</label>
                <div class="col-lg-10">
                    <input type="text" class="form-control" id="name"
                    placeholder="Name">
                </div>
            </div>
            <div class="form-group">
                <label for="image" class="col-lg-2 control-
                label">Avatar</label>
                <div class="col-lg-10">
                    <input type="file" class="form-control" id="image"
                    />
                </div>
            </div>
            <div class="form-group">
                <div class="col-lg-10 col-lg-offset-2">
                    <button type="button" class="btn btn-primary"
                    id="btnRegister">Register</button>
                </div>
            </div>
        </fieldset>
    </div>
```

5. When the player registers by clicking the `Register` button, the player's details need to be sent to the server. To do this, we will write the JavaScript to send details to our `gameHub`:

```
let hubUrl = '/gameHub';
let httpConnection = new signalR.HttpConnection(hubUrl);
```

```
let hubConnection = new signalR.HubConnection(httpConnection);
var playerName = "";
var playerImage = "";
var hash = "#";
hubConnection.start();

$("#btnRegister").click(function () {  //// Fires on button click
        playerName = $('#name').val();   //// Sets the player name
        with the input name.
        playerImage = $('#previewImage').attr('src'); //// Sets the
        player image variable with specified image
        var data = playerName.concat(hash, playerImage); //// The
        registration data to be sent to server.
        hubConnection.invoke('RegisterPlayer', data); //// Invoke
        the "RegisterPlayer" method on gameHub.
    });

$("#image").change(function () { //// Fires when image is changed.
        readURL(this); //// HTML 5 way to read the image as data
        url.
    });

    function readURL(input) {
        if (input.files && input.files[0]) { //// Go in only if
        image is specified.
            var reader = new FileReader();
            reader.onload = imageIsLoaded;
            reader.readAsDataURL(input.files[0]);
        }
    }

    function imageIsLoaded(e) {
        if (e.target.result) {
            $('#previewImage').attr('src', e.target.result); ////
            Sets the image source for preview.
            $("#divPreviewImage").show();
        }
    };
```

6. The player now has a UI to input the name and image, see the preview image, and click `Register`. On clicking the `Register` button, we are sending the concatenated name and image to the `gameHub` on the server through `hubConnection.invoke('RegisterPlayer', data);` So, it's quite simple for the client to make a call to the server. Initialize the `hubConnection` by specifying hub name as we did in the first three lines of the preceding code snippet. Start the connection by `hubConnection.start();`, and then invoke the server hub method by calling the `invoke` method, specifying the hub method name and the parameter it expects. We have not yet created the hub, so let's create the `GameHub` class on the server:

```
/// <summary>
/// The Game Hub class derived from Hub
/// </summary>
public class GameHub : Hub
{
    /// <summary>
    /// To keep the list of all the connected players
        registered with the game hub. We could have
    /// used normal list but used concurrent bag as its thread
        safe.
    /// </summary>
    private static readonly ConcurrentBag<Player> players =
    new ConcurrentBag<Player>();

    /// <summary>
    /// Registers the player with name and image.
    /// </summary>
    /// <param name="nameAndImageData">The name and image data
        sent by the player.</param>
    public void RegisterPlayer(string nameAndImageData)
    {
        var splitData = nameAndImageData?.Split(new char[] {
        '#' }, StringSplitOptions.None);
        string name = splitData[0];
        string image = splitData[1];
        var player = players?.FirstOrDefault(x =>
        x.ConnectionId == Context.ConnectionId);
        if (player == null)
        {
            player = new Player { ConnectionId =
            Context.ConnectionId, Name = name, IsPlaying =
            false, IsSearchingOpponent = false, RegisterTime =
            DateTime.UtcNow, Image = image };
            if (!players.Any(j => j.Name == name))
```

```
        {
            players.Add(player);
        }
    }

    this.OnRegisterationComplete(Context.ConnectionId);
}

/// <summary>
/// Fires on completion of registration.
/// </summary>
/// <param name="connectionId">The connectionId of the
    player which registered</param>
public void OnRegisterationComplete(string connectionId)
{
    //// Notify this connection id that the registration
        is complete.
    this.Clients.Client(connectionId).
    InvokeAsync(Constants.RegistrationComplete);
}
}
```

The code comments make it self-explanatory. The class should derive from the SignalR `Hub` class for it to be recognized as `Hub`.

There are two methods of interest which can be overridden. Notice that both the methods follow the async pattern and hence return `Task`:

- `Task OnConnectedAsync()`: This method fires when a client/player connects to the hub.

- `Task OnDisconnectedAsync(Exception exception)`: This method fires when a client/player disconnects or looses the connection. We will override this method to handle the scenario where the player disconnects.

There are also a few properties that the hub class exposes:

- `Context`: This property is of type `HubCallerContext` and gives us access to the following properties:
  - `Connection`: Gives access to the current connection
  - `User`: Gives access to the `ClaimsPrincipal` of the user who is currently connected
  - `ConnectionId`: Gives the current connection ID string

- **Clients**: This property is of type **IHubClients** and gives us the way to communicate to all the clients via the client proxy
- **Groups**: This property is of type **IGroupManager** and provides a way to add and remove connections to the group asynchronously

To keep the things simple, we are not using a database to keep track of our registered players. Rather we will use an in-memory collection to keep the registered players. We could have used a normal list of players, such as **List<Player>**, but then we would need all the thread safety and use one of the thread safety primitives, such as **lock**, **monitor**, and so on, so we are going with **ConcurrentBag<Player>**, which is thread safe and reasonable for our game development. That explains the declaration of the players collection in the class. We will need to do some housekeeping to add players to this collection when they resister and remove them when they disconnect.

We saw in previous step that the client invoked the **RegisterPlayer** method of the hub on the server, passing in the name and image data. So we defined a **public** method in our hub, named **RegisterPlayer,** accepting the name and image data string concatenated through #. This is just one of the simple ways of accepting the client data for demonstration purposes, we can also use strongly typed parameters. In this method, we split the string on # and extract the name as the first part and the image as the second part. We then check if the player with the current connection ID already exists in our players collection. If it doesn't, we create a **Player** object with default values and add them to our players collection. We are distinguishing the player based on the name for demonstration purposes, but we can add an **Id** property in the **Player** class and make different players have the same name also. After the registration is complete, the server needs to update the player, that the registration is complete and the player can then look for the opponent. To do so, we make a call to the **OnRegistrationComplete** method which invokes a method called **registrationComplete** on the client with the current connection ID. Let's understand the code to invoke the method on the client:

```
this.Clients.Client(connectionId).InvokeAsync(Constants.Registratio
nComplete);
```

On the **Clients** property, we can choose a client having a specific connection ID (in this case, the current connection ID from the **Context**) and then call **InvokeAsync** to invoke a method on the client specifying the method name and parameters as required. In the preceding case method, the name is **registrationComplete** with no parameters.

Now we know how to invoke a server method from the client and also how to invoke the client method from the server. We also know how to select a specific client and invoke a method there. We can invoke the client method from the server, for all the clients, a group of clients, or a specific client, so rest of the coding stuff would be just a repetition of these two concepts.

7. Next, we need to implement the `registrationComplete` method on the client. On registration completion, the registration form should be hidden and the player should be able to find an opponent to play against. To do so, we would write JavaScript code to hide the registration form and show the UI for finding the opponent. On clicking the `Find Opponent` button, we need the server to pair us against an opponent, so we need to invoke a hub method on server to find opponent.

8. The server can respond us with two outcomes:
    * It finds an opponent player to play against. In this case, the game can start so we need to simulate the coin toss, determine the player who can make the first move, and start the game. This would be a game board in the client-user interface.
    * It doesn't find an opponent and asks the player to wait for another player to register and search for an opponent. This would be a no opponent found screen in the client.

In both the cases, the server would do some processing and invoke a method on the client. Since we need a lot of different user interfaces for different scenarios, let's code the HTML markup inside `div` to make it easier to show and hide sections based on the server response. We will add the following code snippet in the body. The comments specify the purpose of each of the `div` elements and markup inside them:

```
<div id="divFindOpponentPlayer"> <!-- Section to display Find
Opponent -->
    <fieldset>
        <legend>Find a player to play against!</legend>
        <div class="form-group">
            <input type="button" class="btn btn-primary"
            id="btnFindOpponentPlayer" value="Find Opponent
            Player" />
        </div>
    </fieldset>
</div>
    <div id="divFindingOpponentPlayer"> <!-- Section to display
    opponent not found, wait -->
    <fieldset>
```

```
                <legend>Its lonely here!</legend>
                <div class="form-group">
                    Looking for an opponent player. Waiting for someone to
                    join!
                </div>
            </fieldset>
        </div>
        <div id="divGameInformation" class="form-group"> <!-- Section to
        display game information-->
            <div class="form-group" id="divGameInfo"></div>
            <div class="form-group" id="divInfo"></div>
        </div>
        <div id="divGame" style="clear:both"> <!-- Section where the game
        board would be displayed -->
            <fieldset>
                <legend>Game On</legend>
                <div id="divGameBoard" style="width:380px"></div>
            </fieldset>
        </div>
```

The following client-side code would take care of *Steps 7* and *8*. Though the comments are self-explanatory, we will quickly see what all stuff is that is going on here. We handle the `registartionComplete` method and display the `Find Opponent Player` section. This section has a button to find an opponent player called `btnFindOpponentPlayer`. We define the event handler of the button to invoke the `FindOpponent` method on the hub. We will see the hub method implementation later, but we know that the hub method would either find an opponent or would not find an opponent, so we have defined the methods `opponentFound` and `opponentNotFound`, respectively, to handle these scenarios. In the `opponentNotFound` method, we just display a section in which we say, we do not have an opponent player. In the `opponentFound` method, we display the game section, game information section, opponent display picture section, and draw the Tic-Tac-Toe game board as a 3×3 grid using CSS styling. All the other sections are hidden:

```
$("#btnFindOpponentPlayer").click(function () {
    hubConnection.invoke('FindOpponent');
});

hubConnection.on('registrationComplete', data => { //// Fires on
registration complete. Invoked by server hub
    $("#divRegister").hide();  // hide the registration div
    $("#divFindOpponentPlayer").show(); // display find opponent
    player div.
});
```

```javascript
hubConnection.on('opponentNotFound', data => { //// Fires when no
opponent is found.
        $('#divFindOpponentPlayer').hide(); //// hide the find
        opponent player section.
        $('#divFindingOpponentPlayer').show(); //// display the
        finding opponent player div.
    });

hubConnection.on('opponentFound', (data, image) => { //// Fires
when opponent player is found.
        $('#divFindOpponentPlayer').hide();
        $('#divFindingOpponentPlayer').hide();
        $('#divGame').show();  //// Show game board section.
        $('#divGameInformation').show(); //// Show game information
        $('#divOpponentPlayer').show(); //// Show opponent player
        image.
        opponentImage = image;  //// sets the opponent player image
        for display
        $('#opponentImage').attr('src', opponentImage); //// Binds
        the opponent player image
        $('#divGameInfo').html("<br/><span><strong> Hey " +
        playerName + "! You are playing against <i>" + data + "</i>
        </strong></span>");  //// displays the information of
        opponent that the player is playing against.
        //// Draw the tic-tac-toe game board, A 3x3 grid :) by
        proper styling.
        for (var i = 0; i < 9; i++) {
            $("#divGameBoard").append("<span class='marker' id=" +
i
            + " style='display:block;border:2px solid
black;height:100px;width:100px;float:left;margin:10px;'>"
            + i + "</span>");
        }
    });
```

First we need to have a Game object to track a game, players involved, moves left, and check if there is a winner. We will have a Game class defined as per the following code. The comments detail the purpose of the methods and the properties defined:

```csharp
internal class Game
{
    /// <summary>
    /// Gets or sets the value indicating whether the
        game is over.
    /// </summary>
    public bool IsOver { get; private set; }
```

```csharp
/// <summary>
/// Gets or sets the value indicating whether the
    game is draw.
/// </summary>
public bool IsDraw { get; private set; }

/// <summary>
/// Gets or sets Player 1 of the game
/// </summary>
public Player Player1 { get; set; }

/// <summary>
/// Gets or sets Player 2 of the game
/// </summary>
public Player Player2 { get; set; }

/// <summary>
/// For internal housekeeping, To keep track of value in each
    of the box in the grid.
/// </summary>
private readonly int[] field = new int[9];

/// <summary>
/// The number of moves left. We start the game with 9 moves
    remaining in a 3x3 grid.
/// </summary>
private int movesLeft = 9;

/// <summary>
/// Initializes a new instance of the
    <see cref="Game"/> class.
/// </summary>
public Game()
{
    //// Initialize the game
    for (var i = 0; i < field.Length; i++)
    {
        field[i] = -1;
    }
}
/// <summary>
/// Place the player number at a given position for a player
/// </summary>
/// <param name="player">The player number would be 0 or
    1</param>
/// <param name="position">The position where player number
    would be placed, should be between 0 and
///8, both inclusive</param>
```

```
/// <returns>Boolean true if game is over and
    we have a winner.</returns>
public bool Play(int player, int position)
{
    if (this.IsOver)
    {
        return false;
    }
    //// Place the player number at the given position
    this.PlacePlayerNumber(player, position);
    //// Check if we have a winner. If this returns true,
    //// game would be over and would have a winner, else game
        would continue.
    return this.CheckWinner();
}
}
```

Now we have the entire game mystery solved with the Game class. We know when the game is over, we have the method to place the player marker, and check the winner. The following server side-code on the GameHub will handle *Steps 7* and *8*:

```
/// <summary>
/// The list of games going on.
/// </summary>
private static readonly ConcurrentBag<Game> games = new
ConcurrentBag<Game>();

/// <summary>
/// To simulate the coin toss. Like heads and tails, 0 belongs to
    one player and 1 to opponent.
/// </summary>
private static readonly Random toss = new Random();

/// <summary>
/// Finds the opponent for the player and sets the Seraching for
    Opponent property of player to true.
/// We will use the connection id from context to identify the
    current player.
/// Once we have 2 players looking to play, we can pair them and
    simulate coin toss to start the game.
/// </summary>
public void FindOpponent()
{
    //// First fetch the player from our players collection having
        current connection id
    var player = players.FirstOrDefault(x => x.ConnectionId ==
```

```
Context.ConnectionId);
if (player == null)
{
    //// Since player would be registered before making this
        call,
    //// we should not reach here. If we are here, something
        somewhere in the flow above is broken.
    return;
}

//// Set that player is seraching for opponent.
player.IsSearchingOpponent = true;

//// We will follow a queue, so find a player who registered
    earlier as opponent.
//// This would only be the case if more than 2 players are
    looking for opponent.
var opponent = players.Where(x => x.ConnectionId !=
Context.ConnectionId && x.IsSearchingOpponent &&
!x.IsPlaying).OrderBy(x =>x.RegisterTime).FirstOrDefault();
if (opponent == null)
{
    //// Could not find any opponent, invoke opponentNotFound
        method in the client.
    Clients.Client(Context.ConnectionId)
    .InvokeAsync(Constants.OpponentNotFound);
    return;
}

//// Set both players as playing.
player.IsPlaying = true;
player.IsSearchingOpponent = false; //// Make him unsearchable
for opponent search

opponent.IsPlaying = true;
opponent.IsSearchingOpponent = false;

 //// Set each other as opponents.
 player.Opponent = opponent;
 opponent.Opponent = player;

//// Notify both players that they can play by invoking
    opponentFound method for both the players.
//// Also pass the opponent name and opoonet image, so that
    they can visualize it.
//// Here we are directly using connection id, but group is a
    good candidate and use here.
Clients.Client(Context.ConnectionId)
```

```
      .InvokeAsync(Constants.OpponentFound, opponent.Name,
      opponent.Image);
      Clients.Client(opponent.ConnectionId)
      .InvokeAsync(Constants.OpponentFound, player.Name,
      player.Image);
        //// Create a new game with these 2 player and add it to
            games collection.
        games.Add(new Game { Player1 = player, Player2 = opponent
  });
    }
```

Here, we have created a games collection to keep track of ongoing games and a `Random` field named toss to simulate the coin toss. How `FindOpponent` works is documented in the comments and is intuitive to understand.

9. Once the game starts, each player has to make a move and then wait for the opponent to make a move, until the game ends. The move is made by clicking on the available grid cells. Here, we need to ensure that cell position that is already marked by one of the players is not changed or marked. So, as soon as a valid cell is marked, we set its CSS class to `notAvailable` so we know that the cell is taken. While clicking on a cell, we will check whether the cell has `notAvailablestyle`. If yes, it cannot be marked. If not, the cell can be marked and we then send the marked position to the server hub. We also see the `waitingForMove`, `moveMade`, `gameOver`, and `opponentDisconnected` events invoked by the server based on the game state. The code is commented and is pretty straightforward. The `moveMade` method in the following code makes use of the `MoveInformation` class, which we will define at the server for sharing move information with both players:

```
  //// Triggers on clicking the grid cell.
  $(document).on('click', '.marker', function () {
      if ($(this).hasClass("notAvailable")) { //// Cell is already
      taken.
      return;
      }

      hubConnection.invoke('MakeAMove', $(this)[0].id); //// Cell is
      valid, send details to hub.
  });

  //// Fires when player has to make a move.
  hubConnection.on('waitingForMove', data => {
      $('#divInfo').html("<br/><span><strong> Your turn <i>" +
      playerName + "</i>! Make a winning move! </strong></span>");
  });
```

```
//// Fires when move is made by either player.
hubConnection.on('moveMade', data => {
    if (data.Image == playerImage) { //// Move made by player.
        $("#" + data.ImagePosition).addClass("notAvailable");
        $("#" + data.ImagePosition).css('background-image',
        'url(' + data.Image + ')');
        $('#divInfo').html("<br/><strong>Waiting for <i>" +
        data.OpponentName + "</i> to make a move.
        </strong>");
    }
    else {
        $("#" + data.ImagePosition).addClass("notAvailable");
        $("#" + data.ImagePosition).css('background-image',
        'url(' + data.Image + ')');
        $('#divInfo').html("<br/><strong>Waiting for <i>" +
        data.OpponentName + "</i> to make a move.
        </strong>");
    }
});

//// Fires when the game ends.
hubConnection.on('gameOver', data => {
    $('#divGame').hide();
    $('#divInfo').html("<br/><span><strong>Hey " + playerName +
    "! " + data + " </strong></span>");
    $('#divGameBoard').html(" ");
    $('#divGameInfo').html(" ");
    $('#divOpponentPlayer').hide();
});

//// Fires when the opponent disconnects.
hubConnection.on('opponentDisconnected', data => {
        $("#divRegister").hide();
        $('#divGame').hide();
        $('#divGameInfo').html(" ");
        $('#divInfo').html("<br/><span><strong>Hey " + playerName +
        "! Your opponent disconnected or left      the battle! You
        are the winner ! Hip Hip Hurray!!!</strong></span>");
    });
```

After every move, both players need to be updated by the server about the move
made, so that both players' game boards are in sync. So, on the server side we will
need an additional model called MoveInformation, which will contain
information on the latest move made by the player and the server will send this
model to both the clients to keep them in sync:

```csharp
/// <summary>
/// While playing the game, players would make moves. This class
    contains the information of those moves.
/// </summary>
internal class MoveInformation
{
    /// <summary>
    /// Gets or sets the opponent name.
    /// </summary>
    public string OpponentName { get; set; }

    /// <summary>
    /// Gets or sets the player who made the move.
    /// </summary>
    public string MoveMadeBy { get; set; }

    /// <summary>
    /// Gets or sets the image position. The position in the game
        board (0-8) where the player placed his
    /// image.
    /// </summary>
    public int ImagePosition { get; set; }

    /// <summary>
    /// Gets or sets the image. The image of the player that he
        placed in the board (0-8)
    /// </summary>
    public string Image { get; set; }
}
```

Finally, we will wire up the remaining methods in the GameHub class to complete the game coding. The MakeAMove method is called every time a player makes a move. Also, we have overidden the OnDisconnectedAsync method to inform a player when their opponent disconnects. In this method, we also keep our players and games list current. The comments in the code explain the workings of the methods:

```csharp
/// <summary>
/// Invoked by the player to make a move on the board.
/// </summary>
/// <param name="position">The position to place
    the player</param>
public void MakeAMove(int position)
{
        //// Lets find a game from our list of games where one of
            the player has the same connection Id as the current
            connection has.
```

```
var game = games?.FirstOrDefault(x =>
x.Player1.ConnectionId == Context.ConnectionId ||
x.Player2.ConnectionId == Context.ConnectionId);

if (game == null || game.IsOver)
{
    //// No such game exist!
    return;
}

//// Designate 0 for player 1
int symbol = 0;
if (game.Player2.ConnectionId == Context.ConnectionId)
{
    //// Designate 1 for player 2.
    symbol = 1;
}

var player = symbol == 0 ? game.Player1 : game.Player2;
if (player.WaitingForMove)
{
    return;
}
//// Update both the players that move is made.
Clients.Client(game.Player1.ConnectionId)
.InvokeAsync(Constants.MoveMade, new MoveInformation {
OpponentName = player.Name, ImagePosition = position,
Image = player.Image });
Clients.Client(game.Player2.ConnectionId)
.InvokeAsync(Constants.MoveMade, new MoveInformation {
OpponentName = player.Name, ImagePosition = position,
Image = player.Image });

//// Place the symbol and look for a winner after every
    move.
if (game.Play(symbol, position))
{
    Remove<Game>(games, game);
    Clients.Client(game.Player1.ConnectionId)
    .InvokeAsync(Constants.GameOver, $"The winner is
    {player.Name}");
    Clients.Client(game.Player2.ConnectionId)
    .InvokeAsync(Constants.GameOver, $"The winner is
    {player.Name}");
    player.IsPlaying = false;
    player.Opponent.IsPlaying = false;
    this.Clients.Client(player.ConnectionId)
    .InvokeAsync(Constants.RegistrationComplete);
```

```
        this.Clients.Client(player.Opponent.ConnectionId)
        .InvokeAsync(Constants.RegistrationComplete);
    }

    //// If no one won and its a tame draw, update the
        players that the game is over and let them
        look for new game to play.
    if (game.IsOver && game.IsDraw)
    {
        Remove<Game>(games, game);
        Clients.Client(game.Player1.ConnectionId)
        .InvokeAsync(Constants.GameOver, "Its a tame
        draw!!!");
        Clients.Client(game.Player2.ConnectionId)
        .InvokeAsync(Constants.GameOver, "Its a tame
        draw!!!");
        player.IsPlaying = false;
        player.Opponent.IsPlaying = false;
        this.Clients.Client(player.ConnectionId)
        .InvokeAsync(Constants.RegistrationComplete);
        this.Clients.Client(player.Opponent.ConnectionId)
        .InvokeAsync(Constants.RegistrationComplete);
    }

    if (!game.IsOver)
    {
        player.WaitingForMove = !player.WaitingForMove;
        player.Opponent.WaitingForMove =
        !player.Opponent.WaitingForMove;
        Clients.Client(player.Opponent.ConnectionId)
        .InvokeAsync(Constants.WaitingForOpponent,
        player.Opponent.Name);
        Clients.Client(player.ConnectionId)
        .InvokeAsync(Constants.WaitingForOpponent,
        player.Opponent.Name);
    }
}
```

With this, we are done with the coding of the game and are ready to run the game app. The detailed source code can be downloaded from `https://github.com/PacktPublishing/. NET-Core-2.0-By-Example`.

Game demo

Now that our app is ready, let's run it and enjoy the game. Press *F5* and the game should be launched in the browser. This will work for both Visual Studio 2017 IDE and Visual Studio Code. Also, since we are running it in our local machine, both players will need to play it on the same machine for the time being. Once we deploy this game in Azure, players can browse the URL from their individual machines. We will see how we can publish an ASP.NET Core 2.0 app to Azure in a later chapter.

This is what the game registration UI looks like:

On clicking **Register**, the find opponent screen is displayed:

On clicking the **Find Opponent Player** button, if a registered player exists, the game starts and this is what the two-player game looks like:

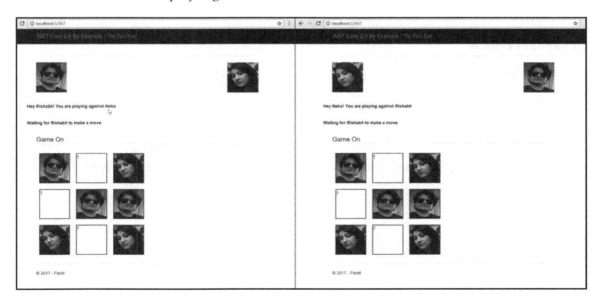

If a player is not available, or you are the lone warrior registered to play, the following screen will be displayed:

We have developed a fully functional two-player Tic-Tac-Toe game, meeting all the requirement specifications. It's time to enjoy your very first ASP.NET Core 2.0 game powered by SignalR Core!

Summary

In this chapter, we learned about the project structure of a typical ASP.NET Core 2.0 app and understood the importance and purpose of each and every file that comes with the default MVC template. We also learned about SignalR and SignalR Core, and developed our very first game, Tic-Tac-Toe, on ASP.NET Core 2.0 based on the given requirements.

In the next chapter, we will deep dive into learning and coding the features of ASP.NET Core 2.0 while developing a real-time chat application for multiple clients called Let's Chat.

4
Let's Chat Web Application

There is an old saying:

"A single conversation with a wise person is worth a month's study of books."

With this thought, let's enable a conversation with our online friends by developing a chat application called Let's Chat in ASP.NET Core 2.0. Over the course of the next three chapters, we will be developing and deploying this chat app. While doing so, we will dive deep into ASP.NET Core 2.0 features, learn their intricacies, and learn how to unit test our ASP.NET Core 2.0 app. We will also learn about containers and deploy our app on the cloud. We will end these three chapters with a quick development and walkthrough of a Chatbot using the Microsoft Bot Framework, which can be easily created in a matter of minutes and can be added to any of your web apps and also integrated with social networks. In this chapter, we will cover the following topics:

- Let's Chat web app requirement specifications
- Let's Chat web app design
- Project setup

With reference to ASP.NET Core 2.0, we will also learn the following:

- Authentication
- Authorization
- ASP.NET Core pipeline
- Middleware
- Dependency registration
- Reading configuration values
- Logging

Let's Chat web app requirement specifications

In this section, we will discuss the requirements for developing our Let's Chat web application in ASP.NET Core 2.0.

As a user, I should be able to fulfill the following requirements for this chat room app:

1. Register myself in the web app
2. Log in to the app
3. Reset the password in case I have forgotten the old one
4. See a list of all the currently logged in users in the chat room
5. See a users joining or leaving the chat room
6. See the display pictures of logged in users, if they exist
7. Chat with all online users at the same time, just like a chat room
8. Access the app from a browser over the internet and chat with any number of online users

To give an example, we are looking at a highly trimmed down version of something like `https://gitter.im/dotnet/cli`, which is a chat room for .NET Core **command-line interface (CLI)** tools.

Now that we have the requirement specifications in place, let's see the activity flow of the app and come up with a flowchart. The following is a rough flowchart of the app workflow:

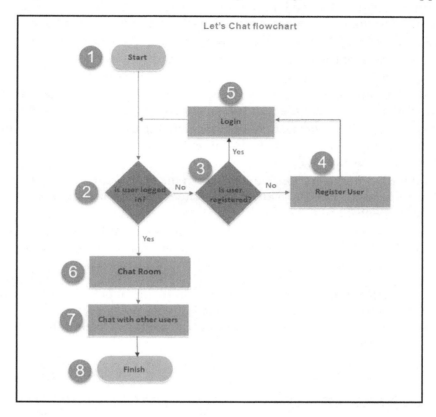

Let's have a look at the flow:

1. **Start**: This is the start of the flow. The user browses the chat URL. It is being conceptualized as a site, as we want to access it from the browser and chat with any number of online users (requirement *Steps 7* and *8*).

2. **Is user logged in**?: At this point, the app checks whether the user is authenticated or not, that is, the user is logged in or not. If the user is logged in, he/she is redirected to the chat room page; otherwise, the user is redirected to the login page. There is also the provision to reset the password (requirement *Steps 2* and *3*).

3. **Is user registered?**: When the user is not logged in, he/she is redirected to the login page, where they need to provide a proper username and password to get authenticated and logged in. But this can happen only if the user has valid credentials, that is, the user is already registered (requirement *Step 1*).

4. **Register User**: If the user is not registered, the app should provide a provision to register the user (requirement *Step 1*).

5. **Login**: This is the landing screen for any unauthenticated user. Already authenticated users are directly navigated to the chat room page. This indicates to other online users that the user has joined the room (requirement *Step 2*).

6. **Chat Room**: Upon successful authentication, the user is redirected to the chat room, where he/she can see the list of online users and chat with all of them (requirements *Steps 4, 5,* and *6*).

7. **Chat with other users**: Once the user is in the chat room, he/she can chat with all the online users and can also see their names and display pictures in the chat (requirements *Steps 6* and *7*).

8. **Finish**: Once the user is done chatting with their friends, he /she can exit the page. This indicates to other online users that the user has left the room (requirement *Step 5*).

As we can see and infer from the flowchart, this is pretty much how every modern online app workflow happens. We also see that chatting happens only in *Steps 6* and *7* of the flowchart. All the other steps are for authentication and setup. We also know that this flow covers all the requirements.

Let's Chat web app – high-level design

In this section, we will look at the flowchart that we created and we will come up with granular modules to constitute the app using ASP.NET Core 2.0. We need to develop the following:

- An authentication and authorization module that takes care of login and authentication of users
- A registration module that takes care of user registration
- A chat room page
- A module that keeps track of all the logged in users and notifies the client chat room pages about the user joining and leaving
- A user information module that keeps track of all the user information, such as display name, display picture, and so on

- A chat hub module that enables a message to be broadcast from each user to the other online users

Sounds easy? Let's see how we can design and implement each of the preceding requirements using ASP.NET Core 2.0:

- **Authentication and authorization module**: This is a core functionality and needed in most modern apps. It makes sense to use something that is already developed, tested, and secure, so that we do not waste our time and energy in rediscovering the wheel. There are a variety of ways by which we can achieve this, such as by creating and using a custom identity provider, or using Facebook, Twitter, Google, or Microsoft authentication providers. We will use Facebook authentication in our app, as it's more likely for the user to have a profile picture in Facebook, which would give a good user experience while chatting. This is done through OAuth (pronounced *oh-auth*), which stands for open authorization and is an open standard for token-based authentication and authorization on the internet. We will discuss this in detail when we implement it in our app. This will take care of *Steps 1* through *5* in our flowchart discussed in the previous section.
- **Chat hub module**: This module will be responsible for enabling real-time chat between all online users and will also track the users as they join and leave the room. The hub will receive messages from clients and then broadcast the received messages to all clients. This will be an implementation on top of the SignalR hub and will be responsible for handling user connections, disconnections, and all the real-time messaging functionality. We have already seen and coded the basics of SignalR in our last app.

Now that we have high-level designs in place, let's deep dive into the details to implement these and learn more about them.

Project setup

In this section, we will start the development of the Let's Chat web app and learn all the required fundamentals and ASP.NET Core 2.0 features in the process.

Create a new ASP.NET Core 2.0 MVC app named Let's Chat, like we did in the *Creating a simple running code* section of `Chapter 1`, *Getting Started*.

Since we need SignalR as well for all the real-time messaging, we need to install the SignalR package in our app. To do so, please follow the steps mentioned in the *Project setup* section of `Chapter 3`, *Building Our First .NET Core Game - Tic -Tac-Toe*.

After installation of SignalR, we are ready to start coding the app. We will start with the authentication and authorization module first and then move on to the Chat hub module.

Authentication and authorization are closely interlinked, but are quite different and are the fundamental concepts of security for distributed applications. It's imperative we understand these concepts so that we can develop a secure application. One of the most defining principles of security is *trust*. When we make our web app available on the internet, it's like keeping our resource in a public area, where hundreds and thousands of people can see it. Do you trust that your resource will be safe? There is a saying, *In God we trust, the rest must bring data* so, it's a big *NO*! Just like stuff left in a public area is not safe, the content we have made available on the internet is not safe and from this comes the need for authentication and authorization. Let's understand authentication and authorization, and then dig into coding the module.

Authentication deals with the process of obtaining some sort of credentials from the users and validates the user's identity based on these credentials. Authorization is the process of specifying the privileges/access rights of the resources to the authenticated resources. Authentication always happens before authorization, even if the app allows anonymous access, as the app would identify the user as an anonymous user first and then grant access. Authorization generally works on the basis of the principle of least privilege.

In research, investigations, and journalism, the *Five Ws and How or 5W1H* methodology of questioning is known to be a highly effective way of gathering the information, so let's use the same approach to understand authentication and authorization:

Question	Authentication	Authorization
What/who?	As per the Oxford dictionary, the meaning of the word authentication in the computing world is *The process or action of verifying the identity of a user or process. It is meant to identify the user/process and whether it is valid.*	As per the Oxford dictionary, the literal meaning of the word authorization is *The action of authorizing.*
Why?	To validate the identity of the user/process on the basis of credentials.	To control or restrict access to your devices/services/resources.

Where/when?	Wherever/whenever I need to restrict or control access to devices/services. But security experts may differ in their answer and say everywhere and at all times.	Wherever/whenever I need to restrict or control access to devices/services. But security experts may differ in their answer and say everywhere and at all times.
How?	Validate the supplied credentials against the stored credentials.	Check the role of the user/process and grant or refuse access to the resource.
Example	Someone knocks at your door. You look out and check you know the person by identifying him/her. This is authentication. The question that comes to mind is *who are you?*	In the same example, after performing authentication (identifying the person), you either let him/her into your house if the person is your friend or relative, or you don't if you don't know them well. This is authorization. The question that comes to mind is *what privileges do you have?*

The following diagram illustrates the authentication and authorization flow:

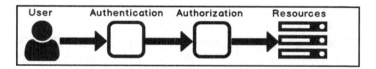

Authentication and authorization are vast topics and if we go into details, there could be a book on them alone, so we will briefly look at the various different implementations and related buzzwords to get the gist of them. The enthusiastic reader may want to read more about authentication and authorization. A few great and reliable resources I can suggest are:

- https://docs.microsoft.com/en-us/aspnet/core/security/authorization/
- https://channel9.msdn.com/Search?term=Advanced%20ASP.
  NET%20Core%20Authorization%20with%20Barry%20Dorrans#pubDate=year
  ch9Searchlang-en=en

Authentication

There has been a variety of implementations for authentication in ASP.NET over the years. Some of the most well-known ones are:

- Windows authentication
- Forms authentication
- Token-based authentication

The following sections discuss these further.

Windows authentication

This uses local Windows users and groups to authenticate. It can be sub-classified into:

- **Basic authentication:** Usernames and passwords are sent as Base64-encoded strings and hence can be easily cracked, so it's a very weak form of authentication and should not be used.
- **Digest authentication:** Issues with basic authentication are solved with digest authentication and the data sent is MD5 hashed. This hashed message is not easy to decipher. However, some browsers don't support it.
- **Integrated authentication**: Kerberos authentication or **NT LAN Manager (NTLM)** authentication. This is the best of the lot, in terms or security as well as support.

Windows authentication is still supported in ASP.NET Core 2.0, but since it is based on Windows, it won't be available on Linux or Macintosh. The app has to be hosted with IIS or HTTP.SYS (a web server for ASP.NET Core, which runs *only* on Windows). This is suited for intranet networks where the servers, clients, and users all belong to the same Windows domain.

Forms authentication

This is cookie/URL-based authentication in which a username and password are stored on the client machine as cookies and are sent encrypted in the URL for every request if the user has turned off cookie support. We can implement this in ASP.NET Core 2.0 as cookie authentication, as illustrated in the following diagram:

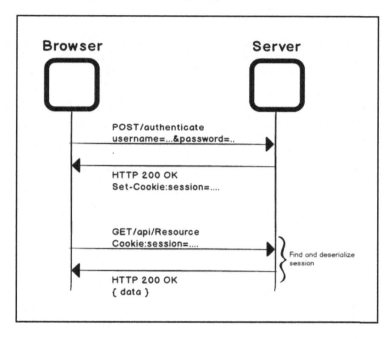

As we can see, once we have the auth-key set with the initial call to authenticate, we just pass the session ID/token from the cookie in every request. It can be used with ASP.NET Core Identity or without it. ASP.NET Core Identity is a membership system that allows us to add login functionality to our web app. Users can create an account and log in with username and password or they can use external social login providers, such as Facebook, Twitter, Google, Microsoft, and so on. We can use SQL Server or other persistence storage mechanisms to store the user details. Since this needs a very detailed understanding, you are advised to read about ASP.NET Identity from Microsoft's official documentation at `https://docs.microsoft.com/en-us/aspnet/core/security/authentication/identity?tabs=visual-studio%2Caspnetcore2x`.

If you have worked with ASP.NET prior to ASP.NET Core, you will find out that the fundamental type `IPrincipal` is more or less the same. It used to be implemented as `user` on `HTTPContext`, which represented the user for a request. Now, we also have a property named `user`, but its type is `ClaimsPrincipal`, which in turn implements `IPrincipal`. This is the shift that ASP.NET Core 2.0 has taken from the previous version of ASP.NET: that is, it has moved to claims-based from a role-based model and claims is the superset of a role. So, the question arises, what is a claim?

Claims are sets of information stored in key value pair form and are used to store user information such as name, address, email address, phone number, and so on. We can use claims as the replacement for roles as we can transfer the role to a claim. For example, I say "I am Rishabh Verma. I live in India. I am the author of this book", where I am claiming that my name is Rishabh Verma, I am claiming that I live in India, and I am claiming that I have the role of author of this book. This is what I mean when I say claims are the superset of roles, as in the preceding statement I have transformed my role of author into a claim.

The following code should nicely explain claims, identity, and principal relations from the preceding statement:

```
IList&lt;Claim&gt; claimCollection = new List&lt;Claim&gt;
{
    new Claim(ClaimTypes.Name, "Rishabh Verma")
    ,new Claim(ClaimTypes.Country, "India")
    ,new Claim(ClaimTypes.Role, "Author")
}

ClaimsIdentity identity = new ClaimsIdentity(claimCollection);
ClaimsPrincipal principal = new ClaimsPrincipal(identity);
```

Token-based authentication

The fundamental concept behind a token-based authentication system is simple. It allows users to enter their username and password in order to obtain a token, and then use this token in every request to fetch a specific resource—without using their username and password again. Once the token has been obtained, the user can offer the token to access the resource for a time period, while the token is valid. This is depicted in the following diagram:

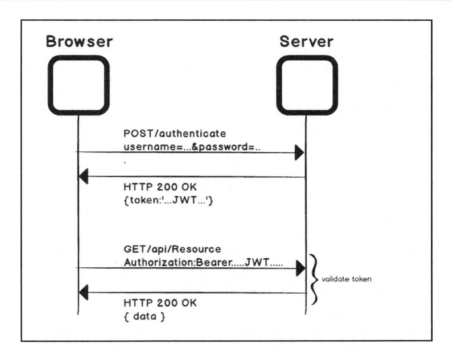

It is stateless and scalable. The server need not store the token in a session or memory (stateless) and hence it is scalable. It is mobile application-ready, secure, and can be used to pass authentication to other systems. Due to the rise of **Single-Page Applications (SPAs)**, **Internet of Things (IoT)**, and web APIs, token-based authentication has gained importance. Although there are different ways to implement the tokens, the **JSON Web Token (JWT)** is more widely used. The JWT is an open standard and has become the de-facto standard token, which defines a compact and self-contained method for securely transmitting information between parties, encoded as a JSON object. The JWT has gained massive popularity due to its compactness, which allows tokens to be easily transmitted through query strings, header attributes, and within the body of requests.

The JWT consists of three parts:

- **Header**: Containing the type of the token and the hashing algorithm.
- **Payload**: Containing the claims of identity.
- **Signature**: Contains the string created using a secret and the combined header and payload. It is used to identify the integrity of the token.

It is in the format xxxxx.yyyyy.zzzzz and a sample token may look like this:

```
eyJhbGciOiJIUzI1NiIsInR5cCI6IkpXVCJ9.eyJuYW1lIjoicmlzaGaGFiaCIsInN1cm5hbWUiOi
J2ZXJtYSISInNpdGGUiOiJodHRwOi8vd3d3LnJpc2hhYmh2ZXJtYS5uZXQiLCJjb2F1dGhvciI6I
k5laGEifQ.Nxhxs024YUyPMVHlsQQWvZ3QN8oXAwL0OAzR6FN62_E
```

You can create the JWT from your data at https://jwt.io/, and can also paste the JWT and check its data.

Let us wrap up our discussion on authentication with a quick discussion of OAuth and OpenID Connect.

- **OAuth 2.0:** It is an open standard for authorization. It is commonly used to provide a way for users to log in to a website (say, our Let's Chat app at http://packtletschat.azurewebsites.net) using a third-party account such as Facebook without having to provide the password of their Facebook account to the Let's Chat app. While we will use it for authentication, it is actually an authorization protocol.

- **OpenID Connect (OIDC):** It is a HTTP-based protocol that uses identity providers to validate that the user is actually who they says they are. It is a very simple protocol and provides protection for passwords. It is a simple layer that works on top of OAuth 2.0 and adds additional security on top of the OAuth protocol. Due to its simplicity, it has found widespread adoption. Google, Facebook, and Stack Exchange are a few of the best-known identity providers. It's important to note that OIDC is a very different protocol to OpenID. The latter is an XML-based protocol that follows similar approaches and goals to OIDC, but in a less developer-friendly way.

Authorization

As discussed earlier, authorization is orthogonal and independent from authentication. Let's have a quick glance at the different types of authorization:

- Simple authorization
- Role-based authorization
- Claim-based authorization

Let's discuss them in the next sections.

Simple authorization

If you have worked with ASP.NET MVC before, you may already be familiar with authorization. The [Authorize] and [AllowAnonymous] attributes are the inbuilt authorization components in the framework. At the simplest level, applying the [Authorize] attribute over a Controller or action restricts the access to the Controller or action to authenticated users only. If you apply the [Authorize] attribute to a Controller, it applies to all the actions:

```
[Authorize]
public class AccountController : Controller
{
    public ActionResult Login()
    {
    }

    public ActionResult Logout()
    {
    }
}
```

In the preceding code, only authenticated users have access to the Login action as well. This doesn't make sense as I want to log in when I am not logged in, and not when I am already logged in. So if you want it to be applied to only a few actions, then apply the attribute to those actions alone. The other way to prevent this situation is to use the [AllowAnnonymous] attribute on the Login action, and that makes it accessible to non-authenticated users as well.

> Treat [AllowAnonymous] like a 0, and [Authorize] as 1. So if you apply [Authorize] on the Controller and [AllowAnonymous] on an action, that action will be accessible anonymously ($1 \times 0 = 0$), while other actions will require authentication. On the contrary, if you apply [AllowAnonymous] on the controller and [Authorize] on an action, all the actions will be accessible anonymously. The reason for this is that anything multiplied by 0 is 0, so if you apply [AllowAnonymous] on the Controller, all other action level attributes are bypassed.

Role-based authorization

When a `ClaimsPrincipal` object is created, like we did previously, there is a property called `IsInRole`. This property provides us access to the `Roles` of the user. Role-based authorization checks are declarative. They can be used in the same way, using the `[Authorize]` attribute that we have seen, by passing in the `Roles` parameter:

```
[Authorize(Roles = "Administrator,ITAdminsitrator")]
public class UserAdministrationController : Controller
{
    ....
}
```

In the preceding example, all the actions of `UserAdministrationController` are accessible to authenticated users with either the `Adminsitrator` or `ITAdministrator` roles. So, we can provide multiple roles as comma-separated values in the `Roles` parameter and they will be treated as an *or* condition. You can further restrict access to only one of the roles by providing the attribute at the action level.

What if I need to have an *and* condition between roles? The following snippet will ensure that actions are accessible only if the authenticated user has both `ITAdministrator` and `Administrator` roles:

```
[Authorize(Roles = "ITAdminsitrator")]
[Authorize(Roles = "Administrator")]
public class UserAdministrationController : Controller
{
    ....
}
```

If we look at the overloads of the `[Authorize]` attribute, there is an overload that accepts the following policy:

```
[Authorize()]
  ▲ 2 of 2 ▼  AuthorizeAttribute(string policy, Properties: [ActiveAuthenticationSchemes = string], [AuthenticationSchemes = string], [Policy = string], [Roles = string])
      ▶  Initializes a new instance of the AuthorizeAttribute class with the specified policy.
      policy: The name of the policy to require for authorization.
```

Policy-based role checks are also supported and can be done at the `Startup` in the `ConfigureServices()` method while configuring authorization:

```
public void ConfigureServices(IServiceCollection services)
{
    services.AddMvc();
    services.AddAuthorization(options =&gt;
    {
        options.AddPolicy("RequireAdminRole", policy =&gt;
        policy.RequireRole("Administrator"));
    });
}

[Authorize(Policy="RequireAdminRole")]
public IActionResult HighPreviligeAction()
{
    return View();
}
```

Claims-based authorization

When you want to authorize based on user claims, then we can use claims-based authorization. A real-world example would be when you are driving a vehicle and the traffic police stop you, suspecting you are younger than 18 years. Then, you take out your driving license and claim that you are a perfectly legal age to drive . The police accept your claim (since it is issued by a valid authority) and let you drive on. This is claims-based authorization. Claims-based authorization checks are also declarative and can be decorated on a controller or action. Claims requirements are policy-based, so like in the previous section, we need to register the policy at startup, expressing the claims requirement. In the preceding example, the code would look like this:

```
services.AddAuthorization(options =&gt;
    {
        options.AddPolicy("RequireClaim", policy =&gt;
        policy.RequireClaim("&lt;&lt;Claim Needed&gt;&gt;"));
    });
```

This discussion should have given you a pretty clear view of authentication and authorization, and you should now be able to dive deep into these topics and broaden and deepen your knowledge on these fundamental concepts.

We also notice that all authentication and authorization is implemented in the `ConfigureServices()` method of the `Startup` class where the pipeline is configured and middleware is added. To complete the discussion, let's quickly understand the ASP.NET Core pipeline, and how it serves the requests. The following diagram illustrates how the request is served by ASP.NET Core in a step-by-step fashion:

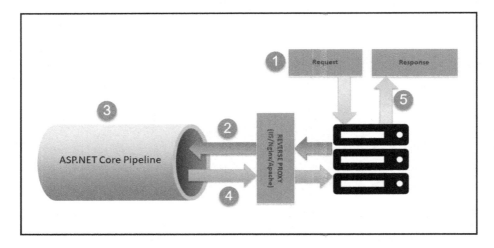

Here is the flow:

1. The browser sends the HTTP request to the server. The request is received by the reverse proxy.
2. The request is forwarded by the reverse proxy to ASP.NET Core.
3. The ASP.NET Core web server receives the request and routes it through its pipeline, through middleware. After passing through middleware, the request is processed by the ASP.NET Core application, which generates the response and passes it back.
4. The ASP.NET Core web server sends the response to the reverse proxy.
5. The HTTP response is sent to the browser.

 A reverse proxy is a type of proxy server that retrieves resources on behalf of a client from one or more servers. It can be defined as a software component that is responsible for receiving requests and forwarding them on to the appropriate web server. The reverse proxy is exposed directly to the internet, whereas the underlying web server is exposed only to the proxy. This setup has several benefits, primarily security and performance for web servers.

Let's look at the details of *Step 3*, as it talks about the ASP.NET Core web server and its pipeline, which is our area of interest. First things first. What is middleware?

Middleware

As per the ASP.NET Core documentation (available at `https://docs.microsoft.com/en-us/aspnet/core/fundamentals/middleware/?tabs=aspnetcore2x`), middleware is a software that is assembled into an application pipeline to handle requests and responses. Each component:

- Chooses whether to pass the request to the next component in the pipeline
- Can perform work before and after the next component in the pipeline is invoked

Request delegates are used to build the request pipeline. The request delegates handle each HTTP request. Request delegates are configured using the `Run`, `Map`, and `Use` extension methods. An individual request delegate can be specified inline as an anonymous method (called **inline middleware**), or it can be defined in a reusable class. These reusable classes and inline anonymous methods are *middleware*. Each middleware component in the request pipeline is responsible for invoking the next component in the pipeline, or short-circuiting the chain as required.

The classical diagram of middleware in the pipeline, which is available at Microsoft's official ASP.NET Core documentation site, is shown here, with the added detail of steps, which makes it extremely lucid. What happens in *Step 3* is shown in the following diagram:

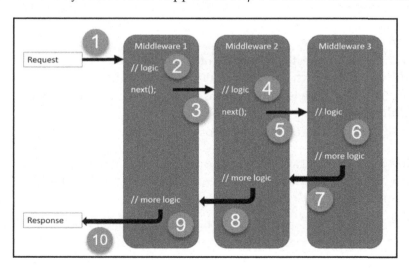

Lets look at it in a step-by-step approach:

1. **Step 1**: The request is received by **Middleware 1**. The pseudo code of **Middleware 1** in the `Configure(IApplicationBuilder app, IHostingEnvironment env)` method of `Startup.cs` would be `UseMiddleware1();`, as it processes the request and invokes the next middleware. Recall that we discussed the `Use`, `Map`, and `Run` methods in brief in `Chapter 3`, *Building Our First .NET Core Game Tic-Tac-Toe*.
2. **Step 2**: The code/logic of **Middleware 1** is executed.
3. **Step 3**: `RequestDelegate`—`next();` is executed, which invokes the next middleware.
4. **Step 4**: The code/logic of **Middleware 2** is executed. The pseudo code of **Middleware 2** in the `Configure(IApplicationBuilder app, IHostingEnvironment env)` method of `Startup.cs` would be `UseMiddleware2();`.
5. **Step 5**: `RequestDelegate`—`next();` is executed, which invokes the next middleware.
6. **Step 6**: The code/logic of **Middleware 3** is executed. Based on this diagram, the request is handled here, but we can chain in as much middleware as we need. The pseudo code of **Middleware 3** in the `Configure(IApplicationBuilder app, IHostingEnvironment env)` method of `Startup.cs` can be either `UseMiddleware3();`, which doesn't call `next();`, or it can simply be `RunMiddleware3();`, which short-circuits the pipeline. Normally, this would be the MVC `Routing` middleware, which would route the request to the MVC `Controller`, which processes the request and returns the response.
7. **Step 7**: As the request is handled in the last step, the response is returned to **Middleware 2**, which can do further processing of the response and return it.
8. **Steps 8 and 9**: Likewise, the response is processed in **Middleware 2** and **Middleware 1**.
9. **Step 10**: The processed response from all middleware is returned.

If we look at the `Configure(IApplicationBuilder app, IHostingEnvironment env)` method in our `Startup.cs` class, we see the following code, which comes with the default MVC template:

```
public void Configure(IApplicationBuilder app, IHostingEnvironment env)
{
    if (env.IsDevelopment())
    {
```

```
        app.UseDeveloperExceptionPage();
        app.UseBrowserLink();
    }
    else
    {
        app.UseExceptionHandler("/Home/Error");
    }

    app.UseStaticFiles();
    app.UseMvc(routes =&gt;
    {
        routes.MapRoute(name: "default",template: "
        {controller=Home}/{action=Index}/{id?}");
    });
}
```

They say that a picture is worth a thousand words, so to understand this code in the context of the pipeline, if we draw the diagram for a non-developer environment (that is, `env.IsDevelopment() == false;`), here is roughly what it would look like:

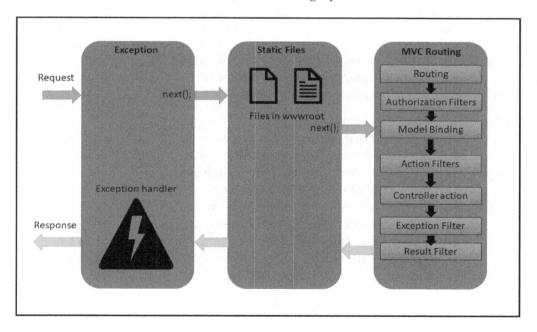

We can see that, based on the code for the `else` case, the request first goes through the exception middleware through `app.UseExceptionHandler("/Home/Error");`. This is done to ensure that if any part of the code encounters the exception in the pipeline, it is handled by the exception handler, so it's kept first. From the diagram, we can note that during the request processing, the middleware does nothing, but just invokes the next middleware in the chain. This can be seen from the ASP.NET Core source code, which is freely available for everyone to see and learn from GitHub (`https://github.com/aspnet`). I would highly encourage readers to browse the code and see the implementation for a better understanding of the way things have been implemented by the ASP.NET Core team.

Next in line is the static file middleware, which serves static files such as `css`, `js`, `images`, and so on placed in the `wwwroot` folder. These should be served fast as it makes sense to keep this middleware early in the pipeline. If a request for a static file comes, the static file middleware serves the request and *short-circuits* the pipeline, so that other unnecessary code is not executed while serving the static file contents. This is configured through `app.UseStaticFiles();`. Then comes the MVC routing, which routes the incoming request to its desired controller action. We see that there are a number of items that are executed in this middleware. We will go into detail concerning each of these items in later sections and chapters, but the important stuff to note here is that the request is served from the controller action and then routed back through the same pipeline. The static file middleware has no role while a non-static file request is being served, and that becomes evident from the diagram. If there is an exception, it would be handled by the exception handler and the response is served back.

> The first `app.Run` delegate terminates the pipeline. That is, after this, even if you add any further middleware or code, it will not be executed. Multiple request delegates or middleware can be chained using `app.Use`. The `next` parameter represents the next delegate in the pipeline. We can short-circuit the pipeline by not invoking the `next` action. Never call `next.Invoke` after the response has been sent to the client. Changes to `HttpResponse` after the response has started will throw an exception. The order in which middleware components are added in the `Configure` method defines the order in which they are invoked on the requests, and the reverse order for the response.

Hopefully, by now we have a relatively good understanding of the ASP.NET Core pipeline and middleware. Before we write middleware of our own and learn how to plug it into our pipeline, let's first learn about Dependency Injection, as it will be used extensively in whatever ASP.NET Core application that we write.

Dependency Injection

Dependency Injection (**DI**) is a software design pattern that enables us to develop loosely coupled code and is a great way to reduce tight coupling between software components. The **D** of the **SOLID** design principles stands for **Dependency Inversion Principle** (**DIP**), which states that *"high-level modules should not depend upon low-level modules. Both should depend on abstractions"*. That is, it depends on abstractions, not on concrete implementations. If we speak in the language of the code, the class should not use new or static helper methods to populate its dependencies; it should rather have them injected. If you ever heard your architect or lead utter *"program to interfaces, not implementations"*, it's because he/she wants you to use DI. DI is the implementation of DIP.

DI enables better:

- Testability
- Maintainability
- Reusability

I am not great at dishing out examples, but let me give it a try with a real-world scenario. Suppose there is a boy who wants to get married. To get married, he needs a girl, so he is dependent on a girl for marriage. The pseudo code for this scenario would be roughly as follows:

```
public class Boy : IBoy
{
    //// Get married. First get the girl friend and then marry her.
    public void GetMarried()
    {
        IGirl girl = this.GetGirl(); //// Returns null, if boy doesn't
        have a girl-friend.
        //// Marry with girl.
    }
}
```

We notice that the Boy class has hard coupling with the girl class, as it gets a specific instance of the girl class in the marriage method and marries her. This hard coupling represents that the boy already has a girlfriend and so boy and girl are tightly linked. Well, most boys are not lucky (or unlucky, depending upon how you see it), enough to have a girlfriend. Also, the preceding code might not work for all scenarios, such as if the boy doesn't have a girlfriend or if the parents find a girl for the boy.

A better way of implementing the preceding code would be to remove the hard-coupling of the girl by injecting the `girl` object from outside. With this, the `GetMarried` method is generic as it, removes the hard-coupling of the `girl` class, and will work for all boys, depending on the `girl` object passed:

```
public class Boy : IBoy
{
    //// Get married. The girl object passed can be boy's girlfriend or
        any girl selected by his parents
    public void GetMarried(IGirl girl)
    {
        //// Marry with girl.
    }
}
```

This is the simplest example of DI, in which rather than creating a new instance of a dependent object, we inject the dependency from outside. There are various ways in which dependency can be injected. We will discuss only a few here, with reference to classes and interfaces, as follows.

Let us suppose we have two classes:

- `CoreClass` is the main class implementing the `ICore` interface
- `DependencyClass` is the class implementing the `IDependency` interface, so that `CoreClass` is dependent on `DependencyClass`:

  ```
  public class CoreClass : ICore
  {
      public CoreClass()
      {
      }

      //// Class Methods. Hidden for brevity
  }

  public class DependencyClass : IDependency
  {
      public DependencyClass()
      {
      }

      //// Class methods. Hidden for brevity
  }
  ```

Taking the preceding classes and interfaces as a reference, we can inject the dependency in the following ways:

- **Constructor injection**: In constructor injection, the dependency object is injected at the time of constructing the object, that is, in the constructor of the class. This way, the dependency is clearly spelled out at the time of the object's creation. The disadvantages are that once the object is created, the dependency cannot be changed and since the dependency is injected in the constructor, the class doesn't have a default parameterless constructor. The constructor-injected code for the preceding class would look like this:

```
public class CoreClass : ICore
{
    private readonly IDependency dependency;
    public CoreClass(IDependency dependency)
    {
        this.dependency = dependency;
    }

    //// Class Methods. Hidden for brevity
}
```

- **Property setter injection**: In property injection, the dependency object is injected as a property setter. This way, the default construction of the class continues to exist and the dependency can be changed, even after object's creation, by just setting the property. The disadvantage is that since the dependency is not injected at the time of the object creation, the dependency to be set can be missed and hence may result in runtime errors. The property injected code would look like this:

```
public class CoreClass : ICore
{
    public CoreClass()
    {
    }

    public IDependency Dependency {get;set;}
    //// Class Methods. Hidden for brevity
}
```

In the preceding `CoreClass` class, there is a property named `Dependency` of type `IDependency` that is needed for the class to function correctly. However, if the developer just initializes `CoreClass` by creating a new instance of it and forgets to set the `Dependency` property, we may encounter a runtime exception. In contrast, in constructor injection, since the dependency is passed at the time of the object's creation, we are never at risk of such issues.

We have seen how dependencies can be injected. Imagine a system where we have numerous classes in which dependency needs to be injected. If we follow any one the preceding approaches for injection and create the objects at every place where they are needed, it will become spaghetti code or become completely messed up. It is therefore meaningful to have classes to create these classes and inject dependencies as needed. These classes are called containers, DI containers, **Inversion of Control (IoC)** containers. A container can be thought of as a factory that is responsible for providing instances of types that are requested from it. If a given type has declared that it has dependencies, and the container has been configured to provide the dependency types, it will create the dependencies as part of creating the requested instance. In this way, complex dependency graphs can be provided to classes without the need for any hardcoded object construction. In addition to creating objects with their dependencies, containers typically manage object lifetimes within the application.

ASP.NET Core comes with a very simple built-in container (the `IServiceProvider` interface) that supports constructor injection by default. ASP.NET's container refers to the types it manages as services. These services can be injected into the container in the `ConfigureServices` method of the ASP.NET Core application's `Startup` class.

There are certain facts about the inbuilt ASP.NET Core container that we need to be aware of to make correct use of DI in the app.

The constructor for the dependency that should be resolved must have a `public` access modifier.

There should be only one constructor that gets resolved with a given set of parameters. Constructor overloads are supported, but only one overload can exist, whose arguments can all be fulfilled by DI. If multiple constructors exist, you may encounter `InvalidOperationException`.

Notice the signature of the `ConfigureServices` method in the `Startup` class:

```
// This method gets called by the runtime. Use this method to add services
to the container.
public void ConfigureServices(IServiceCollection services)
{
    //// Code excluded for brevity.
}
```

This method exposes the `IServicesCollection`, where we can add our own services/types as needed. This can be done by the following extension methods in the `Microsoft.Extensions.DependencyInjection` namespace:

- `AddTransient`: Use this extension method to instantiate types that should be created each time they are requested. This should be used for lightweight, stateless services.
- `AddScoped`: Use this extension method to instantiate types that should be created once per request. Types that are based on requests should be instantiated on a per-request basis and hence should be created by this method.
- `AddSingleton`: Use this extension method to create types that should be instantiated only once and should be used throughout the life cycle of the application. A common example of this scenario is caching. One instance is good enough for the application.

My architect calls these *every time, sometimes, and one time*, respectively. Transients are created every time they are requested; scoped are created once per request, so sometimes. Singletons are created once in the lifetime of the application, so one time. Nice way to remember!

 On a lighter note and to digest the concept: the **Prime Minister (PM)** of a nation can be a good example of a singleton. Irrespective of where and how many times he/she is needed, there is one and only one PM, so the PM is a singleton. Likewise, examples of transient and scoped can be formed. This is left as an exercise and teaser to readers to come up with real-world examples of transient and scoped.

Each of these extension methods have seven or more overloads to provide flexibility and cater to different needs, such as passing the concrete instance or providing a factory method to create the object. Readers should have a good look at the overloads and make effective use of these methods. The easiest way to do so is either to use *F12* on one of these extension methods in Visual Studio and read the method documentation, or use the object browser of Visual Studio, or browse the source code on GitHub (`https://github.com/PacktPublishing/.NET-Core-2.0-By-Example`).

I will list a few of the ways by which we can inject the types/services:

```
services.AddSingleton&lt;IHttpContextAccessor, HttpContextAccessor&gt;();
//// Will inject HttpContextAccessor where IHttpContextAccessor is used
    but only one instance.
services.AddSingleton&lt;HttpContextAccessor&gt;();

//// Directly inject HttpContextAccessor as a singleton
services.AddSingleton&lt;Connection&gt;((serviceProvider) =&gt;
this.CreateConnection(serviceProvider));

//// Singleton using factory method overload using service provider.
    Same overloads apply to transient and scoped as well.
services.AddTransient&lt;IUserRepository, UserRepository&gt;();

//// A new instance of UserRepository would be created and passed,
    whenever it is requested.
services.AddScoped&lt;IScopedService, ScopedService&gt;();
//// Would be created and passed, once per request.
```

This concludes our discussion on DI. For a more detailed and extensive dive into DI in ASP.NET Core 2.0, please visit `https://docs.microsoft.com/en-us/aspnet/core/fundamentals/dependency-injection`.

How do you write custom middleware?

Now is the right time to create simple middleware of our own and plug it into the pipeline, so that all this theory that we have gone through ends with a practical example.

We can write either inline middleware or a neatly written class which can be configured at the startup. We will write both:

```
public void Configure(IApplicationBuilder app)
{
    app.Run(async context =&gt;
    {
```

```
        await context.Response.WriteAsync(".NET Core 2.0 By Example");
    });
}
```

This is the simplest middleware that one can write. This is the `Run` middleware and short-circuits the pipeline after execution, and just sends a response with the message " .NET Core 2.0 By Example". It has been plugged with this code into the `Configure` method of `Startup.cs/`.

Having seen inline middleware, let's write the more serious middleware that you would write in your app.

Let's begin by creating a class called `MyFirstMiddleware`.

Since middleware is just a request delegate that processes the request/response and then invokes the next one in the chain, the following is how we would create the class for middleware. Notice the next request delegate is expected to be resolved by DI. It's a pretty simple class, consisting of:

- A `readonly` field to hold the reference to the next `RequestDelegate`.
- A constructor that expects the next `RequestDelegate` to be executed as the parameter. During construction, it sets the field with the reference of the next request delegate.
- An `Invoke` method that takes an `HttpContext` object to fiddle with and then passes it along to the next middleware.

Let's have a look at the code:

```
public class MyFirstMiddleware
{
    //// To hold the next middleware in the pipeline.
    private readonly RequestDelegate next;

    public MyFirstMiddleware(RequestDelegate next)
    {
        this.next = next;
    }
    public async Task Invoke(HttpContext httpContext)
    {
        // Execute the logic, that doesn't write to response.

        // Call the next delegate in the pipeline
        await this.next(httpContext);
    }
}
```

With this, we have our simple middleware code ready. However, we are yet to plug it into our app pipeline. To do so, we will create an extension method of `IApplicationBuilder`, which internally uses the `UseMiddleware&lt;T&gt;` method to register the middleware, as shown here:

```
public static class MyFirstMiddlewareExtensions
{
    public static IApplicationBuilder UseMyFirstMiddleware(this
    IApplicationBuilder builder)
    {
        return builder.UseMiddleware&lt;MyFirstMiddlewareExtensions&gt;();
    }
}
```

Finally, to plug it into our pipeline, go to the `Configure` method of the `Startup` class and add the middleware with a simple single line of code, `app.UseMyFirstMiddleware();`.

With this, we have created our very first middleware and plugged it into our app pipeline. Sweet, short, and simple!

Next, we will look at the configuration providers in ASP.NET Core and how we can read configuration and use it in our app.

Extension methods in C# allow us to extend an existing type with new functionality, and add new methods to it, without having to derive or recompile the old type. Extension methods are a special kind of static method, but they are called as if they are instance methods on the extended type. The most common extension methods are the `LINQ` standard query operators. ASP.NET Core makes extensive use of extension methods for registering services.

Configuration

When we develop ASP.NET Core web apps, we will quickly realize that we need to change a few settings at runtime. To give an example, consider a web application that makes API calls to the service. When you develop the web app, the service is deployed in some development server and when you deploy it in production, the service URL is different, so the URL should not be hardcoded in the application. Instead, it should be read from the configuration, so that it can be changed without having to recompile the code. Another often used example is that of database connection strings, if the app makes use of them. This section takes a look at how we can accomplish this in ASP.NET Core.

The ASP.NET Core configuration model has three main constructs of interest:

- `ConfigurationProvider`
- `ConfigurationRoot`
- `ConfigurationBuilder`

As shown in the following screenshot, the map diagram is constructed from
`Microsoft.Extensions.Configuration`:

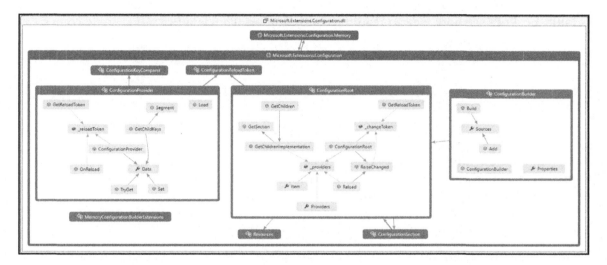

`ConfigurationProvider` is abstracted from the developer and hence we would not see it,
but it's good to know that there is support for multiple configuration providers. A few of
the important ones are:

- **JSON file**: Reads the JSON file in the app's `Startup` folder and configures the
  application
- **Command-line arguments**: While launching the app, command-line arguments
  can be passed as a key value to configure the application
- **Environment variables**: Setting the environment variables, the provider reads the
  environment variable and takes care of configuration
- **Azure Key Vault**: We will cover this in later chapters when we discuss Azure,
  but as the name suggests, it is a key vault.

So in a single app, we can choose to read a few configurations from the JSON file, a few from the command line, and so on. When we add multiple providers, it's important to consider the order in which we add them, as that defines the order in which the configuration values are added to the underlying dictionary. Configuration values from later providers will overwrite values with the same key from earlier providers. Also, we can notice in the diagram that there is a `GetReloadToken` method in `ConfigurationProvider` and a `Reload` method in `ConfigurationRoot` as well. If we read the documentation (using *F12* in Visual Studio), we know that the configuration system supports reloading the configuration without having to restart the web app, which is fantastic. Let's see how we can read the configuration. The default `Startup.cs` comes with the following code:

```
public Startup(IConfiguration configuration)
{
    Configuration = configuration;
}

public IConfiguration Configuration { get; }
```

Notice that we already have the `IConfiguration` interface injected in the `Startup` constructor, which sets the `Configuration` property of the `Startup`. Also notice that when we create an app from the template, `appsettings.json` is included by default. Essentially, the default code has already wired up JSON-based configuration for us and we can leverage its goodness without having to code anything extra.

To make effective use of the `Configuration` property, lets do *F12* (go to definition) on `IConfiguration` and check out its properties. The following is the code that comes up in Visual Studio:

```
//
// Summary:
// Represents a set of key/value application configuration
    properties.
[DefaultMember("Item")]
public interface IConfiguration
{
    //
    // Summary:
    // Gets or sets a configuration value. //
    // Parameters:
    // key:
    // The configuration key. //
    // Returns:
    // The configuration value.
    string this[string key] { get; set; }
```

```
//
// Summary:
// Gets the immediate descendant configuration sub-sections. //
// Returns:
// The configuration sub-sections.
IEnumerable&lt;IConfigurationSection&gt; GetChildren();

//
// Summary:
// Returns a Microsoft.Extensions.Primitives.IChangeToken that
   can be used to observe
// when this configuration is reloaded. //
// Returns:
// A Microsoft.Extensions.Primitives.IChangeToken.
IChangeToken GetReloadToken();
//
// Summary:
// Gets a configuration sub-section with the specified key. //
// Parameters:
// key:
// The key of the configuration section. //
// Returns:
// The
   Microsoft.Extensions.Configuration.IConfigurationSection. //
// Remarks:
// This method will never return null. If no matching sub-
   section is found with
// the specified key, an empty
   Microsoft.Extensions.Configuration.IConfigurationSection
// will be returned.
IConfigurationSection GetSection(string key);
}
```

So, we see that we can get the value of a key through the indexer property, passing in the key to look up. We can get children, get a reload token, or get a specific section by giving the key. This documentation makes our task of using the configuration extremely easy. Let's see an example. First, define the config that we want to read, as shown here:

```
{
"Book": ".NET Core 2.0 By Example",
  "Genere": {
    "Name": "Technical level 200"
  },
  "Authors": [
    {
      "Name": "Rishabh Verma",
      "Experience": "10"
```

```
    },
    {
      "Name": "Neha Shrivastava",
      "Experience": "7"
    }
  ]
}
```

The code to read the values would be:

```
var book = Configuration["Book"];
var genereName = Configuration["Genere:Name"];
var author1Name = Configuration["Authors:0:Name"];
var author1Experience = Configuration["Authors:0: Experience "];
var author2Name = Configuration["Authors:1:Name"];
var author2Experience = Configuration["Authors:1:Experience"];
```

Notice that we used a zero-based index to access the contents of an array. The rest of the keys are read just by passing in the correct key to the `Configuration` indexer, as we have just seen.

We generally use different configuration settings for different environments. For example, Development, Test, Staging, and Production may all have different configuration settings. The `CreateDefaultBuilder` extension method in an ASP.NET Core 2.0 app adds configuration providers for reading JSON files and environment variables in the following order:

1. `appsettings.json`
2. `appsettings.<EnvironmentName>.json`
3. Environment variables

Here, `appsettings.<EnvironmentName>.json` would overwrite the key values defined in `appsettings.json` and the environment variables would overwrite the key values defined before them.

This didn't need any code changes in our `Startup` class. However, if we wish to use any other named config file, then we will need the code to be changed. The following example uses `config.json` as the configuration file, followed by `config.Development.json`:

```
public Startup(IHostingEnvironment env)
{
    var builder = new ConfigurationBuilder()
        .SetBasePath(env.ContentRootPath)
        .AddJsonFile("config.json")
        .AddJsonFile($"config.{env.EnvironmentName}.json");
```

```
Configuration = builder.Build();
}
```

A thoughtful programmer would say that in my appsettings.json, there may be a variety of sections for caching, database connection strings, service URLs, and so on. Why should I pass on all these values to every place? For example, what has caching to do with the database connection strings section or the service URL? Looks like there is no separation of concerns, and a clear violation of the **I** of **SOLID: Interface Segregation Principle**. Why should caching depend on IConfiguration when it needs just a subsection of it? To prevent these violations, it is *not* recommended to use the preceding way to access settings if configurations are to be read outside of Startup.cs.

We should instead use what is called the Options pattern. Using it is simple: first create a simple **Plain Old CLR Object (POCO)** class and then use it by registering it as a service and consume it wherever we need. It's a simple and dumb class with properties and no logic or smartness.

The POCO class for the preceding example would be:

```
public class BookDetails
{
    public string Book { get; set; }
    public Genere Genere { get; set; }
    public Author[] Authors { get; set; }
}

public class Genere
{
    public string Name { get; set; }
}

public class Author
{
    public string Name { get; set; }
    public string Experience { get; set; }
}
```

To register it, we go to the ConfigureServices method in Startup.cs and add the following line:

```
services.Configure&lt;BookDetails&gt;(Configuration);
```

BookDetails will be populated and added to the container. To use it in the controller, the following code would suffice:

```
private readonly BookDetails details;

public HomeController(IOptions&lt;BookDetails&gt; options)
{
    this.details = options.Value;
}
```

The properties can now be used from the strongly typed object, details. If you wish to overwrite certain properties after the configuration is bound, you can do the following in the ConfigureService method:

```
services.Configure&lt;BookDetails&gt;(Configuration);
services.Configure&lt;BookDetails&gt;(opt =&gt; {opt.Name = "Roslyn via
C#";});
```

This changes the name of the book to "Roslyn Via C#". This is a last-one-wins approach, in which what is done last prevails.

Another question that comes to mind is what if my configuration value changes, do I restart my app like in the old days when modifying the web.config used to restart the app? No, we have this covered in ASP.NET Core. For this, we need to use IOptionsSnapshot, which is designed to support the reloading of configuration data when the configuration file changes. Using IOptionsSnapshot with the reloadOnChange flag set to true, the options are bound to the configuration and reloaded when the file changes.

From the preceding sample, we just need to change IOptions to IOptionsSnapshot and add a flag, reloadOnChange, to true while adding the JSON file in the AddJsonFile method.

Let's take a step back and look at our Program.cs, which is the entry point of the application:

```
public static void Main(string[] args)
{
    BuildWebHost(args).Run();
}

public static IWebHost BuildWebHost(string[] args) =&gt;
        WebHost.CreateDefaultBuilder(args)
        .UseStartup&lt;Startup&gt;()
        .Build();
}
```

The `CreateDefaultBuilder` loads optional configurations from
`appsettings.json`, `appsettings.{Environment}.json`, User Secrets (in
the Development environment), environment variables, and command-line arguments. The
`CommandLine` configuration provider is called last. Calling the provider last allows the
command-line arguments passed at runtime to override the configuration set by the other
configuration providers called earlier, by the last-one-wins approach. Also, it is important
to note that `reloadOnChange` is enabled for the `appsettings` file and so command-line
arguments are overridden if a matching configuration value in an `appsettings` file is
changed after the app starts.

When we work in enterprise applications, we will realize that there are a variety of
configuration settings, such as secrets, passwords, and so on, that should not be kept in
configuration files and hence should be kept out of the application code. Also, as a best
practice, we should not be using production secrets in our development environment. In
production also, these should be read from Azure Key Vault, which we will look at in later
chapters. In the development environment, we can use the Secret Manager tool to safeguard
secrets.

Before seeing how to use User Secrets, a question comes to mind: is that why we don't use
environment variables to keep secrets away from the application, as it is supported by
ASP.NET Core and is also there by default in the template code? Yes, we can use
environment variables. However, environment variables are stored as plain text and can be
accessed from any third-party code, so we can use them in local development but should
not rely on them for production deployments.

The Secret Manager tool is just a fancy name given to store the secrets of a .NET Core
project outside of the code base during development. The data stored is *not* encrypted. The
only advantage this approach provides is that the secrets would not be part of the code and
hence will not be checked in the source control, and so the secret will remain a secret during
development. The secret is stored in a JSON file, which is kept in the user profile folder. To
set up the User Secret tool, edit the `.csproj` file and add the following line in the
`ItemGroup` node:

```
&lt;DotNetCliToolReference
Include="Microsoft.Extensions.SecretManager.Tools" Version="2.0.0" /&gt;
```

So the final code looks like this:

```
&lt;ItemGroup&gt;
    &lt;DotNetCliToolReference
    Include="Microsoft.VisualStudio.Web.CodeGeneration.Tools"
    Version="2.0.0" /&gt;
    &lt;DotNetCliToolReference
    Include="Microsoft.Extensions.SecretManager.Tools" Version="2.0.0"
    /&gt;
&lt;/ItemGroup&gt;
```

Save the `.csproj` file. This will restore the package we just added. Now, right-click the project in the **Solution Explorer** and select **Manage User Secrets**. This will add a new node named `UserSecretId` in the `PropertyGroup`. Save the file. A file named `secrets.json` will open up in Visual Studio. Hover over it and see the path. It will be `%AppData%\microsoft\UserSecrets\&lt;userSecretsId&gt;\secrets.json`.

Now we can add key value-pairs in the JSON file, just like we did for the configuration file. To read them, we need to add a couple of lines of code in our startup, as shown here:

```
public Startup(IHostingEnvironment env)
{
    var builder = new ConfigurationBuilder()
        .SetBasePath(env.ContentRootPath)
        .AddJsonFile("config.json")
        .AddJsonFile($"config.{env.EnvironmentName}.json");

    Configuration = builder.Build();
}
```

After this, we can access the secret, just like we access anything else from the configuration:

```
var secretValue = Configuration["SecretKey"];
```

This concludes our configuration discussion. Let's check out how we can do logging.

Logging

ASP.NET Core supports the logging API, which works with a wide variety of logging providers. We can write logs to one or more locations and we can also plug in third-party logging frameworks, such as NLog, Serilog, and so on. In this section, we will look at out-of-the box logging, as it is sufficient for the logging needs of most apps.

Let's see the architecture of the logging infrastructure. The code map diagram for logging is shown here:

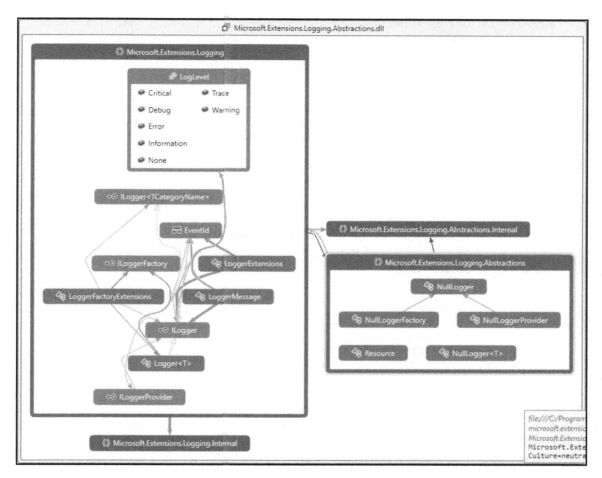

As we can see, it consists of the following main components:

- ILogger/ ILogger<TCategoryName>: We will use this in our app to log messages. We can see it has the IsEnabled() method to check whether logging is enabled and Log to write the log.
- ILoggerFactory: It has a method to add a provider and logger.
- ILoggerProvider: It has a method to create the logger and it will control the output location of the log.

We also notice the `EventId`, `LogLevel` enumeration, and extensions for registering the logging.

We can configure logging at the time of building the `WebHost` in the `Program.cs` file, as shown here:

```
public static IWebHost BuildWebHost(string[] args) =>
        WebHost.CreateDefaultBuilder(args)
            .UseStartup<Startup>()
            .ConfigureLogging((hostingContext, logging) => {
             logging.AddConfiguration(hostingContext.
             Configuration.GetSection("Logging"));
             logging.AddConsole();
             logging.AddDebug();
        })
            .Build();
```

This code configures the logging to read the logging configuration section provided in `appsettings.json` and adds console and debug logging. Alternatively, we can inject `ILoggerFactory` as a parameter in the `Configure` method of `Startup.cs` and configure `loggerFactory`, as shown here:

```
public void Configure(IApplicationBuilder app, IHostingEnvironment env,
ILoggerFactory loggerFactory)
{
    loggerFactory.AddConsole();
    loggerFactory.AddDebug();
    //// Other methods omitted for brevity.
}
```

Like any other type or service in the ASP.NET Core application, the logger is also injected into a class or controller through DI. Here we inject `ILogger<T>`, where `T` is the name of the class. The type parameter `T` is used to define the *category* as it follows the `ILogger<TCategoryName>` interface.

For example, to write a log message in an ASP.NET Core controller, `HomeController`, we would inject the `ILogger<HomeController>` and call one of the logging extension methods on `ILogger`:

```
public class HomeController: Controller
{
    private readonly ILogger<HomeController> logger;

    public HomeController(ILogger<HomeController> logger)
    {
        this.logger = logger;
```

```
    }

    public IActionResult Index()
    {
        logger.LogInformation($"Calling {nameof(this.Index)}");
        return View();
    }
}
```

This will write a log message to each output of the configured logging providers. The following is what it would look like in the console:

ASP.NET Core includes numerous logging providers out of the box, which we can use to write log messages to various locations:

- **Console provider**: To write log messages to the console
- **Debug provider**: To write log messages to the **Debug** window while debugging in Visual Studio
- **EventSource provider**: To write log messages using Event Tracing for Windows
- **Event Log provider**: To write log messages to the Windows event log

There is support for third-party structured logging as well, which is greatly useful, as it makes finding and diagnosing issues easier in production. Structured logging involves associating key-value pairs with each log entry, instead of a simple string of messages. We will not delve into this discussion, but it's good to know and the reader should take it up as an exercise to explore and implement structured logging with ASP.NET Core apps.

A *category* is included with each log that is created. We specify the category while creating an ILogger object. The category may be any string, but the convention is to use the qualified name of the class from which the logs are written, like we did in our previous example. We can also specify the log level, which indicates the degree of severity or importance of the log. For example, typically we use an information log when a method executes normally, a warning log when a method returns a 404 return code, and an error log when an unexpected exception is caught. Log methods that include the level in the method name are extension methods for ILogger , such asLogError,LogWarning, LogInformation, and LogTrace. Behind the scenes, these methods call the Log method whcih takes a LogLevel parameter. ASP.NET Core defines the following log levels, ordered here from least to highest severity. The documentation of the code makes it intuitive to understand:

```
//
// Summary:
// Defines logging severity levels.
public enum LogLevel
{
    //
    // Summary:
    // Logs that contain the most detailed messages. These messages
        may contain sensitive
    // application data. These messages are disabled by default and
        should never be
    // enabled in a production environment.
    Trace = 0,
    //
    // Summary:
    // Logs that are used for interactive investigation during
        development. These logs
    // should primarily contain information useful for debugging
        and have no long-term
    // value.
    Debug = 1,
    //
    // Summary:
    // Logs that track the general flow of the application. These
        logs should have long-term
    // value.
    Information = 2,
    //
    // Summary:
    // Logs that highlight an abnormal or unexpected event in the
        application flow,
    // but do not otherwise cause the application execution to
```

```
        stop.
      Warning = 3,
      //
      // Summary:
      // Logs that highlight when the current flow of execution is
         stopped due to a failure.
      // These should indicate a failure in the current activity, not
         an application-wide
      // failure.
      Error = 4,
      //
      // Summary:
      // Logs that describe an unrecoverable application or system
         crash, or a catastrophic
      // failure that requires immediate attention.
      Critical = 5,
      //
      // Summary:
      // Not used for writing log messages. Specifies that a logging
         category should not
      // write any messages.
      None = 6
   }
```

We can set minimum trace levels while configuring the logger as well, with the following code, which creates the WebHost in the Program.cs file:

```
.ConfigureLogging(logging =&gt; logging.SetMinimumLevel(LogLevel.Warning))
```

We can also do scope-based logging; that is, logging, on a logical group of operations within a scope in order to attach same data to each log. The BeginScope method is specifically made for this purpose and the following example shows the sample usage:

```
using (this.logger.BeginScope($"Logging scope demo"))
{
    this.logger.LogInformation($"Calling {nameof(this.Index)}");
    return View();
}
```

Before we conclude, let's have a look at the configuration for Logging in the appSettings.json file. Consider the following Logging configuration:

```
{
  "Logging": {
    "IncludeScopes": false,
    "Debug": {
      "LogLevel": {
        "Default": "Information"
      }
    },
    "Console": {
      "LogLevel": {
        "Microsoft.AspNetCore.Mvc.Razor": "Error",
        "Default": "Information"
      }
    },
    "LogLevel": {
      "Default": "Debug"
    }
  }
}
```

The preceding configuration defines four logging filters. The following is the interpretation of the configuration:

1. Scope-based logging is disabled, as we have IncludeScopes as false. One of the primary use cases of scope-based logging comes in transactional data access or operations, where you may want to attach the same identifier to all the operations that happen in the transaction.
2. The default log level of the Debug log provider is Information for all categories.
3. The default log level of the Console log provider is Information for all categories.
4. The log level of categories beginning with Microsoft.AspNetCore.Mvc.Razor is Error for the Console log provider.
5. The default log level for all log providers for all categories is Debug.

For a detailed and deep dive into logging in ASP.NET Core 2.0, readers should visit https://docs.microsoft.com/en-us/aspnet/core/fundamentals/logging/?tabs=aspnetcore2x.

With this, we conclude our discussion of logging, and this chapter as well.

Summary

In this chapter, we discussed the Let's Chat web application, its requirements and high-level design, and did the project setup to get started with coding. After doing the project setup, we learned about ASP.NET Core fundamentals, such as authentication, authorization, middleware, Dependency Injection, configuration, and logging.

In the next chapter, we will complete the fundamentals and then dive into coding the Let's Chat application.

5

Developing the Let's Chat Web Application

In the previous chapter, we got the requirements and high level design of the Let's Chat web application. We got started with the Let's Chat web application by setting up project. We learned about the fundamental concepts of ASP.NET Core in the process. In this chapter, we will develop the Let's Chat web application and learn about a few more concepts of ASP.NET Core. We will cover the following topics in this chapter:

- ASP.NET Core 2.0 fundamentals
- Implementing authentication through Facebook

ASP.NET Core 2.0 fundamentals

This section is a continuation of our journey of learning ASP.NET Core 2.0 fundamentals that we started in the previous chapter. We will (re)visit the fundamentals, so that we can use them correctly while coding the app. In this section, we will take a quick lap around MVC and we will further discuss routing, filters, error handling, and so on. Let's start with MVC.

Quick lap around MVC

MVC stands for **Model-View-Controller**. The intent of this pattern is to achieve separation of concerns. In general terms, we can draw an analogy of MVC with *"Division of labour"*. In this architectural pattern, the application is divided into three distinct components: the Model, the View, and the Controller. When a user requests a resource in the server, it is routed to a Controller which works with the Model to perform user actions and/or CRUD (**Create**, **Read**, **Update**, **Delete**) operations. The Controller then chooses the View to display the user interface to the user, and provides it with the required Model data. The following diagram displays the three main components:

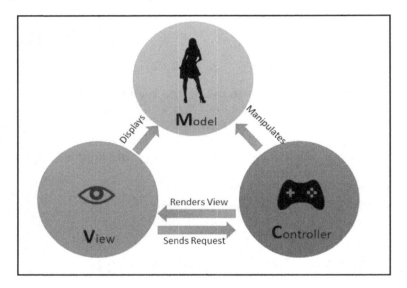

We see that in the diagram, both the View and the Controller depend on the Model. However, the Model depends on neither of them. This is one of the key benefits of the pattern and also the golden rule for correct implementation of MVC. Using this separation, we can build and test the Model independently of the visual presentation. The **S** of the **SOLID** design principle, **single responsibility principle** (**SRP**), is at the heart of MVC. It also reiterates the **don't repeat yourself** (**DRY**) principle. MVC is all about the separation of concerns to have better test-ability and maintainability. The responsibility of each of the components is clearly laid out:

- **Model** is the central component of this architectural pattern and represents the data. It maintains the data of the application.

- **View** is the visual component and is the user interface for the model; that is, it displays the data of the model to the end user and also enables them to edit the data.
- **Controller** is the controller of the request; that is, the request handler. Typically, users interact with the View for displaying, editing, adding, and deleting the data. This raises a corresponding URL request. This request is handled by a Controller. The Controller renders the appropriate View with the Model data as a response:

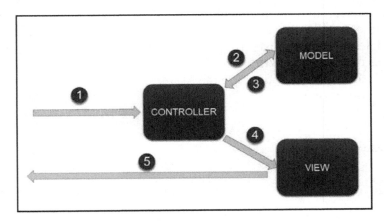

The preceding diagram sums up the general working of the MVC pattern:

1. The client sends a request, which is routed to a **CONTROLLER**
2. The **CONTROLLER** uses the **MODEL** to perform some *business* operations
3. The **MODEL** returns the result of the operations back to the **CONTROLLER**
4. The **CONTROLLER** decides which **VIEW** is to be rendered and sends it the model (data) that must be rendered
5. The **VIEW** renders the output and sends the response back to the client

Let's see an analogy of MVC in the real world, so that the new users of MVC find it linkable. Let's think about a magazine. If I were to *loosely* fit a magazine cover in the MVC pattern, it would be as follows: the user sees the magazine. What we see as the cover of the magazine is the **View** (user interface). We see some text and an image; for example, a fashion model or a sports star in the View. This is the **Model** (data), and the photographer/editor would be the **Controller** as they have manipulated the data and displayed it in the cover. This hopefully demonstrates the gist of MVC.

A couple of trivia questions. When was MVC invented? The answer roughly would be 1979 (December 10). Who invented it? A Smalltalk programmer, named Trygve Reenskaug (read about him at: `https://en.wikipedia.org/wiki/Trygve_Reenskaug`), who maintains a web page to explain the history of MVC in his own words at: `http://heim.ifi.uio.no/~trygver/themes/mvc/mvc-index.html`. It's worth a read!

So far, we have discussed MVC as an architectural pattern. Since we are learning ASP.NET Core, let's talk about the ASP.NET Core MVC framework. The ASP.NET Core MVC is a lightweight, open source, and highly testable presentation framework, that has been tailor-made for use with ASP.NET Core. It gives full control over the generated HTML markup and follows the latest web standards. To use it is pretty simple as well. We just need to add MVC in a services container, by writing `AddMVC` in the `ConfigureServices` method of `Startup.cs`, and then configure the pipeline to start using it by writing `UseMVC`, as shown in the following code snippets:

```
public void ConfigureServices(IServiceCollection services)
{
    services.AddMvc();
}

public void Configure(IApplicationBuilder app, IHostingEnvironment env)
{
    if (env.IsDevelopment())
    {
        app.UseDeveloperExceptionPage();
        app.UseBrowserLink();
    }
    else
    {
        app.UseExceptionHandler("/Home/Error");
    }
    app.UseStaticFiles();
    app.UseMvc(routes =>
    {
        routes.MapRoute(
            name: "default",
            template: "{controller=Home}/{action=Index}/{id?}");
    });
}
```

`UseMvc` has two overloads:

- `UseMvc()`: This works only with attribute-based routes, which we will visit in a while.
- `UseMvc(Action<IRouteBuilder> configureRoutes)`: This works with both conventional and attribute- based routes. It has a `callback` method to configure the routes. We have used this overload in the preceding sample.

This can be seen from the documentation of the API, which defines the `UseMvc` extension methods. The code can be seen at GitHub at: `https://github.com/aspnet/Mvc/blob/760c8f38678118734399c58c2dac981ea6e47046/src/Microsoft.AspNetCore.Mvc.Core/Builder/MvcApplicationBuilderExtensions.cs.`

There is one more extension method, `UseMvcWithDefaultRoute`, which can be used to configure MVC to work with a default route named `default` and `template` as `'{controller=Home}/{action=Index}/{id?}'`.

By using any of the preceding extension methods to use MVC middleware, we can start leveraging the goodness of ASP.NET Core MVC. Recall that by doing so, we are entering the last middleware/section of the request pipeline, as shown in the following diagram:

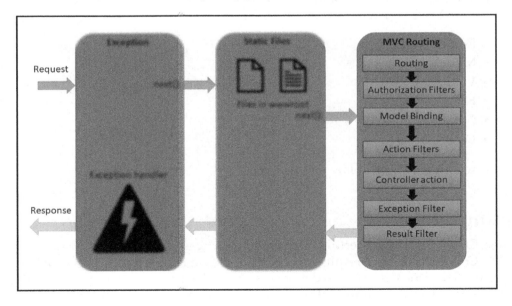

We saw this diagram in the previous chapter as well. However, the clarification of this section, other middleware in the pipeline blurred out to indicate we are focusing on MVC middleware. Let's have a look at this in detail.

The middleware resides in the `Microsoft.AspNetCore.Builder` namespace in the `Microsoft.AspNetCore.Mvc.Core` assembly. Let's look at the code map diagram:

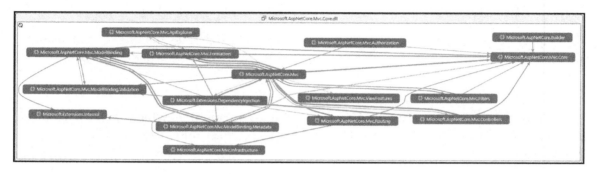

As we can see, there is so much that we can't even see the association and inheritance relationships between the different components. Don't worry about this complexity; it's already baked in the framework and we just need to learn and use things of interest. ASP.NET Core MVC is rich in features and includes the following:

- Routing
- Model binding
- Validation
- Filters
- Controller
- Error handling

We will discuss them in the following sections.

Routing

ASP.NET Core MVC is a powerful URL-mapping software component as it stands on top of ASP.NET Core routing. As a result, we can build apps that have easily understandable and searchable URLs. This way, we can define our app's URL naming patterns that work well for **search engine optimization (SEO)** and link generation, without having to worry about how the files are physically organized in the server. In the ASP.NET Core MVC framework, routing is defined in the `Microsoft.AspNetCore.Mvc.Routing` namespace.

Let's look at the code map diagram for routing:

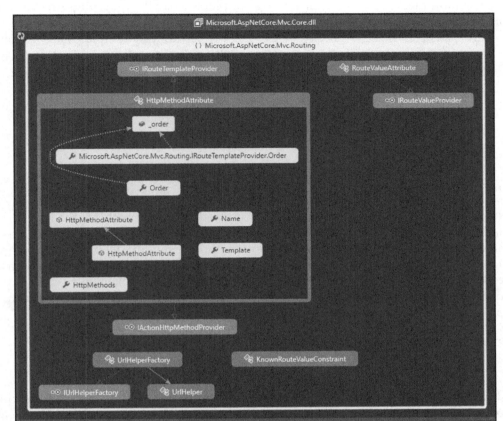

We see `HttpMethodAtribute`, which has the properties `Name`, `Template`, `HttpMethods`, and `Order` apart from the constructor. We see `UrlHelperFactory`, `UrlHelper`, `RouteValueAttribute`, and `KnownRouteValueConstraint` with their properties, constructors, and methods. Routing is the mechanism through which incoming requests are mapped to controllers and actions, that is, the controller and action can be deduced from the request URL.

For example, consider the request URL as `http://localhost:9596/packt/Books/Index`.

This maps to the books controller and index action. This mapping of controller and action from the request URL is the job of routing.

We already discussed that MVC is itself injected as a middleware in the request pipeline. The routing middleware makes use of routing templates to do the mapping. An example of a simple routing template is shown in the following code:

`packt/{controller=Home}/{action=Index}/{id?}`. Routing templates use literals and tokens. Literals are matched exactly to the text in URL, whereas tokens are replaced when matching a route. Tokens are enclosed in `{}`. In the preceding example, we have three tokens:

- **Controller token:** `{controller=Home}`
- **Action token:** `{action=Index}`
- **ID token:** `{id?}`

And `packt` is the literal which would be matched with the requested URL.

Matching a template requires a controller token and action token, as this is the key information routing middleware needs to locate the controller and action. Other tokens in the URL are mapped to the parameters of action methods using model binding, which we will see later. When adding a route mapping, default values can be provided for tokens. In the preceding example, `Home` is the default value of the controller token and `Index` is the value of the action token. Templates can also provide optional tokens for action parameters, such as `{id?}`. `?`, which here indicates that it is optional.

Now suppose a client requests the following URL:

```
http://localhost:9596/packt/Books/Index/2
```

This URL would match the preceding template and would invoke the `Index` action with the `id` value as 2 on the `Books` controller. So, the code of `BooksController` would be roughly like:

```
public class BooksController: Controller
{
    public IActionResult Index(int id)
    {
        return this.View();
    }
}
```

The following client requests would also be served:

- `http://localhost:9596/packt/Books/Index`: The `id` parameter is optional
- `http://localhost:9596/packt/Books`: The default value of the `Index` would be used for the action
- `http://localhost:9596/packt`: The default value of the `Home` would be used for the controller and the `Index` for the action

These were all happy path scenarios, but what if the URL is `http://localhost:9596/packt/Books/Index/.NETCore2.0ByExample`?

In this case, the controller would resolve to `BooksController`, and the action would resolve to `Index`. However, the last parameter is defined as `int`, which is not what we want. To ensure that `id` is always an integer for the mapping, we can use route constraint, as shown here:

```
packt/{controller=Home}/{action=Index}/{id:int?}
```

This ensures that the route maps to action only if `id` is specified as an optional `int`; otherwise, the URL would not map to this route. There are lots of constraints that can be used, such as:

- `:bool`
- `:datetime`
- `:decimal`
- `:guid`
- `:int`
- `:length(min,max)`

The comprehensive list of constraints can be seen in Microsoft route constraint reference at: `https://docs.microsoft.com/en-us/aspnet/core/fundamentals/routing#route-constraint-reference`.

 The URL strings are case-insensitive, so `packt` and `Packt` are treated the same.

The following is the code map diagram of `RouterMiddleware` and the extensions to use for this middleware:

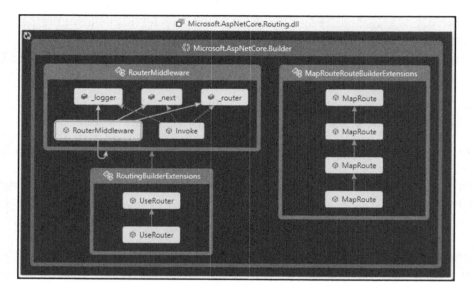

Now that we know about routing middleware and how the routing template works, let's look at the types of routing. Broadly speaking, there are the following types of routing:

- Convention-based routing
- Attribute routing
- Mixed routing; that is, a combination of the preceding two types

Convention-based routing enables us to define the URL formats, which are understood by the application. Convention-based routing also lets us define how each of the URL formats maps to a specific action method on a controller. Once a request is received, the routing engine parses the URL and matches it to one of the defined URL formats. Based on the url format, the controller and action method is mapped and invoked by the routing engine. The code example that can be used in the `UseMvc` method that takes the `routeBuilder` action as a parameter in the `Configure` method of Startup.cs is as follows:

```
routes.MapRoute(
          name: "default",
          template:
          "packt/{controller=Home}/{action=Index}/{id?}"
       );
```

The preceding method adds a route named "default". We can specify multiple named routes and templates, and these would be executed in the order in which they are defined.

The MapRoute method has several overloads. These can be seen in the following documentation:

```
//
// Summary:
// Provides extension methods for
Microsoft.AspNetCore.Routing.IRouteBuilder to
// add routes.
public static class MapRouteRouteBuilderExtensions
{
    //
    // Summary: Adds a route to the
       Microsoft.AspNetCore.Routing.IRouteBuilder with the specified
    // name and template.
    //
    // Parameters:
    // routeBuilder: The Microsoft.AspNetCore.Routing.IRouteBuilder to
       add the route to.
    // name: The name of the route.
    // template: The URL pattern of the route.
    // Returns: A reference to this instance after the operation has
       completed.
    public static IRouteBuilder MapRoute(this IRouteBuilder
    routeBuilder, string name, string template);
    //
    // Summary: Adds a route to the
       Microsoft.AspNetCore.Routing.IRouteBuilder with the specified
    // name, template, and default values.
    //
    // Parameters:
    // routeBuilder: The Microsoft.AspNetCore.Routing.IRouteBuilder to
       add the route to
    // name: The name of the route
    // template: The URL pattern of the route
    // defaults: An object that contains default values for route
       parameters. The object's properties
    // represent the names and values of the default values.
    // Returns: A reference to this instance after the operation has
       completed.
    public static IRouteBuilder MapRoute(this IRouteBuilder
    routeBuilder, string name, string template, object defaults);
    //
    // Summary: Adds a route to the
       Microsoft.AspNetCore.Routing.IRouteBuilder with the specified
```

```
// name, template, default values, and constraints.
//
// Parameters:
// routeBuilder: The Microsoft.AspNetCore.Routing.IRouteBuilder to
   add the route to.
// name: The name of the route.
// template: The URL pattern of the route.
//
// defaults:
// An object that contains default values for route parameters. The
   object's properties
// represent the names and values of the default values.
//
// constraints:
// An object that contains constraints for the route. The object's
   properties represent
// the names and values of the constraints.
//
// Returns:
// A reference to this instance after the operation has completed.
public static IRouteBuilder MapRoute(this IRouteBuilder
routeBuilder, string name, string template, object defaults, object
constraints);
//
// Summary:
// Adds a route to the Microsoft.AspNetCore.Routing.IRouteBuilder
   with the specified
// name, template, default values, and data tokens.
//
// Parameters:
// routeBuilder:
// The Microsoft.AspNetCore.Routing.IRouteBuilder to add the route
   to.
//
// name:
// The name of the route.
//
// template:
// The URL pattern of the route.
//
// defaults:
// An object that contains default values for route parameters. The
   object's properties
// represent the names and values of the default values.
//
// constraints:
// An object that contains constraints for the route. The object's
   properties represent
```

```
    // the names and values of the constraints.
    //
    // dataTokens:
    // An object that contains data tokens for the route. The object's
       properties represent
    // the names and values of the data tokens.
    //
    // Returns:
    // A reference to this instance after the operation has completed.
    public static IRouteBuilder MapRoute(this IRouteBuilder
    routeBuilder, string name, string template, object defaults, object
    constraints, object dataTokens);
}
```

Attribute routing can be used to describe routing information by decorating the attributes on the controller and actions. This means that the route definitions of the controller are placed adjacent to the controller and action tokens with which they're associated. This is done by using the Route attribute, which contains the route of the controller, as shown in the following code:

```
[Route("packt/[controller]")]
public class BooksController : Controller
{
   [HttpGet("{id}")]
   public IActionResult GetBook(int id)
   {
     //// Code hidden for brevity.
   }
}
```

We can also use any of the Http verbs, such as HttpGet, HttpPut, HttpPost, HttpDelete, and so on, to specify the attribute-based routes. The following code snippet illustrates the route specified for the Index action. Also note that we have multiple HttpGet attributes applied to the action, showing that multiple routes can map to a single action:

```
[Route("packt/[controller]")]
public class BooksController : Controller
{
   [HttpGet("index")]
   [HttpGet("~/")]
   [HttpGet("")]
```

```
public IActionResult Index()
{
  //// Code hidden for brevity.
}
}
```

These `HttpGet` attributes with routes are referring to the following URL path. For example, if we are passing a blank inside `HttpGet`, it is taking us to the `http://localhost:9596/packt/Books` path and if we are passing `HttpGet("index")`, it will refer until the index page:

- `[HttpGet("index")]` matches
  `http://localhost:9596/packt/Books/index`
- `[HttpGet("")]` matches `http://localhost:9596/packt/Books`; that is, the default `action` of `controller`
- `[HttpGet("~/")]` matches `http://localhost:9596/packt/Books`; that is, the default `action` of `controller`

Since we can have multiple routes, ordering can be applied to the route attributes to execute a general route or specific route as needed. The framework would look at the `Order` property and execute the routes in ascending order. The default `Order` of 0 would execute, followed by the route that is immediately higher than it, and so on.

Mixed routing is a perfectly valid scenario as based on the requirements; we may have convention-based routing in some controllers and actions and attribute routing for others. However, we cannot have both for the same action. If an action uses attribute routing, no convention-based routes can map to that action. Placing a route attribute on the controller or the action makes it attribute routed. Actions that define attribute routes cannot be reached through the conventional routes and vice-versa.

Next in the pipeline, after the request is routed, it maps to a controller action. We will close our discussion on routing here. The next hop on the request pipeline diagram is the authorization filter. We will skip it for now and discuss it when we discuss filters later in the chapter. Let's discuss model binding now, which comes into the picture after the authorization filter.

The request may be a PUT, POST, DELETE, or GET operation and, based on the operation it is meant to handle, the action may have parameters, which need to be populated by the framework from the client request data. The component that does this conversion is called the model binder. Let's have a look at it.

Model binding

As discussed, model binding maps the data from HTTP requests to action method parameters. These parameters, like any other C# method, can be simple types, such as int, long, decimal, string, or the complex classes. ASP.NET Core MVC has abstracted this logic away from the developers so that they need not worry about this request data to parameter conversion. This conversion is done by the framework in a predefined order. Let's look at how the framework does this. The following is the code map diagram of the model binding subsystem:

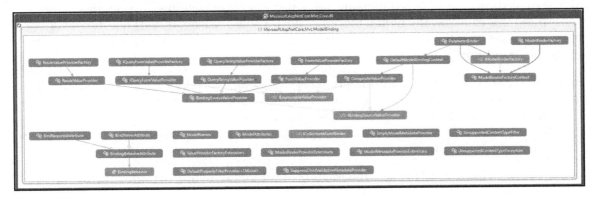

Important things to notice in the diagram are:

- ParameterBinder
- ValueProvider factories
- Value providers
- Attributes
- Extensions

The framework tries to bind the request data to the action parameters by name. To do so, it looks at the values for each parameter using the parameter name and the names of its public settable properties. In the preceding `GetBook` request URL example, the only action parameter was named `id`, which the framework binds to the value with the same name in the route values. The ASP.NET Core MVC framework uses three primary value providers or data sources to map HTTP request data to action parameters, in the following order:

1. **Form values (using** `FormValueProvider`**)**: The values in the form that came in the HTTP request body. These would generally be in `HttpPost` or `HttpPut`

2. **Route values (using** `RouteValueProvider`**)**: The values provided by the routing subsystem, which executes just before model binding is used

3. **Query string (using** `QueryStringValueProvider`**)**: The values found in the request URL query string are used

All the preceding data is stored in name value pairs in corresponding dictionaries. If, after performing this exercise, the model binding fails for some reason, it does not throw an exception; it just sets the `IsValid` property of `ModelState` to `false`. It's up to the action method to handle such scenarios.

Apart from the default model binding, the framework also provides a customized way to accomplish model binding by using attributes that we noted in the preceding code map diagram. We can use these attributes to alter the binding behavior of the property of a complex object, which is used as an action parameter, or to the parameter itself directly. Let's look at these attributes:

- `[BindNever]`: This tells the model binder to ignore this parameter from binding
- `[BindRequired]`: This attribute adds a model state error if the binding fails
- `[FromBody]`: This tells the model binder to bind the data from the request body
- `[FromForm]`: This tells the model binder that the value should be fetched through the form data
- `[FromHeader]`: This tells the model binder that value should be fetched through a header

- [FromQuery]: This tells the model binder that the value should be fetched through a query string
- [FromRoute]: This tells the model binder that the value should be fetched through the route data
- [FromServices]: This tells the model binder that dependency injection should be used to bind the parameter
- [ModelBinder]: This attribute is used to override the default model binder, binding the source and name

The next hop of the request is validation, so let's have a look at validation.

Validation

Validation is one of the key operations for any app working with data. Before we persist the data to the persistent store (database/filesystem), we should ensure the sanctity of the data, its format, type, size, and check if it complies to our rules and doesn't pose any potential security threat. This is ensured through validation. This can be done at both the client and server side. I am a firm believer that validation should be performed at both the client and server side. The validation has been abstracted from the developers into validation attributes, which reduces the amount of code needed to perform the validation. Validation attributes are C# attributes that derive from ValidationAttribute. Most of the commonly used validation attributes can be found in the System.ComponentModel.DataAnnotations namespace. In case the already provided attribute does not suffice our needs, we can do either of the following:

- Create a new custom validation attribute that derives from ValidationAttribute
- Implement the interface IValidatableObject in our model class

The following code map diagram illustrates both the `ValidationAttribute` as well as the `IValidatableObject` interface:

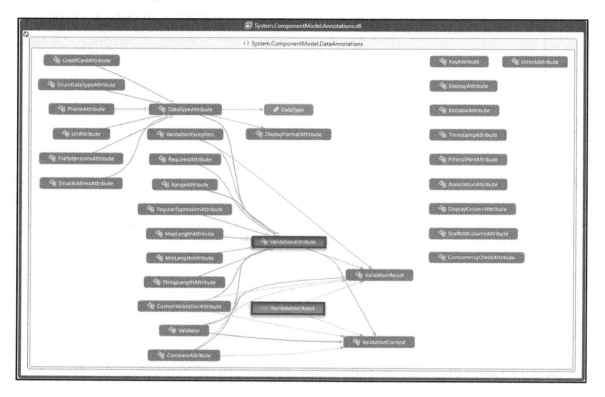

`IValidatableObject` is a simple interface with just the `Validate` method, while `ValidationAttribute` has a lot more to offer for customization and has `IsValid`, `Validate`, and `GetValidationResult` methods along with properties to meet the validation needs. We also see that there are numerous attributes already defined and derived from `ValidationAttribute`. Some of the most important ones are:

- `UrlAttribute`: Validates that the property has a valid URL.
- `PhoneAttribute`: Validates that the property has a telephone format.
- `FileExtensionsAttribute`: Validates that the file extensions are valid as per the predefined set of file extensions.
- `EmailAddressAttribute`: Validates that the property has a valid email format.

- `CreditCardAttribute`: Validates that the property has a credit card format.
- `DataTypeAttribute`: Validates that the property has a valid data type, as specified by passing the `DataType` enumeration value. The `DataType` enumeration value can be seen at the top part of the preceding image.
- `RangeAttribute`: Validates that the property value falls within the specified range.
- `RegularExpressionAttribute`: Validates that the property value matches the given regular expression.
- `RequiredAttribute`: Makes a property mandatory and hence the user would always have to provide its value.
- `CompareAttribute`: Validates two properties in a model match.
- `StringLengthAttribute`: Validates that the string property value length does not exceed the maximum length.

Applying only validation attributes to the model properties is not sufficient to perform the validation; we should ensure that on the server side in our action method, we also perform the `ModelState.IsValid` check to ensure that the input data validation passed or failed and act accordingly for pass and failed cases. The ASP.NET MVC Core framework sets the `ModelState` dictionary with errors after it performs the model binding from the HTTP request; if the validation does not pass, `ModelState.IsValid` would be false even if there is one validation error. This happens before the action execution starts, so we have the validation result available as soon as we enter the action method code. The framework, by default, continues validating properties until it reaches a maximum count of 200. This number is configurable though by writing the following code in the `ConfigureServices` method of the `Startup.cs` method, which sets the maximum count to 20:

```
services.AddMvc(options => options.MaxModelValidationErrors = 20);
```

In case we wish to perform some validations after the model binding and validations are completed, we can do so by manually invoking the validation using: `TryValidateModel(<<model to validate>>)`.

All this time, what we saw was the server-side validation, which involves a round trip to the server and hence takes time, so to do an additional validation in the client side makes sense so that if the validation fails, we do not even send the request to the server. We will have a quick discussion about client-side validation when we look at the Views, later in the chapter. Now that we have the concept and theory in mind, let's do a quick implementation of the validation. Suppose we want to validate the book information, such as name, author, description, publisher, pages, release date, price, and so on, before saving the book information to the database. To do so, let's create a model and controller. The model would look like this:

```
public class Book
{
    public int Id {get;set;}
    [Required]
    [StringLength(100)]
    public string Name {get;set;}

    [Required]
    [StringLength(50)]
    public string Author {get;set;}

    [Required]
    [StringLength(1000)]
    public string Description {get;set;}

    [Required]
    [StringLength(50)]
    public string Publisher {get;set;}
    //// No point of having required attribute here as its a value type
        and has a default value.
    public int Pages {get;set;}

    [DataType(DataType.Date)]
    public DateTime ReleaseDate {get;set;}
    [Range(0, 499.99)]
    public decimal Price {get;set;}
}
```

And the controller would look like this:

```
public class BooksController: Controller
{
    [HttpPost]
    public IActionResult SaveBookInfo(Book model)
    {
        if(this.ModelState.IsValid)
        {
            /// Code for successful validation.
        }
        else
        {
            //// Code for failed validation.
            return this.View(model);
        }
    }
}
```

As we can see, there are two paths in the `SaveBookInfo` method. If `ModelState.IsValid` is true, the data is valid and the data can be saved to the persistent storage; otherwise, we return to the same `View`. Generally, the `View` would have a validation summary that would display the validation errors.

That's it! It is this easy to implement server-side validation. This concludes our discussion on validation. Let's move on to filters.

Filters

Filters in ASP.NET Core MVC are the places where we can run the code before or after the action execution in the request processing pipeline. Filters run within the MVC action invocation pipeline, also known as **filter pipeline**. This pipeline comes into View after the framework chooses the action to be executed.

The following list view code map diagram illustrates the actors involved in filters:

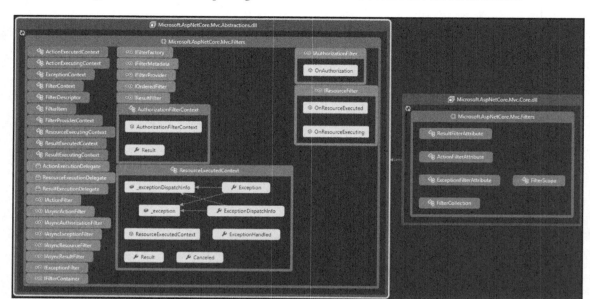

On the right, we have attributes defined, which are abstract classes. On the left, there are abstractions and context classes. The filters execute at different stages in the action execution pipeline, based on the type of filter, which can be:

- **Authorization filters**: These are the implementation of `IAuthorizationFilter`/`IAsyncAuthorizationFilter` and are run first to determine if the current user is authorized or not. They can short circuit the pipeline if the user in unauthorized.

- **Resource filters**: These are the implementation of `IResourceFilter`/`IAsyncResourceFilter` and are run immediately after the authorization filters. When these filters execute, model binding has not taken place in the pipeline so they can be used to alter the model binding. The most common use of these filters is that of caching.

- **Action filters**: These filters are the implementation of `IActionFilter` / `IAsyncActionFilter` or `ActionFilterAttribute` and are run immediately before and after an action execution. Due to their location in the pipeline, they are well-suited for any manipulation to action method parameters as well as to returned results from the action.

- **Exception filters**: These filters are the implementation of `IExceptionFilter` / `IAsyncExceptionFilter` or `ExceptionFilterAttribute` and are used to apply exception handling to the code before the response is written.
- **Result filters**: These are the implementation of `IResultFilter` / `IAsyncResultFilter` or `ResultFilterAttribute` and are run immediately before and after the execution of individual action results. They are run only if the action method successfully executes.

If we look closely, we can notice that there are multiple ways to implement the filter. There is filter interface, then there is async filter interface, and we have abstract attribute classes that we can implement. The framework first checks if the filter implements an async interface. If it does, it calls the async methods of the filter. If not, it calls the non-async methods, so either an async or synchronous interface should be implemented. If we implement both, only the async implementation would be called. This is also the case when we implement the abstract class. To summarize, the following is what the filter pipeline looks like:

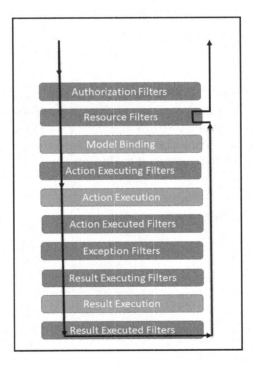

We should write our custom filters based on the preceding flow, so that the desired operation code can be written at the right place in the filter pipeline. Next, we will see an implementation of the sample filter and different ways to implement a filter.

1. Derive from `Attribute` and implement `IActionFilter`—filters are implemented as attributes and hence we need to derive from `Attribute` and implement `IActionFilter` for the class to be treated as a filter:

```
using Microsoft.AspNetCore.Mvc.Filters; //// required namespace

public class BookPublishingFilter: Attribute, IActionFilter
{
    public void OnActionexecuting(ActionExecutingContext context)
    {
        //// Write code to be executed, before the action method is
            called.
    }

    public void OnActionexecuted(ActionExecutedContext context)
    {
        //// Code to be executed, after the action method is called.
    }
}
```

2. Derive from `ActionFilterAttribute`—the `ActionFilterAttribute` class already derives from the `Attribute` class and implements `IActionFilter` and hence we can directly derive from `ActionFilterAttribute` and create a filter attribute. So, the preceding code would remain the same apart from the base class and interface with which we need to derive:

```
using Microsoft.AspNetCore.Mvc.Filters; //// required namespace

public class BookPublishingFilter: ActionFilterAttribute
{
    public void OnActionexecuting(ActionExecutingContext context)
    {
        //// Write code to be executed, before the action method is
            called.
    }

    public void OnActionexecuted(ActionExecutedContext context)
    {
        //// Code to be executed, after the action method is called.
    }
}
```

There are few other ways to define the action filters, but we will not discuss them here. They can be seen from the reference link shared towards the end of the section. Likewise, Exception filters can be created by deriving from `ExceptionFilterAttribute`, `ResultFilter` by deriving from `ResultFilterAttribute`, and so on.

For consuming the filters, they can be registered globally in the `ConfigureServices` method in the `Startup.cs` or by decorating the filter attribute in the controller or action, which is shown as follows:

```
//// Register the filter globally. This would be invoked for all
    controller actions.
public void ConfigureServices(IServiceCollection services)
{
    services.AddMvc(options =>
    {
        options.Filters.Add(typeof(BookPublishingFilter)); // by type
        //// Use either above line or below line, not both. Here both
            are shown to demonstrate ways in which it can be done.
        options.Filters.Add(new BookPublishingFilter()); // an instance
    });
}

//// Register the filter only at action where it is needed. If it is
    applied in controller, it applies to all actions.
[BookPublishingFilter]
public IActionResult GetUnpublishedBooks()
{
}
```

Since the filters can be registered both globally and at action level also, a definite question comes to mind, which is: in what order do they execute? The answer is simple:

- The action executing method of global filters runs first, then of action executing methods of filters registered at controller runs, and finally action executing methods of filters registered at action level.
- While returning from action, the order is the other way round. The action executed method of filter registered at action level runs first, then action executed method of filter registered at controller level, and finally the action executed method of filter registered globally.
- This is also referred to as Nesting Doll or Russian Doll model.
- This is the default behaviour. ASP.NET Core provides a way to override the default order of execution by implementing `IOrderedFilter`, which exposes an `Order` property, specifying which can override the default order of execution.

For a detailed and thorough discussion on filters, please read the documentation of filter at: `https://docs.microsoft.com/en-us/aspnet/core/mvc/controllers/filters`.

With this note, we will move on to our next topic: Controllers.

Controllers

Broadly speaking, a controller is a class with a group of methods called actions. An action, also known as an action method, is a method that handles the request. As per the convention used by the ASP.NET Core MVC framework, a controller is a class that:

- Is instantiable; that is, an instance of that class can be created
- Resides in the project's root-level folder, named `Controllers`
- Inherits from an abstract class, `Microsoft.AspNetCore.Mvc.Controller`

The framework is flexible and would also treat an instantiable class as a controller if any one or more of the following holds good:

- The class is decorated with the `[Controller]` attribute
- The class name is suffixed with `Controller`, such as `HomeController`
- The class derives from a class, whose name ends with `Controller`

An important thing to note here is that we have a controller defined, even if we do not derive our controller from the `Controller` class. As discussed earlier, the role of a controller is to validate the request data and return the result in the form of a View or data. In the ASP.NET Core MVC project structure, we can see a `Controllers` folder at the project root level, as shown here:

Let's have a look at the code map diagram of the `Controller` class to understand it better:

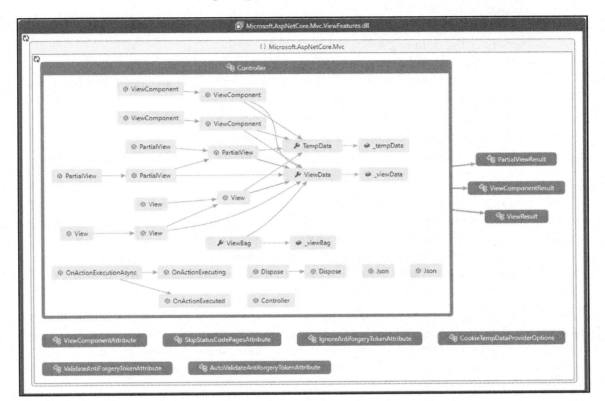

The diagram reveals that the `Controller` class itself derives from the `ControllerBase` class, by which it gets access to `HttpContext` and `ControllerContext` properties. It has properties for `TempData`, `ViewData`, and `ViewBag`, which we will discuss when we discuss the Views in the next chapter. The class contains a bunch of methods, mostly for returning action results and executing action filters. Let's have a look at them:

- `PartialView`: Creates a `Microsoft.AspNetCore.Mvc.PartialViewResult` object that renders a partial View to the response

- `View`: **Creates a** `Microsoft.AspNetCore.Mvc.ViewResult` object that renders a View to the response
- `Json`: **Creates a** `Microsoft.AspNetCore.Mvc.JsonResult` object that serializes the data to JSON
- `ViewComponent`: **Creates a** `Microsoft.AspNetCore.Mvc.ViewComponentResult` by specifying the name of a View component to render
- `OnActionExecuting`: **Called before the action method is invoked**
- `OnActionExecuted`: **Called after the action method is invoked**
- `OnActionExecutionAsync`: **Called before the action method is invoked in an async implementation**

Not all methods defined in the `Controller` class are actions. Only `public` methods which are not decorated with the `[NonAction]` attribute are actions. An action method can return anything, but generally, we will see them return an instance of `IActionResult` (or `Task<IActionResult>` for `async` methods). An action method decides the kind of response it would return; it may be a View or formatted response data, such as JSON, or anything else.

With the intent of separation of concerns and loose coupling, the `Controller` class should always have the dependencies injected to it, rather than creating the instance of it. If a type or service is required for only one action method, we can use the injection of a service directly in the action by using the `[FromServices]` attribute that we saw earlier; otherwise, the construction injection should be used.

We will end our lap around MVC with an overview of error handling.

Error handling

Error handling is a particularly important piece in any reliable and stable software application, and ASP.NET Core applications are no different. The error handling strategy differs while the app is under development and when it is deployed. While developing, the developer wants to see highly detailed error messages so that he/she can go to the crux of the issue and fix it.

However, such a level of detailing would not be great in production as the end user would not understand any of that and it would give hackers too much information, which they could utilize to compromise your app. Also, the end user would rather appreciate a user-friendly message than some stack trace, which would be Greek to them.

So, we display a developer exception page in the development environment and a more user-friendly error screen in the production environment. The old school ASP.NET programmers may be able to link this to the custom errors flag in the ancient versions of ASP.NET. Let's see how we can configure these pages.

To configure an app to display an error page to display the detailed exception, we need to have the `Microsoft.AspNetCore.Diagnostics` namespace. We need to add the following code in our `Configure` method of `Startup.cs`. Notice that this should be added before adding any other middleware, so that all the exceptions from the subsequently executed middleware are caught:

```
if (env.IsDevelopment())
{
    app.UseDeveloperExceptionPage();
}
else
{
    app.UseExceptionHandler("/error");
}
```

In case of an exception in the development environment, the developer exception page would be displayed, as shown in the following screenshot. I used the classical and easiest code to simulate the exception here—divide by zero:

Notice that it has four tabs:

- **Stack**: Displays the stack trace of the error
- **Query**: Displays the query string of the request
- **Cookies**: Displays the cookies associated with a request, if any
- **Headers**: Displays the header of the request, as shown in the following screenshot:

Stack	Query	Cookies	Headers	
Variable		Value		
Accept		text/html, application/xhtml+xml, image/jxr, */*		
Accept-Encoding		gzip, deflate		
Accept-Language		en-US		
Connection		Keep-Alive		
Host		localhost:52846		
User-Agent		Mozilla/5.0 (Windows NT 10.0; Win64; x64) AppleWebKit/537.36 (KHTML, like Gecko) Chrome/52.0.2743.116 Safari/537.36 Edge/15.15063		

In a non-development environment, we will see a generic error page, as shown in the following screenshot:

Error.

An error occurred while processing your request.

Request ID: |9ad91bef-458e37c27fd3ccc7.

Development Mode

Swapping to **Development** environment will display more detailed information about the error that occurred.

Development environment should not be enabled in deployed applications, as it can result in sensitive information from exceptions being displayed to end users. For local debugging, development environment can be enabled by setting the **ASPNETCORE_ENVIRONMENT** environment variable to **Development**, and restarting the application.

Please note, an error in an error page can also throw an exception, which, if not properly handled, can crash your app. So, we should try and keep the error page content static.

If any exceptions occur during the app startup, they can only be handled in the hosting layer. When the error occurs after the host address / port binding, hosting can only show an error page for such captured startup errors. If any port/address binding fails for any reason, such as the address/port is already in use, the hosting layer logs a critical exception, the dotnet process crashes, and no error page is displayed.

MVC error handling continues to work as it does, by using exception filters for exceptions and Model validations for validation failures. We have already seen these in our quick lap around MVC. We have one more important component of MVC, the visual element, Views, to discuss. We will discuss this when we do the implementation of our chat UI and Chat hub in the next chapter.

This wraps up our quick lap around MVC. With all the fundamentals in place, we are now ready to dive into coding. We will begin by implementing authentication in our application, which we will do in the following section.

Implementing authentication through Facebook

Enough of the theory and samples. Time for us to convert the requirements into reality. We will start with the authentication module first. Recall that based on our discussion in the last chapter, this module needs to support a secure login, a forgotten password, as well as register user functionality. Once we are done with it, we will have completed a substantial part of our app, as per the following flowchart:

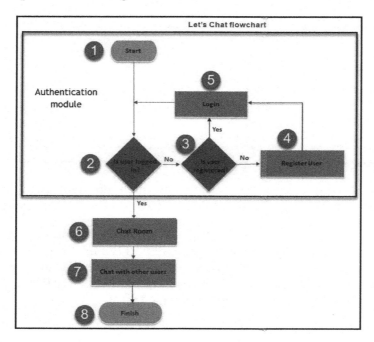

We are going to leverage Facebook authentication to implement this module of our system. We could have used any of the other providers as well, such as Twitter, Google, Microsoft, and so on, but since it's a fun chat app, Facebook is most appropriate. In `Chapter 7`, *To the Cloud*, we will see how we can support multiple authentication providers and let the user decide which provider they wish to use for authentication. To code this module, we will perform the following steps:

1. To integrate Facebook with our app, we first need to create a Facebook App ID. So, go to `https://developers.facebook.com/apps/` and click on **Add a New App** button. Please note, this requires us to sign in to our Facebook account, so you need to have a Facebook account to do this activity. If you don't have a Facebook account, please create one. On clicking the button, the following screen will display:

2. Enter **Display Name** and **Contact Email**, and click on the **Create App ID** button. It will display a **Completely Automated Public Turing Test to tell Computers and Humans Apart (CAPTCHA)** verification page. On successful verification, the App ID will get created and a products page will be displayed, as shown in the following screenshot:

Select a product

Account Kit

Seamless account creation. No more passwords.

Facebook Login

The world's number one social login product.

Audience Network

Monetize your mobile app or website with native ads from 3 million Facebook advertisers.

Analytics

Understand how people engage with your business across apps, devices, platforms and websites.

Messenger

Customize the way you interact with people on Messenger.

Webhooks

Subscribe to changes and receive updates in real time without calling the API.

Marketing API

Integrate Facebook Marketing API with your app.

App Center

Get your game discovered by being listed as a featured game on Facebook.

Web Payments

Accept in-app payments through Facebook's secure payment system.

Instagram

Integrate your app with the Instagram API to let businesses use your app with their Instagram accounts.

Messenger Expression

Let people on Messenger express themselves more creatively through your app.

Looking for something else?

There are many more integration possibilities that we can help you with.

Expand Additional Products

3. We need to choose **Facebook Login**, so click on the **Setup** button, which will display when we hover over **Facebook Login**. On clicking **Setup**, Facebook will display a select platform page, as shown in the following screenshot:

4. Choose **Web** and then enter the website URL in the next screen. This is the URL of your web app. Once we run our app using Visual Studio or dotnet run, we can see the URL (or we will directly see launchSettings.json or project properties). Copy the URL and paste it in the Site URL field, as shown in the following screenshot:

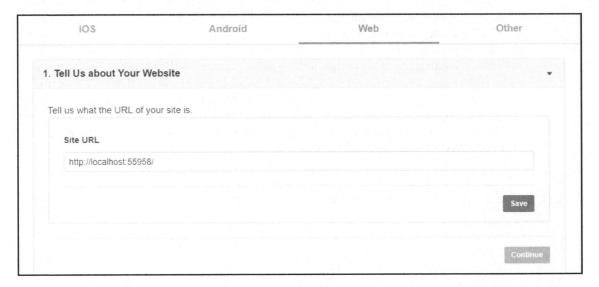

5. Click the **Save** button. Now, click on the **Facebook Login** on the left navigation panel in the **PRODUCTS** section and make the following selections:

OAuth redirect URIs should be correct; otherwise, the flow will not work. There is no point in putting the lock on the door and keeping the key alongside, similarly, there is no point in using authentication and using an HTTP protocol for OAuth. The URI should be using an HTTPS protocol. This is a demo app, so I have used the HTTP protocol. However, for any non-demo app, we should always use HTTPS. We can provide multiple URLs in the OAuth redirect URIs, so once we publish the app to Azure, we would need to add one more URL here. With this, our Facebook app is set up. We need an App ID and App Secret, which we will copy by navigating to the **Dashboard** of the app we just created. This can be done by clicking on the **Dashboard** in the left-hand side navigation. Copy the **App ID** and **App Secret** in a notepad for our use:

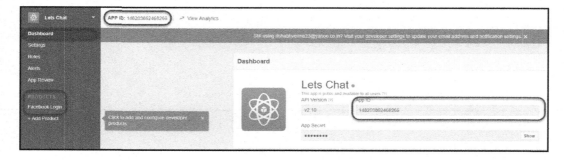

With this, we are done with the app setup in Facebook. We will come back to the portal again when we make our app public and publish it to Azure. For now, we will start coding. As discussed earlier, we will make use of middleware to perform authentication. The pattern to use middleware is also very simple. First, add the middleware in the `ConfigureServices` method and then use it in the `Configure` method of `Startup.cs`. The framework takes care of most of the heavy lifting, so the coding part is quite simple as well, as we will see.

6. We will use Facebook and cookie authentication. To use them, we add the following using directives in `Startup.cs`:

```
using Microsoft.AspNetCore.Authentication.Facebook;
using Microsoft.AspNetCore.Authentication.Cookies;
```

7. We need to use the App ID and App Secret to integrate Facebook authentication with our web app. To do so, we need to read the values of the App ID and App Secret. This can be done through reading from the `appsettings.json` or from the User Secret Manager tool in development. Essentially, these secrets should be kept way from the application code and real apps deployed on Azure should be fetched from the Azure Key-vault. We will use the User Secret Manager tool as well as Key-vault in `Chapter 7`, *To the Cloud*. For the sake of simplicity, in this demo, we will make use of `asppsettings.json` to read these values (though its not recommended for actual systems), as shown here:

```
"FacebookAuthenticationAppId": "148203862468266",
"FacebookAuthenticationAppSecret": "<<App Secret>>"  //// Your App
    Secret goes here.
```

8. In the `ConfigureServices` method of `Startup.cs`, we will write the following lines of code to add the authentication middleware and read the App ID and App Secret from configuration, by using the following code:

```
//// Configure Authentication, we will challenge the user, via
Facebook and sign in via Cookie ////authentication, so setting the
appropriate values.
services.AddAuthentication(options =>
{
  options.DefaultChallengeScheme =
  FacebookDefaults.AuthenticationScheme;
  options.DefaultSignInScheme =
  CookieAuthenticationDefaults.AuthenticationScheme;
  options.DefaultAuthenticateScheme =
  CookieAuthenticationDefaults.AuthenticationScheme;
}).AddFacebook(options =>
```

```
{
    options.AppId =
    this.Configuration["FacebookAuthenticationAppId"]; //// AppId
    options.AppSecret =
    this.Configuration["FacebookAuthenticationAppSecret"]; // App
    Secret
}).AddCookie();
```

The comments make it very clear that we would challenge the user through Facebook and sign in using cookie authentication. We have configured Facebook to use the App ID and App Secret from the `appsettings` and also added cookie authentication. Also, to keep the application secure, it's highly recommended that we always enforce SSL; that is, use HTTPS. We can do so with the following line of code, while adding MVC:

```
//// Since HTTPS is secure, lets make it mandatory, by using the
RequireHttpsAttribute Filter
services.AddMvc(options =>
{
    options.Filters.Add(new RequireHttpsAttribute());
});
```

9. In the `Configure` method of `Startup.cs`, write the following code between `app.UseStaticFiles` and `app.UseMvc`:

```
app.UseAuthentication();
```

This ordering is important and will ensure that static resources, such as `js`, `css`, and `image` files, will not have to go through authentication. They would be served without authentication, while before any other page access request or authentication can kick in. If we run the app now, the authentication would still not kick in. We need to decorate the controller/controller action(s) with the `[Authorize]` attribute, which we only want the authenticated user to access. We can also configure this at the global level. We saw the sample for this in the last chapter.

10. We will decorate the `Index` action of `HomeController` with the `[Authorize]` attribute, so that we can challenge the user if he/she is not logged in, as shown here:

```
public class HomeController : Controller
{
    [Authorize]
    public IActionResult Index()
    {
```

```
                    return this.View();
                }
            }
```

Now, if we run the app and we have followed all the steps correctly so far, we will see the Facebook login page, as shown here:

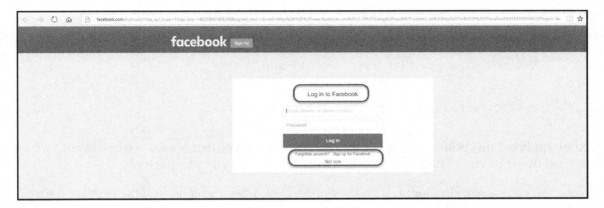

It will also ask for permission to use the user profile, as shown here:

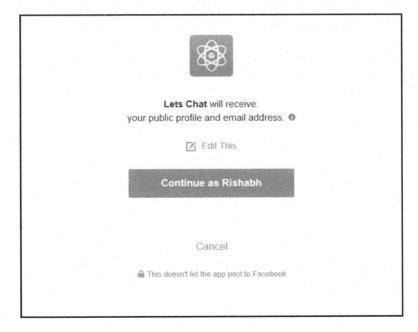

Click on **Continue as** <your name> and we will be navigated to the Index page.

It's not a scaleable model to put [Authorize] on every controller as it is susceptible to mistakes. New developers adding a new controller may forget to do so and it may not be caught unless someone browses the URL for that controller, so it is recommended that we configure authentication in the ConfigureServices method of Startup.cs, as shown here:

```
services.AddMvc(config =>
{
    var policy = new AuthorizationPolicyBuilder()
                    .RequireAuthenticatedUser()
                    .Build();
    config.Filters.Add(new AuthorizeFilter(policy));
});
```

After applying this policy, wherever we need non-authenticated access, we can insert the [AllowAnonymous] attribute. This is safer from a security perspective.

Now, we have a working login, with the option to register a user as well the provision to reset the password, if the user forgot it, without doing any custom coding. We can safely rely on Facebook to take care of this stuff. We will wrap up this module by seeing how we can do an explicit sign in and sign out, so that if we wish to sign out or sign in explicitly by clicking on a link or button, we can handle it. To do so, we will add a new controller called AuthenticationController with two actions, SignIn and SignOut, as shown here:

```
[Route("authentication")]
public class AuthenticationController : Controller
{
    private readonly ILogger<AuthenticationController> logger;

    public AuthenticationController(ILogger<AuthenticationController>
    logger)
    {
        this.logger = logger;
    }

    [Route("signin")]
    public IActionResult SignIn()
    {
        logger.LogInformation($"Calling {nameof(this.SignIn)}");
        return Challenge(new AuthenticationProperties { RedirectUri =
        "/" });
    }

    [Route("signout")]
```

```
[HttpPost]
public async Task<IActionResult> SignOut()
{
    await
    HttpContext.SignOutAsync(CookieAuthenticationDefaults
    .AuthenticationScheme);
    return RedirectToAction("Index", "Home");
}
}
```

The code is simple but an explanation is important, as we have used a lot of things here:

- We have used attribute routing at the controller level, by using the `[Route("authentication")]` attribute. This may seem unnecessary as its name is the same as that of the controller, but the intent is to demonstrate how the `Route` attribute is used at a controller level. Had we used `[Route("auth")]`, all requests to /auth/ would redirect to this controller.

- Next, we see that the `AuthenticationController` derives from the `Controller` class. This is mandatory when we create any controller; it should derive from the `Controller` class. We can have it derive from some other class, say `BaseController`, but then `BaseController` should derive from the `Controller` class.

- Next, we see we have a field of type `ILogger<AuthenticationController>` called `logger`, which would be used to do the logging with the `AuthenticationController` as the category.

- Then, we have the constructor for the `AuthenticationController`. This takes in a dependency of `ILogger<AuthenticationController>`, which is injected by default by the framework. This demonstrates DI.

- There is an action created with the name `SignIn`. Note that it also uses attribute routing, as it's decorated with `[Route("signin")]`. The return type of this action is `IActionResult`. As is evident, the first line of action is for logging the information. The important thing in this action is that its returns a `ChallengeResult`, taking in the `AuthenticationProperties` as the parameter. It's important to set the `RedirectUri` as it is responsible for redirecting the page to the appropriate page after authentication. `ChallengeResult` would use the configured challenge scheme, Facebook, in this case.

- The last action is `SignOut`. Again, it uses attributebased routing. It would be served when a `POST` request comes as it is decorated with the `[HttpPost]` attribute. We also note the `async` keyword to demonstrate that we can have `async` controller actions. It uses the `SignOutAsync` method of `HttpContext` and signs out using the cookie authentication scheme. Post sign out, it redirects the user to the `Index` action of the `Home` controller. If the `Index` action of the `Home` controller has the `[Authorize]` attribute applied, it may take the user to the login screen and if cookies are not cleared from the browser, you may have the user logged back in.

In the View, we will do the following. If the user is not signed in, show him the `Sign In` button, or show him the `Sign Out` button. This can be done easily in the `_Layout.cshtml` by the writing the following code:

```
@if (User.Identity.IsAuthenticated) /// If user is authenticated
{
   <li>
     <br/>
         <form method="post" asp-controller="Authentication" asp-
         action="SignOut">
           <button type="submit" class="btn btn-primary">Sign
           Out</button>
         </form>
   </li>
}
else
{
   <li><a asp-area="" class="btn btn-primary" asp-
   controller="Authentication" asp-action="SignIn">Sign In</a></li>
   }
```

By doing this in `_Layout.cshtml`, we ensure this functionality is common across all the pages. The `@prefix` on Razor tells the RazorEngine that it is C# code. We first check if the user is authenticated; if yes, `User.Identity.IsAuthenticated` would be `true`. Inside this condition, we display the `Sign Out` button inside a `form` tag. The `form` tag is important, as we are doing a submit action on the `Sign Out` button, so on clicking it, the form would be posted to the server. This call should never ever be `HttpGet`. The `form` tag uses the `post` method and uses tag helpers to specify the controller and action as `Authentication` and `SignOut`, respectively.

HTTP method definitions (`https://www.w3.org/Protocols/rfc2616/rfc2616-sec9.html`) recommend the usage of `HttpPost` methods over `HttpGet` methods for security reasons (`https://www.w3.org/Protocols/rfc2616/rfc2616-sec15.html#sec15.1.3`), when the data is being submitted to the server, as per the following excerpt:
If your of services use the HTTP protocol, then you **SHOULD NOT** use `GET`-based forms for the submission of sensitive data. Otherwise, this will cause the data to be encoded in the Request-URI. The request URI will be logged somewhere by existing servers, proxies, and user agents, and it might be accessible to third parties. Servers can use `POST`-based form submission instead.

This completes our authentication module, and we are ready to develop the SignalR Chat hub module.

Summary

In this chapter, we brushed up on the fundamentals of MVC and looked at the features of ASP.NET Core MVC. Post learning the fundamentals, we developed the authentication module for our Let's Chat app using Facebook. We checked that we can log in, sign out, register a new user, as well as reset the password, using the work already done by Facebook, with minimal lines of code in our ASP.NET Core 2.0 app. In the next chapter, we will develop the SignalR Chat hub module and complete the Let's Chat web app. We will also learn about unit testing and deployment for the ASP.NET Core 2.0 app.

6
Testing and Deploying – The Let's Chat Web Application

In the previous chapter, we developed the authentication module of our Let's Chat web application. In this chapter, we will develop the Chat hub module using SignalR and wrap up the coding of our web application. After that, we will have a demonstration of how it works, and learn to test and deploy it. We will learn about Docker containers and how they may be helpful. Finally, we will develop an ASP.NET Core-based Chatbot and integrate it with the Let's Chat application and Facebook. The motivation behind this chapter is to understand the testing deployment model of .NET Core applications, the Live Unit Testing feature of Visual Studio 2017, and containers, and get a sneak peek into developing a simple Bot, based on the Microsoft Bot Framework. In this chapter, we will cover the following:

- Chat hub module
- Testing overview
- Introduction to containers
- Bot 101

Chat hub module

Now that we have the authentication module in place, a user can log in to our Let's Chat web application using Facebook. We still need to develop the Chat module so that the user can see their friends online and chat with them. In this section, we will develop the Chat hub module using SignalR. We have already developed a Tic-Tac-Toe game using SignalR. Hence, we are already familiar with how to develop a SignalR hub and get the communication going back and forth between clients and server, so this should be relatively easier for us. On the client side, we will make use of Razor pages. ASP.NET Core 2.0 introduced a new feature called Razor pages, which makes the coding of page-focused scenarios much easier. If you have worked on earlier versions of ASP.NET, you will have seen or heard about ASP.NET Web forms (`.aspx`) applications, which had web forms at the heart of development. This is more or less on the same lines in the MVC world and makes it really productive to develop quick demos and **proof of concepts** (**PoCs**). We will quickly do a detour through Razor, views, and Razor pages, and then jump into the coding of the Chat hub module.

View, in a **Model-View-Controller** (**MVC**) pattern, handles the application data presentation and user interaction. Specifically, in the context of ASP.NET MVC, View is just an HTML template with Razor markup. Razor markup... huh! Let's have a look at the Razor primer, before we understand View.

Razor primer

Razor is a markup syntax for embedding server-based code in a web page. Developers familiar with PHP will find themselves at home while working with Razor, as the syntax is very similar. Razor syntax consists of Razor markup, C#, and HTML. Since it contains C# as well as HTML, files containing Razor syntax generally have a `.cshtml` extension. The @ symbol is of great importance in Razor syntax and it is used to transition from HTML to C#. OK! But how does Razor work? A `.cshtml` file can have Razor, C#, and HTML. The server first runs the Razor markup and C#, which ultimately would translate into HTML that the browser can understand and render. This HTML is then combined with the remaining HTML content and sent back to the browser. The following are reserved keywords in Razor:

- `functions`
- `inherits`
- `model`
- `page`
- `section`

Language-specific keywords (for C# in `.cshtml` and VB in `.vbhtml`) remain as-is in Razor code blocks, and hence are not given special mention. It must be noted that when an `@` symbol is followed by a Razor reserved keyword, it gets translated into Razor-specific markup; otherwise, it transitions into plain C#. Let's have a quick look at the Razor syntax:

Point to learn	Example	Remarks
@ with Razor reserved keyword	`@model` `@page`	When an @ symbol is followed by a Razor reserved keyword, it transitions into Razor-specific markup. Otherwise, it transitions into plain C#.
Escape @ character	`<span>@@Name</span>` is rendered in HTML as `<span>@Name</span>`	The HTML attributes and content containing email addresses don't treat @ as a transition character. To escape an @ symbol in Razor markup, use a second @ symbol.
Implicit Razor expression	`<p>@DateTime.Now</p>`	@ followed by C# code.
Spaces not allowed	`@DateTime.Now - TimeSpan.FromDays(2)`	Rendered as `29/12/2017 - TimeSpan.FromDays(2)` as there are spaces between.
Generics are *not* supported	`<p>@SomeMethod<int>()</p>`	<> would be interpreted as an HTML tag, hence not supported in implicit expression.
Explicit Razor syntax	`@(DateTime.Now.AddDays(1))`	Any content inside @() brackets is evaluated and rendered to output.
Expression encoding	`@("<span>Hello DotNet 2.0 By Example</span>")`	Renders the HTML as `&lt;span&gt;Hello DotNet 2.0 By Example&lt;/span&gt;`, which is shown in the browser as `<span>Hello DotNet 2.0 By Example</span>`.
Without expression encoding	`@Html.Raw("<span> Hello .NET Core 2.0 </span>")` is rendered as `<span>Hello .NET Core 2.0</span>`	This results in security vulnerabilities such as malicious user input and cross site scripting and hence must be used with the utmost care. Make a rule of thumb to avoid using `@Html.Raw` unless you are 110% sure that it can under no circumstances compromise on security and would never be user input.

Razor code blocks	`@{`
	`ViewData["Title"] = "Let's Chat";`
	`}`
		Razor code blocks start with @ and are enclosed by {}. Unlike expressions, C# code inside code blocks isn't rendered.

Explicit line transition	`@:Name: @User.Name` would render as Name: `<<Value of User.Name>>`	To render the rest of an entire line as HTML inside a code block, use the @: syntax.

`@If-else if-else`	`@if (condition){`
	`}else if (some condition) {`
	`} else { }`
		@ is needed only before starting `if`.

`@switch`	`@switch(value)` `{ case 1:break;default:break; }`	Simple syntax for `switch` case.
`@for`	`@for (var i = 0; i < array.Length; i++){}`	Use `@for`.
`@foreach`	`@foreach (var item in array) {}`	Use `@foreach`.
`@while`	`@{var i=0;}` `@while (i < array.Length) {}`	Use `@while`.

`@do while`	`@{ var i = 0; }`
	`@do {`
	`     }while(i< array.Length)`
		Use `@do...while`.

`@using`	`@using (Html.BeginForm()) {` `@* Entire form content *@}@using System.Linq`	Used to create HTML helpers that contain additional content. The example renders a form tag. Can also be used as a `using` directive and it adds the C# `using` directive to the generated view.

`@try, catch, finally`	`@try{}`
	`catch(Exception ex){}`
	`finally{}`
		use `@try` and similar to C# syntax.

`@lock`	`@lock(syncLock)` `{// DO critical work here}`	Same as C#, to protect the critical region. Use `@lock`.
Comments	• `<!-- HTML Comment-->` • `/* C# Comment *//// C# comment` • `@* Razor multiline comment *@`	Razor supports both HTML and C# comments.
`@model`	`@model HomeViewModel`	The `@model` directive specifies the type of the model passed to a view and is used extensively in strongly typed views.
`@inherits`	`@inherits BaseRazorPage` Now the view will have access to all the protected and public properties, fields and methods of the `BaseRazorPage` class	`@inherits` directive provides full control of the class the view inherits.

@inject	`@inject IHtmlLocalizer`	The `@inject` directive enables the Razor page to inject a service from the service container into a view.
@functions	`@functions { public string GetTime(){` `    return    DateTime.Now.ToString();` `}}` `<div> Current Time : @GetTime()</div>`	The `@functions` directive enables a Razor page to add function-level content to a view.
@section	`@section Scripts { <script type="text/javascript" src="~/scripts/main.js"></script> }`	The `@section` directive is used in conjunction with the layout page to enable views to render contents in different parts of the HTML page such as header, footer, body, and so on.

Tag Helpers

Tag Helpers are a new feature introduced in ASP.NET Core that enables server-side code to participate in creating and rendering HTML elements in Razor files. Tag Helpers are C# classes that participate in view generation by manipulating HTML elements. By using Tag Helpers, we can add additional attributes to HTML elements, change the content, or replace them entirely. In simple terms, Tag Helper's code that helps us to build our `.cshtml` forms without needing to write Razor syntax. For example, if we were to write an anchor tag in Razor we would write it like:

```
@Html.ActionLink("Read my book", "Read", "Book")
```

where `Read` is the action in `Book` controller and the text between anchor tag would be `"Read my book"`. Using Tag Helper, it becomes very easy to write the same anchor tag as:

```
<a asp-action="Read" asp-controller="Book">Read my book</a>
```

This is both very easy to write as well as easy to understand, and looks more neat and easily maintainable as well, as it looks like HTML. Visual Studio has great tooling support for Tag Helpers and it highlights all the HTML elements that use Tag Helpers, thus making it easier to identify them and also provide rich intellisense to explore and use them as needed. Notice that all the Tag Helper attributes start with `asp-` and their naming is self-explanatory. There are a number of inbuilt Tag Helpers that come with the framework and writing a new one is also pretty straightforward. Let's have a quick look at a few inbuilt Tag Helpers and then we will conclude this discussion by creating one custom Tag Helper as well. The following table lists a few of the inbuilt Tag Helpers:

Tag Helper	Example
Anchor	`<a asp-action="Index" asp-controller="Home">Back to Home</a>` anchor Tag Helper has few other properties that could be set, such as `asp-fragment`, `asp-route`, `asp-path`. This defines the anchor tag.
Label	`<label asp-for="Name"></label>` defines a label for a control.
Input	`<input type="text" asp-for="Name"/>` Earlier we used to have multiple Razor helpers for different types of input (`checkbox`, `select`, `radio`, `text`). Now we have just two helper attributes `asp-for` and `asp-format`.

Form	`<form asp-action="Create" asp-anti-forgery="true" asp-controller="Person"></form>` `action` and `controller` are defined, as well as the `ValidateAntiForgeryToken` is taken care of ! Wonderful!
Text area	`<textarea asp-for="Description"></textarea>`.
Select	`<select asp-for="SelectedBook" asp-items="Model.Books"></select>`.
Image	`<img src="~/content/images/image.png" alt="profile image" asp-append-version="true"/>` Used for cache-busting the image as the Tag Helper appends the hash of the image as the query string parameter such as `<img src="/content/images/image.png?v=Z6p6D366_nQ2fQqUso0F24gWy2ZekXjHz83WvYbaiOOk" alt="profile image"/>`.
Cache	`<cache expires-after="@TimeSpan.FromMinutes(5)"></cache>` The content inside the `cache` tag is cached in server memory unless explicitly disabled.
Link and Script	These are the most interesting Tag Helpers of the lot as they have cache busting as well as fallback mechanisms implemented in them, such as `<link rel="stylesheet" href="//ajax.aspnetcdn.com/ajax/bootstrap/3.0.0/css/bootstrap.min.css" asp-fallback-href="~/lib/bootstrap/css/bootstrap.min.css" asp-fallback-test-class="hidden" asp-fallback-test-property="visibility" asp-fallback-test-value="hidden" />`
Validation	`<span asp-validation-for="Description"></span>`.
Environment	`<environment names="Staging,Production"></environment>`. This is a special helper as contents of helper gets rendered only if the deployed environment name matches the names property of the Environment tag.

As we can see, Tag Helpers provide a great boost in productivity while coding `.cshtml` files. The Visual Studio tooling with IntelliSense makes this experience even more efficient. In ASP.NET Core 2.0, Application Insights is also enabled by using a Tag Helper in the background. Next let's create a custom Tag Helper. Creating a custom Tag Helper needs these steps to be followed:

1. Create a custom class which derives from the `Microsoft.AspNet.Razor.TagHelper.TagHelper` class
2. Create the properties in the class to hold the attribute values
3. Restrict the Tag Helper to be applicable only to a certain type of HTML element by decorating the class with the `HtmlTargetElement` attribute
4. Override the `ProcessAsync` method and set the attributes as needed
5. Add a line to `_ViewImports.cshtml` for the Razor views to recognize the Tag Helpers

Since we are not using Tag Helpers right now, we will not go into details, but as we can see, it's quite straightforward and easy. Now that we have visited the fundamentals of Razor syntax and Tag Helpers, we will quickly recap views.

Views

In the MVC pattern, a View is meant to display the application data to the user and handle user interaction. View helps us to implement the separation of concern design principle in MVC applications, by separating the user interface from business logic. It is an HTML page with additional Razor markup apart from the HTML markup, as we have seen earlier in this chapter. The `.cshtml` files are Views and treated as web pages. For example, if we create a simple MVC application, it creates a View under the `Views` folder and each View is associated with a controller. In the following example, `HomeController` is calling three Views—`Index`, `About`, and `Contact` . Inside the `Views` folder, we have a sub-folder with the controller name (`Home`) and this folder contains all views used in `HomeController`. This is shown in the following screenshot:

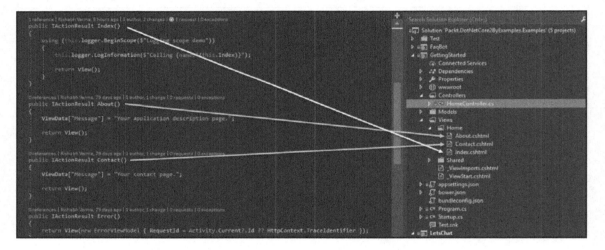

The most commonly used components of Views are:

1. **Layouts**: These are like the master page and are used to maintain consistency among all web pages. For example, we see common content used in all the pages such as header, footer, menu, and so on.

2. **Partial views**: Partial Views are useful for re-usability. If we have some content which needs to be displayed in more than one screen, or if we have a page which doesn't have any logic or code to execute and has only content to display, we can have them as partial Views.

3. **View Components**: These are similar to partial Views and help us to reuse the code, but the difference is that a partial View only binds the model, and View components can interact with data and business logic, as they have a mini controller. A common example of a View component is the shopping cart of any e-commerce website. It renders content using database interaction.

Next, we will look into a new feature introduced in ASP.NET Core 2.0 called Razor pages.

Razor pages

Razor pages are lightweight pages with the added functionality of handling requests directly without a controller. This makes them extremely useful to create a quick application, or a proof of concept or for presenting cool demonstrations to an audience. To make a View page into a Razor page, we need to add the @page directive. It should be the first directive on the page. For example:

```
@page
<h1>Hello from .NET Core 2.0 By Example</h1>
```

Razor pages are useful when we need a View with small logic. For smaller logic, the return on investment would be better for Razor pages than that for creating a controller, actions, and view. In Razor pages, we can add logic inside the page or we can simply create code behind page.cshtml.cs, to write code. The question that came to my mind is: *Are we moving forward, or moving back to the web form code-behind world?*.

Creating a Razor page is very simple. Right-click on the project and click **Add | New Item** and select **Razor Page,** as shown here:

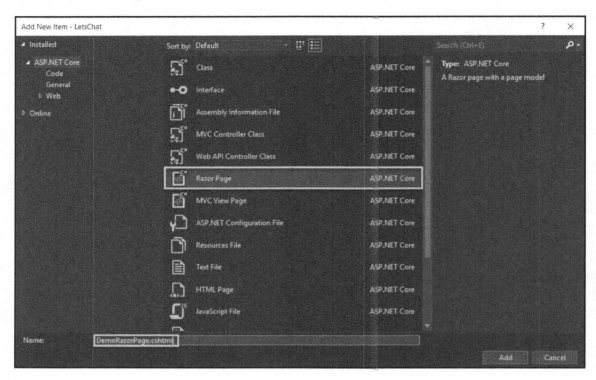

In this example, the `DemoRazorPage.cshtml` has `DemoRazorPage.cshtml.cs` and `DemoRazorPageModel` associated with it. We can go ahead and write code as needed, without needing to worry about creating a controller, then its action methods, and finally adding a view in the specific location. Super productive!

In the image, `DemoRazorPage.cshtml` file is the Razor page,
and `DemoRazorPage.cshtml.cs` is the code behind the file of the Razor page, which uses `DemoRazorPageModel` as the model.

With this, we have touched upon all the basic and most frequently used features of ASP.NET Core. We will now move on to code the Chat hub module.

Coding the Chat hub module

Now let's code the Chat hub module for our Let's Chat web application. We have already seen how to create a simple real-time web application using SignalR, while developing a Tic-Tac-Toe game, so we would not spend much time on things we have already seen. Recall that we already have authentication implemented using Facebook and we have user details, such as the display name and profile picture. We need to develop the following as part of our Chat hub module:

- List all online users connected to the Chat hub
- Update the online list of users, as and when someone joins or leaves the chat room
- Any chat message sent in the room goes to all the connected users

Quite clearly, to meet these requirements, we would need to track the users, so that a connected user shows in the online list and disappears from the list when they leave the chat room. We would first create a class named `UserInformation` to hold the user details such as `name`, display picture URL (`imageURL`), and `connection identifier`, as defined here:

```
/// <summary>
/// The class to hold the user information.
/// </summary>
public class UserInformation
{
    /// <summary>
    /// Initializes a new instance of the <see
        cref="UserInformation"/> class.
    /// </summary>
    /// <param name="connectionId">The connection identifier.
        </param>
    /// <param name="name">The name of user.</param>
    /// <param name="imageUrl">The url of user's profile picture.
        </param>
    public UserInformation(string connectionId, string name, string
```

```
imageUrl)
{
    this.ConnectionId = connectionId;
    this.Name = name;
    this.ImageUrl = imageUrl;
}

/// <summary>
/// Gets the image path of the user
/// </summary>
public string ImageUrl { get; }

/// <summary>
/// Gets the connection identifier.
/// </summary>
public string ConnectionId { get; }

/// <summary>
/// Gets the name of user.
/// </summary>
public string Name { get; }
}
```

Next, let's create an interface named `IUserTracker` with three methods for user tracking:

- **Get all online users**: This would be used to display all the users that are connected to the chat
- **Add user**: This would be used to add a user-to-user tracker data store and should be called when a user joins the chat room
- **Remove user**: This would be used to remove a user from the user tracker data store and should be called when a user leaves the chat room

The code is as shown here and the comments should make the code comprehensive:

```
/// <summary>
/// Contract for user tracking.
/// </summary>
public interface IUserTracker
{
    /// <summary>
    /// Gets all the online users (connected to chat hub)
    /// </summary>
    /// <returns>A collection of online user information</returns>
    Task<IEnumerable<UserInformation>> GetAllOnlineUsersAsync();
    /// <summary>
    /// Add user to User Tracker data store. This would be called
```

```
            when a user joins the chat hub.
/// </summary>
/// <param name="connection">The hub connection context.
    </param>
/// <param name="userInfo">The user information</param>
/// <returns>The task.</returns>
Task AddUserAsync(HubConnectionContext connection,
UserInformation userInfo);

/// <summary>
/// Removes user from User Tracker data store. This would be
    called when a user leaves the chat hub.
/// </summary>
/// <param name="connection">The hub connection context.
    </param>
/// <returns>The task.</returns>
Task RemoveUserAsync(HubConnectionContext connection);
}
```

We created an interface so that we could leverage Dependency Injection to inject the user tracking component, wherever we need it. Though we have worked with SignalR already, we have not come across the HubConnectionContext class, which we have used in the interface. So, let's have a quick look at it. The HubConnectionContext class resides in the Microsoft.AspNetCore.SignalR.Core assembly under the Microsoft.AspNet.SignalR namespace. It encapsulates all the information about a SignalR connection. The following code map diagram shows the HubConnectionContext class and its properties:

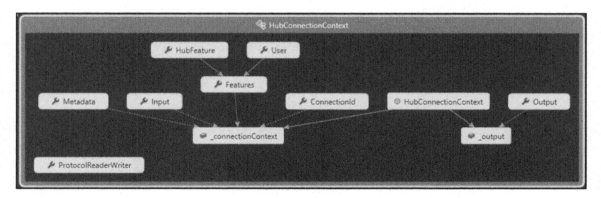

The code is as shown here:

```
namespace Microsoft.AspNetCore.SignalR
{
```

```
public class HubConnectionContext
{
    public HubConnectionContext(WritableChannel<HubMessage> output,
    ConnectionContext connectionContext);

    public virtual string ConnectionId { get; }
    public virtual ClaimsPrincipal User { get; }
    public virtual IFeatureCollection Features { get; }
    public virtual IDictionary<object, object> Metadata { get; }
    public virtual HubProtocolReaderWriter ProtocolReaderWriter {
    get; set; }
    public virtual WritableChannel<HubMessage> Output { get; }
}
}
```

There would be an extension method to get the HttpContext from
HubConnectionContext.

We use the HubConnectionContext class to keep track of the user and connection in our
UserTracker class, which we will implement next. Let's implement the IUserTracker
interface in our UserTracker class, as shown here:

```
/// <summary>
/// The User Tracker class for tracking users that are connected to
///     chat.
/// </summary>
public class UserTracker : IUserTracker
{
    /// <summary>
    /// The private storage for keeping the track of online users
    ///     connected to chat hub.
    /// We are going to register the User Tracker as singleton, so
    ///     no need to make it as static as it would be resued once the
    ///     class is initialized.
    /// </summary>
    private readonly ConcurrentDictionary<HubConnectionContext,
    UserInformation> onlineUserStore = new
    ConcurrentDictionary<HubConnectionContext, UserInformation>();

    /// <summary>
    /// Add user to User Tracker data store. This would be called
    ///     when a user joins the chat hub.
    /// </summary>
    /// <param name="connection">The hub connection context.
    ///     </param>
    /// <param name="userInfo">The user information</param>
    /// <returns>The task.</returns>
```

```
public async Task AddUserAsync(HubConnectionContext connection,
UserInformation userInfo)
{
    //// Add the connection and user to the local storage.
    onlineUserStore.TryAdd(connection, userInfo);
    await Task.CompletedTask;
}

/// <summary>
/// Gets all the online users (connected to chat hub)
/// </summary>
/// <returns>A collection of online user information</returns>
public async Task<IEnumerable<UserInformation>>
GetAllOnlineUsersAsync() => await
Task.FromResult(onlineUserStore.Values.AsEnumerable());

/// <summary>
/// Removes user from User Tracker data store. This would be
    called when a user leaves the chat hub.
/// </summary>
/// <param name="connection">The hub connection context.
    </param>
/// <returns>The task.</returns>
public async Task RemoveUserAsync(HubConnectionContext
connection)
{
    //// Remove the connection and user from the local storage.
    if (onlineUserStore.TryRemove(connection, out var
    userInfo))
    {
        await Task.CompletedTask;
    }
}
}
```

With this, our user tracker component is created. It has a backup store (concurrent dictionary), where we will add the connection and user details when a user joins the chat room, and remove the entry from it when the user leaves the chat room. We can keep the concurrent dictionary as static as well, but we will use dependency registration to register our UserTracker class as a singleton, so we can be sure that the same instance of class would be used for all the user connections. To register our UserTracker as a singleton, we would write the following lines of code in the ConfigureServices method of the Startup.cs class:

```
//// Register IUserTracker as singleton.
services.AddSingleton(typeof(IUserTracker), typeof(UserTracker));
```

```
services.AddSignalR();    //// Adds SignalR goodness in the container.
```

Next, we will code the Chat hub, which will use the `UserTracker` class, and SignalR goodness to complete our chat room. To do so, let's create a class named `ChatHub` derived from the `Hub` class, with the following code:

```
/// <summary>
/// The Chat hub class.
/// </summary>
[Authorize]
public class ChatHub : Hub
{
    /// <summary>
    /// The user tracker to keep track of online users.
    /// </summary>
    private IUserTracker userTracker;

    /// <summary>
    /// Initializes a new instance of the <see cref="ChatHub"/>
        class.
    /// </summary>
    /// <param name="userTracker">The user tracker.</param>
    public ChatHub(IUserTracker userTracker)
    {
        this.userTracker = userTracker;
    }
}
```

There are important points to note here:

1. The class `ChatHub` derives from the `Microsoft.AspNetCore.SignalR.Hub` class.
2. The class `ChatHub` is decorated with the `[Authorize]` attribute, which means only an authenticated and authorized user can access the hub.
3. The constructor of `ChatHub` uses `IUserTracker` as a dependency, which would be injected through Dependency Injection.

The `Microsoft.AspNetCore.SignalR.Hub` class has a property called `Context` of type `HubCallerContext`, which contains the SignalR connection identifier, user claim information, and `HubConnectionContext`. We can leverage the `Context` property to extract the user information from our Chat hub. To do so, we would need a helper/extension method, which takes in `HubCallerContext` and returns the `UserInformation` object that we created earlier. The following code snippet shows a helper class, which contains a method to translate the `HubCallerContext` to `UserInformation`:

```
/// <summary>
/// The Helper class.
/// </summary>
public static class Helper
{
    /// <summary>
    /// Gets the user information from the Hub caller context.
    /// </summary>
    /// <param name="context">The Hub Caller Context.</param>
    /// <returns>The user Information.</returns>
    public static UserInformation
    GetUserInformationFromContext(HubCallerContext context)
    {
        Claim nameIdentifierClaim =
        context.User.Claims.FirstOrDefault(j => j.Type ==
        "http://schemas.xmlsoap.org/ws/2005/05/
        identity/claims/nameidentifier")
        ; //// Make it a constant.
        var userId = nameIdentifierClaim.Value; //// Get user Id.
        var imageUrl =
        $"https://graph.facebook.com/{userId}/picture?type=square";
        //// Get FB image.
        return new UserInformation(context.ConnectionId,
        context.User.Identity.Name, imageUrl);
    }
}
```

With this structure, we are now in a position to track online users, as and when they join or leave our chat room, by overriding the `OnConnectedAsync` and `OnDiconnectedAsync` virtual methods, which are exposed by the `Microsoft.AspNetCore.SignalR.Hub` class. We would also need to add an additional method to fetch a list of all the connected users. We can do this easily by writing the following code in our `ChatHub` class:

```
/// <summary>
/// Gets all the connected user list.
/// </summary>
```

```
/// <returns>The collection of online users.</returns>
public async Task<IEnumerable<UserInformation>>
GetOnlineUsersAsync()
{
    return await userTracker.GetAllOnlineUsersAsync();
}

/// <summary>
/// Fires on client connected.
/// </summary>
/// <returns>The task.</returns>
public override async Task OnConnectedAsync()
{
    var user = Helper.GetUserInformationFromContext(Context);
    await this.userTracker.AddUserAsync(Context.Connection,
    user);
    await Clients.All.InvokeAsync("UsersJoined", new
    UserInformation[] { user });
    //// On connection, refresh online list.
    await Clients.All.InvokeAsync("SetUsersOnline", await
    GetOnlineUsersAsync());
    await base.OnConnectedAsync();
}

/// <summary>
/// Fires when client disconnects.
/// </summary>
/// <param name="exception">The exception.</param>
/// <returns>The task.</returns>
public override async Task OnDisconnectedAsync(Exception
exception)
{
    var user = Helper.GetUserInformationFromContext(Context);
    await Clients.All.InvokeAsync("UsersLeft", new
    UserInformation[] { user });
    await this.userTracker.RemoveUserAsync(Context.Connection);
    //// On disconnection, refresh online list.
    await Clients.All.InvokeAsync("SetUsersOnline", await
    GetOnlineUsersAsync());
    await base.OnDisconnectedAsync(exception);
}
/// <summary>
/// Sends the message to all the connected clients.
/// </summary>
/// <param name="message">The message to be sent.</param>
/// <returns>A task.</returns>
public async Task Send(string message)
{
```

```
        UserInformation user =
        Helper.GetUserInformationFromContext(Context);
        await Clients.All.InvokeAsync("Send", user.Name, message,
        user.ImageUrl);
    }
```

The code is simple to understand. However, for the sake of clarity and completeness, we will do a quick walk-through of the preceding code. There are four methods:

- GetOnlineUsersAsync: This method returns all the online users as stored in the UserTracker store. This method would be used to display online users in the chat room page.

- OnConnectedAsync: This method is fired when a user connects to the Chat hub, that is, joins the chat room. In this method, we first fetch the user information by calling the Helper class method, GetUserInformationFromContext, passing the Context property of hub, which contains information about the current connection. After getting the user information, we add the connection and user information in the UserTracker store. Next, we need to notify all connected clients that a new user is now available for chat, so we fire the UsersJoined method on all the clients. We will see this method in a short while. This method takes an array of UserInformation as a parameter. This way, we can display to all the connected clients that a new user has joined the chat room. Finally, we need to update the list displaying the online users, so we invoke the client method, SetUsersOnline, on all the connected clients, passing in the list of connected users.

- OnDisconnectedAsync: This method is the exact opposite of the OnConnectedAsync method and is fired when a user disconnects from the Chat hub, that is, leaves the chat room. In this method, we first fetch the user information by calling the Helper class method, GetUserInformationFromContext, passing the Context property of hub, which contains information about the current connection. After getting the user information, we need to notify all the connected clients that the user is no longer available for chat, so we fire the UsersLeft method on all the clients. We will see this method in a short while. This method takes an array of UserInformation as a parameter. This way, we can display to all the connected clients that a user has left the chat room. Next, we remove the connection and user information from the UserTracker store. Finally, we need to update the list displaying the online users, so we invoke the client method, SetUsersOnline, on all the connected clients, passing in a list of connected users.

- Send: The last method that we see is called `Send`. As the name suggests, this method is used to send the message to all the connected clients, along with the username and image URL. In this method, we first get the user information from the `Context` like we did in the preceding methods, and then invoke the client method, `Send`, on all connected clients, passing in the username and image URL of the user who has typed the message. We will see the details of the `Send` method shortly, when we explore client-side methods.

We will wrap our server-side coding of the Chat hub by configuring the HTTP pipeline to intercept and map any request having `chatHub` to our `ChatHub` class. To do so, we will write the following code in the `Configure` method of `Startup.cs` between `app.UseAuthentication` and `app.UseMvc`:

```
//// Use - SignalR & let it know to intercept and map any request having
chatHub.
app.UseSignalR(routes =>
{
    routes.MapHub<ChatHub>("chatHub");
});
```

This wraps up our server-side coding. Next, we will look at the client-side coding that we will do in our View. The user interface code is quite straightforward and so we will not go into details. The reader can browse the source code and see the user interface code and the used `.css` classes. We will look at the client-side JavaScript code that would be needed to complete the chat room experience. As a matter of best practice, all the JavaScript/jQuery coding should be done in a separate `.js` file and referenced in the View. For the sake of simplicity, I shall be showing the inline JavaScript in the View itself. So let's code the client-side stuff:

We begin by ensuring that the following references for CSS and JavaScript are present in the `_Layout.cshtml` file, so that they would be available in our View as well:

```
<script src="~/lib/jquery/dist/jquery.js"></script>
<link href="~/css/site.css" rel="stylesheet" />
<script src="~/js/signalr-client-1.0.0-alpha1-final.js"></script>
<script src="~/js/signalr-clientES5-1.0.0-alpha1-final.js"></script>
<script src="~/js/signalr-msgpackprotocol-1.0.0-alpha1-final.js"></script>
```

In the `Index.cshtml` of our `HomeController` class, create a `<script>` node and initialize the SignalR hub connection in the bottom of the page as shown here:

```
<script type="text/javascript">
    let hubUrl = '/chatHub';
    let httpConnection = new signalR.HttpConnection(hubUrl);
```

```
    let hubConnection = new signalR.HubConnection(httpConnection);
</script>
```

Next, we need to define the following methods that we saw previously, while doing the server side coding:

- `SetUsersOnline`: This method displays connected users in the left panel.
- `UsersJoined`: This method is fired when a user joins the chat room. This method displays information to the effect that the user has joined the room.
- `UsersLeft`: This method is fired when a user leaves the chat room. This method displays information to the effect that the user has left the room.
- `Send`: This method is called when a user types a message and clicks on the `Send` button.

The pseudo code for the preceding methods is as follows. The detailed and complete code can be seen from the source code repository URL (`https://github.com/PacktPublishing/.NET-Core-2.0-By-Example`) shared with the book:

```
hubConnection.on('SetUsersOnline', usersOnline => {
    if (usersOnline.length > 0) {
        $('#onlineUsers').innerText = '';
        $.each(usersOnline, function (i, user) {
            //// Display users in the panel.
        });
    }
});

hubConnection.on('UsersJoined', users => {
    if (users != null && typeof (users) != undefined) {
        appendLine(users.name + ' joined the chat room', 'green');
        //// Display that user joined the chat room.
    }
});

hubConnection.on('UsersLeft', users => {
    if (users != null && typeof (users) != undefined) {
        appendLine(users.name + ' left the chat room', 'red');
        //// Display that user left the chat room.
        document.getElementById(users.connectionId).outerHTML = '';
    }
});
```

While doing any client-side development or any web page/View design using Bootstrap, you can make use of Bootstrap theme sites such as `https://bootswatch.com/default/`, which gives the preceding code as needed, and can be used with minimal changes. We can spin up a web page or a complete site in a matter of hours. Do try it out! It's very handy!

Once we are done with the user interface and client-side coding, our Let's Chat application is ready to be used. Let's run the application. This is what the user interface of the Let's Chat application looks like:

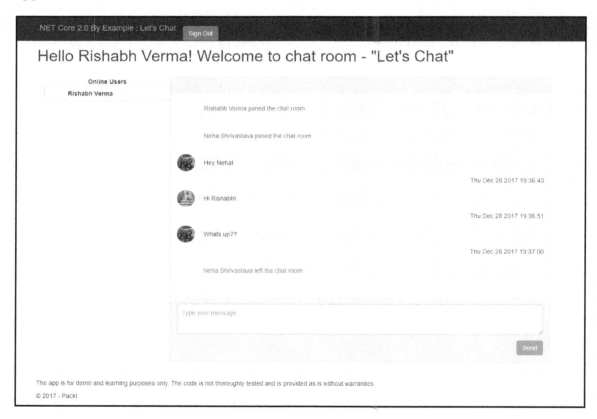

Let's look at it from top to bottom:

1. It recognizes the logged in user and hence is able to display **Hello** {User Name} (**Rishabh Verma** in the screenshot), so our authentication module is working fine.
2. On the left, it displays **Online Users**, which lists just one name, so it is able to track users that are connected to the chat room.
3. In the Chat area, we can see **Rishabh Verma joined the chat room**, **Neha Shrivastava joined the chat room**, so our IUserTracker class is working fine in conjunction with the authentication module.
4. The Facebook profile pictures of users display with their message.
5. It also displays text if a user leaves the chat room.

With this, our Let's Chat application code is complete. Next, we will do unit testing to ensure that issues or bugs in the code are caught at the time of development itself, and we thus ship and deploy a quality product. In the process, we will also learn about testing with reference to ASP.NET Core 2.0.

Testing overview

The famous Java programmer, Bruce Eckel, come up with a slogan which highlights the importance of testing software:

If it ain't tested, it's broken.

Though a confident programmer may challenge this, it beautifully highlights the ability to determine that code works as expected over and over again, without any exception. How do we know that the code that we are shipping to the end user or customer is of good quality and all the user requirements would work? By testing? Yes, by testing, we can be confident that the software works as per customer requirements and specifications. If there are any discrepancies between expected and actual behavior, it is referred to as a bug/defect in the software. The earlier the discrepancies are caught, the more easily they can be fixed before the software is shipped; and the results is good quality. No wonder software testers are also referred to as quality control analysts in various software firms. The mantra for a good software tester would be:

In God we trust, the rest we test.

We will not go into types of testing in any depth, as that would make another chapter in itself. We will look at them briefly, and then write our unit tests, which every good developer should write after writing any software program. Software testing is conducted at various levels:

- **Unit testing**: While coding, the developer conducts tests on a unit of a program to validate that the code they have written is error-free. We will write a few unit tests shortly.
- **Integration testing**: In a team where a number of developers are working, there may be different components that the developers are working on. Even if all developers perform unit testing and ensure that their units are working fine, there is still a need to ensure that, upon integration of these components, they work without any error. This is achieved through integration testing.
- **System testing**: The entire software product is tested as a whole. This is accomplished using one or more of the following:
    - **Functionality testing**: Test all the functionality of the software against the business requirement document.
    - **Performance testing**: To test how performant the software is. It tests the average time, resource utilization, and so on, taken by the software to complete a desired business use case. This is done by means of load testing and stress testing, where the software is put under high user and data load.
    - **Security testing**: Tests how secure the software is against common and well-known security threats.
    - **Accessibility testing**: Tests if the user interface is accessible and user-friendly to specially-abled people or not.
- **User acceptance testing**: When the software is ready to be handed over to the customer, it goes through a round of testing by the customer for user interaction and response.
- **Regression testing**: Whenever a piece of code is added/updated in the software to add a new functionality or fix an existing functionality, it is tested to detect if there are any side-effects from the newly added/updated code.

Of all these different types of testing (and many more not listed here), we would focus on unit testing, as that is done by the developer coding the functionality.

Unit testing

.NET Core has been designed with testability in mind. .NET Core 2.0 has unit test project templates for VB, F#, and C#. We can also pick the testing framework of our choice amongst xUnit, NUnit, and MSTest.

Unit tests that test single programming parts are the most minimal-level tests. Unit tests should just test code inside the developer's control, and ought to not test infrastructure concerns, for example databases, filesystems, or network resources. Unit tests might be composed utilizing **test-driven development** (**TDD**) or they can be added to existing code to affirm its accuracy. The naming convention of `Test` class names should end with `Test` and reside in the same namespace as the class being tested. For instance, the unit tests for the `Microsoft.Example.AspNetCore` class would be in the `Microsoft.Example.AspNetCoreTest` class in the test assembly. Also, unit test method names must be descriptive about *what is being tested*, *under what conditions*, and *what the expectations are*. A good unit test has three main parts to it in the following specified order:

1. Arrange
2. Act
3. Assert

We first arrange the code and then act on it and then do a series of asserts to check if the actual output matches the expected output. Let's have a look at them in detail:

1. **Arrange:** All the parameter building, and method invocations needed for making a call in the act section must be declared in the arrange section.
2. **Act:** The act stage should be one statement and as simple as possible. This one statement should be a call to the method that we are trying to test.
3. **Assert:** The only reason method invocation may fail is if the method itself throws an exception, else, there should always be some state change or output from any meaningful method invocation. When we write the act statement, we anticipate an output and then do assertions if the actual output is the same as expected. If the method under test should throw an exception under normal circumstances, we can do assertions on the type of exception and the error message that should be thrown.

We should be watchful, while writing unit test cases, that we don't inject any dependencies on the infrastructure. Infrastructure dependencies should be taken care of in integration test cases, not in unit tests. We can maintain a strategic distance from these shrouded dependencies in our application code by following the Explicit Dependencies Principle and utilizing Dependency Injection to request our dependencies on the framework. We can likewise keep our unit tests in a different project from our integration tests and guarantee our unit test project doesn't have references to the framework.

Testing using xUnit

In this section we will learn to write unit and integration tests for our controllers. There are a number of options available to us for choosing the test framework. We will use xUnit for all our unit tests and Moq for mocking objects. Let's create a xUnit test project by doing the following:

1. Open the Let's Chat project in Visual Studio 2017
2. Create a new folder named `Test`
3. Right-click the `Test` folder and click **Add | New Project**
4. Select **xUnit Test Project (.NET Core)** under **Visual C#** project templates, as shown here:

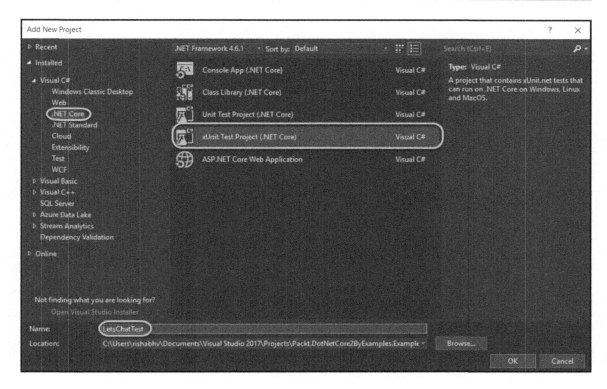

5. Delete the default test class that gets created with the template
6. Create a test class inside this project `AuthenticationControllerUnitTests` for the unit test

We need to add some NuGet packages. Right-click the project in VS 2017 to edit the project file and add the references manually, or use the NuGet Package Manager to add these packages:

```
// This package contains dependencies to ASP.NET Core
<PackageReference Include="Microsoft.AspNetCore.All" Version="2.0.0" />
// This package is useful for the integration testing, to build a test host
for the project to test.
<PackageReference Include="Microsoft.AspNetCore.TestHost" Version="2.0.0"
/>
// Moq is used to create fake objects
<PackageReference Include="Moq" Version="4.7.63" />
```

With this, we are now ready to write our unit tests. Let's start doing this, but before we do that, here's some quick theory about xUnit and Moq.

The documentation from the xUnit website and Wikipedia tells us that xUnit.net is a free, open source, community-focused unit testing tool for the .NET Framework. It is the latest technology for unit testing C#, F#, Visual Basic .NET, and other .NET languages. All xUnit frameworks share the following basic component architecture:

- **Test runner**: It is an executable program that runs tests implemented using an xUnit framework and reports the test results.
- **Test case**: It is the most elementary class. All unit tests are inherited from here.
- **Test fixtures:** Test fixures (also known as a test context) are the set of preconditions or state needed to run a test. The developer should set up a known good state before the tests, and return to the original state after the tests.
- **Test suites:** It is a set of tests that all share the same fixture. The order of the tests shouldn't matter.

xUnit.net includes support for two different major types of unit test:

1. **Facts**: Tests which are always true. They test invariant conditions, that is, data-independent tests.
2. **Theories**: Tests which are only true for a particular set of data.

Moq is a mocking framework for C#/.NET. It is used in unit testing to isolate the class under test from its dependencies, and ensure that the proper methods on the dependent objects are being called.

Recall that in unit tests, we only test a unit or a layer/part of the software in isolation and hence do not bother about external dependencies, so we assume they work fine and just mock them using the mocking framework of our choice.

Let's put this theory into action by writing a unit test for the following action in `AuthenticationController`:

```
public class AuthenticationController : Controller
{
    private readonly ILogger<AuthenticationController> logger;

    public
    AuthenticationController(ILogger<AuthenticationController>
    logger)
    {
        this.logger = logger;
```

```
    }

    [Route("signin")]
    public IActionResult SignIn()
    {
        logger.LogInformation($"Calling {nameof(this.SignIn)}");
        return Challenge(new AuthenticationProperties { RedirectUri
        = "/" });
    }
}
```

The unit test code depends on how the method to be tested is written. To understand this, let's write a unit test for a SignIn action. To test the SignIn method, we need to invoke the SignIn action in AuthenticationController. To do so, we need an instance of the AuthenticationController class, on which the SignIn action can be invoked. To create the instance of AuthenticationController, we need a logger object, as the AuthenticationController constructor expects it as a parameter. Since we are only testing the SignIn action, we do not bother about the logger and so we can mock it. Let's do it:

```
/// <summary>
/// Authentication Controller Unit Test - Notice the naming
    convention {ControllerName}Test
/// </summary>
public class AuthenticationControllerTest
{
    /// <summary>
    /// Mock the dependency needed to initialize the controller.
    /// </summary>
    private Mock<ILogger<AuthenticationController>> mockedLogger =
    new Mock<ILogger<AuthenticationController>>();

    /// <summary>
    /// Tests the SignIn action.
    /// </summary>
    [Fact]
    public void SignIn_Pass_Test()
    {
        // Arrange - Initialize the controller. Notice the mocked
            logger object passed as the parameter.
        var controller = new
        AuthenticationController(mockedLogger.Object);

        // Act - Invoke the method to be tested.
        var actionResult = controller.SignIn();
```

```
        // Assert - Make assertions if actual output is same as
            expected output.
        Assert.NotNull(actionResult);
        Assert.IsType<ChallengeResult>(actionResult);
        Assert.Equal(((ChallengeResult)actionResult).
        Properties.Items.Count, 1);
    }
}
```

Reading the comments would explain the unit test code. The previous example shows how easy it is to write a unit test. Through depending upon the method to be tested, things can get complicated, but most of it would be around mocking the objects and, with some experience on the mocking framework and binging around, mocking should not be a difficult task. The unit test for the SignOut action would be a bit complicated in terms of mocking as it uses HttpContext. The unit test for the SignOut action is left to the reader as an exercise. Let's explore a new feature introduced in Visual Studio 2017 called Live Unit Testing.

Live Unit Testing

It may disappoint you but **Live Unit Testing (LUT)** is available only in the Visual Studio 2017 Enterprise edition and not in the Community edition. What is Live Unit Testing? It's a new productivity feature, introduced in the Visual Studio 2017 Enterprise edition, that provides real-time feedback directly in the Visual Studio editor on how code changes are impacting unit tests and code coverage. All this happens live, while you write the code and hence it is called Live Unit Testing. This will help in maintaining the quality by keeping tests passing as changes are made. It will also remind us when we need to write additional unit tests, as we are making bug fixes or adding features.

To start Live Unit Testing:

1. Go to the **Test** menu item
2. Click **Live Unit Testing**
3. Click **Start,** as shown here:

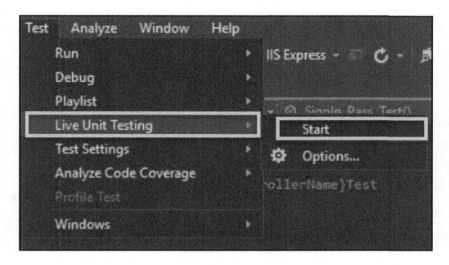

On clicking this, your CPU usage may go higher as Visual Studio spawns the MSBuild and tests runner processes in the background. In a short while, the editor will display the code coverage of the individual lines of code that are covered by the unit test. The following image displays the lines of code in AuthenticationController that are covered by the unit test. On clicking the right icon, it displays the tests covering this line of code and also provides the option to run and debug the test:

Similarly, if we open the test file, it will show the indicator there as well. Super cool, right!

If we navigate to **Test | Live Unit Testing** now, we would see the options to **Stop** and **Pause**. So, in case we wish to save our resources after getting the data once, we can pause or stop Live Unit Testing:

There are numerous icons which indicates the code coverage status of individual lines of code. These are:

- **Red cross**: Indicates that the line is covered by at least one failing test

- **Green check mark**: Indicates that the line is covered by only passing tests

- **Blue dash**: Indicates that the line is not covered by any test

If you see a clock-like icon just below any of these icons, it indicates that the data is not up to date. With this productivity enhancing feature, we conclude our discussion on basic unit testing. Next we will learn about containers and how we can do the deployment and testing of our .NET Core 2.0 applications in containers.

Introduction to containers

Think of a container as just another process running in the machine; it's just that they offer a lot more isolation than a normal process does. So, we define a container as an isolated process. A container can have its own filesystem, own network IP address, own hostname, own registry, own unique resources and so on. A question that would come to mind is: *Why Containers?* In the modern world, where new software comes in and changes overnight, there are numerous challenges in:

1. **Discovering the software**: There is no single point at which to find all software. A few are available as executables on the developer sites, a few in platform-specific application stores, a few as package managers, and so on and so forth.
2. **Installing the software**: Software can be installed on specific OS, CPU architectures, OS versions, and build versions with the relevant prerequisites. Over a period of time, this becomes messy and confusing.
3. **Running the software**: We have all faced the issue where *I am unable to find that software that I downloaded*. Applications that are installed and updated in the registry are easy to find but the ones that run as stand alone executables are more likely to missed. On top of that, we have licensing, upgrades, documentation, paths, and so on to take care of if we wish to run the software. On top of it, are we 100% sure that the executable that we are running is secure and would not cause a security breach if it's run on the machine?

These slightly over exaggerated points highlight that there are challenges a plenty in discovering, installing, and running software. Containers are about software and relieve much of this pain. Just as shipping containers allow goods to be transported by ship, train, or truck regardless of the cargo inside, software containers act as a standard unit of software that can contain different code and dependencies. Containerizing software this way enables developers and IT professionals to deploy them across environments, with little or no modification. Containers also isolate applications from each other on a shared OS. Containerized applications run on top of a container host that in turn runs on the OS (Linux or Windows). Containers therefore have a significantly smaller footprint than **virtual machine (VM)** images. There is a myth that containers are replacements for VMs, which is incorrect. Containers require fewer resources than VMs, and hence a server can host more containers than VMs, making choice easier when there is a confusion. There are a number of containers available in the market today such as LXC, Docker, and so on. We will use Docker as our container, and will discuss it next.

Docker

Docker is an open source project for automating the deployment of applications as portable, self-sufficient containers that can run on the cloud or on-premise. Docker is also a company that promotes and evolves this technology. Docker works in collaboration with cloud, Linux, and Windows vendors, including Microsoft. Docker image containers run natively on Linux and Windows. Windows images run only on Windows hosts and Linux images run only on Linux hosts. The host is a server or a VM. Docker containers package an application with everything it needs to run: code, runtime, system tools, system libraries—anything we would install on a server for the application to run. A container is an isolated place where an application can run without affecting the rest of the system, and vice versa. This makes them an ideal way to package and run applications in production environments. Additionally, as discussed previously, Docker containers are lightweight which enables scaling applications quickly by spinning up new instances.

Before we deploy our Let's Chat application in Docker, let's get familiar with Docker terminology from Microsoft's official documentation site, (https://docs.microsoft.com/en-us/dotnet/standard/microservices-architecture/container-docker-introduction/docker-terminology):

- **Container image**: It is a package with all the dependencies and information needed to create a container. An image includes all the dependencies such as frameworks, deployment, and the execution configuration to be used by a container at runtime. An image is immutable once it has been created.
- **Container**: An instance of a Docker image is called a container. It represents the execution of a single application, process, or service. It consists of the contents of a Docker image, an execution environment, and a standard set of instructions. When scaling a service, we create multiple instances of a container from the same image.
- **Tag**: A mark or label applied to images, so that different images or versions can be identified.
- **Dockerfile**: It is a text file that contains instructions to build a Docker image.
- **Build**: The action of building a container image, based on the information and context provided by its Docker file, and additional files in the folder where the image is built. We can build images with the Docker docker build command.
- **Repository**: A collection of related Docker images, labeled with a tag that indicates the image version.

- **Registry**: A service that provides access to repositories. The default registry for most public images is the Docker Hub (owned by Docker as an organization). A registry usually contains repositories from multiple teams. Companies often have private registries to store and manage images they've created; the Azure Container Registry is another example.
- **Docker Hub**: A public registry to upload images and work with them. Docker Hub provides Docker image hosting, public or private registries, build triggers and web hooks, and integration with GitHub and Bitbucket.
- **Azure Container Registry**: A public resource for working with Docker images and its components in Azure. This provides a registry that is close to deployments in Azure and that gives control over access, making it possible to use Azure Active Directory groups and permissions.
- **Compose**: A command-line tool and YAML file format with metadata for defining and running multi-container applications. We define a single application based on multiple images with one or more `.yml` files that can override values depending on the environment. After creating the definitions, we can deploy the whole multi-container application with a single command (`docker-compose up`) that creates a container per image on the Docker host.

This is just a basic introduction to Docker to get us started. There is a lot to be learned, so much so that a complete book can be written on Docker itself. So, interested and curious readers should spend quality time in familiarizing themselves with Docker from the Docker documentation site, or Microsoft's documentation on Docker.

Now that we have some context about Docker, let's try and deploy our Let's Chat application in a Docker container, using the tooling provided by Visual Studio 2017. To do so, we will follow these steps:

1. If you have used Visual Studio 2017 and worked along with the chapters thus far, you already have Docker support enabled with the Visual Studio installation. If not, you would need to modify the Visual Studio 2017 installation and choose the **.NET Core cross-platform development** workload.
2. Next, we will need to install Docker for Windows from `https://docs.docker.com/docker-for-windows/install/`. It's a simple installation in which you just need to do **Next | OK | Finish** stuff, so we will not discuss it here. As of writing this chapter, 17.12 is the latest version.

3. Once the installation is successful, we would see a dialog as shown here:

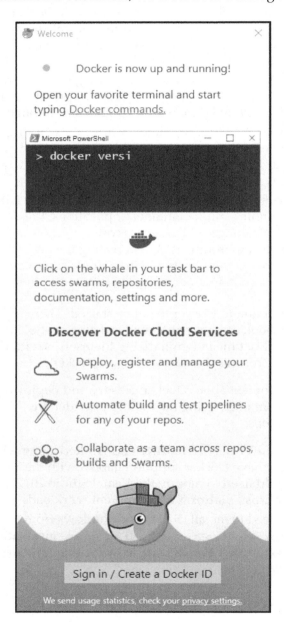

4. Next, we would need to share the drive in our local machine with Docker, where the images can be built and run. To do this, right-click on the Docker system tray icon and click **Settings,** as shown here:

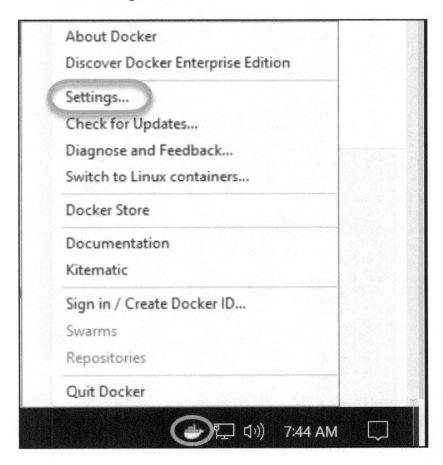

4. Share the drive where the images will run from in the **Shared Drives** tab of **Settings**.
5. Now, open the Let's Chat project in Visual Studio 2017.
6. Right-click on `LetsChat.csproj` and choose **Add | Docker Support**.
7. Visual Studio would do all the heavy lifting for us and add a Docker file amongst a few others as shown here:

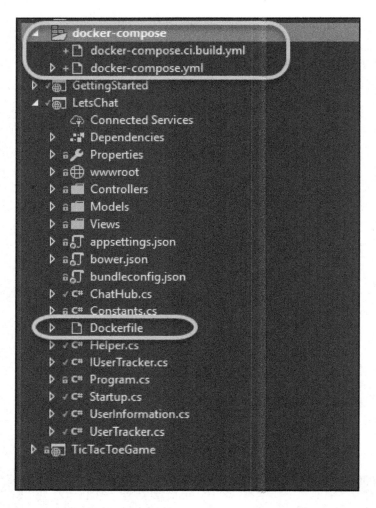

8. We can also see that the **Start** button in the command bar has changed to **Docker,** as shown here:

9. With this, we are done with our steps. Just click on the **Docker** button (or press *F5*) and the application will run in the Docker container.

We will see in `Chapter 10`, *Functional Programming with F#* how we can deploy the application in the cloud, as well as how we can deploy Docker containers in Azure. This wraps up our discussion on Docker containers. We will conclude this chapter by learning to develop a FAQ Bot using the Microsoft Bot Framework.

Bot 101

A Chatbot, also known as talkbot, chatterbot, Bot, or IM bot, is a computer program which conducts a conversation through auditory or textual methods. Such programs are often designed to convincingly simulate how a human would behave as a conversational partner, thereby passing the Turing test. Chatbots are typically used in dialog systems for various practical purposes, including customer service or information acquisition. You would have noticed that various sites offer live chat with agents as it helps them gain better customer experience and business. In this section, we will see how we can quickly create a simple Chatbot to answer the basic questions. This section is completely informational and just provides a basic 100-level awareness of how a simple Chatbot can be created and the related technology. Curious and enthusiastic readers can explore other avenues from this basic knowledge. Let's learn to develop a simple FAQ Bot, which will answer simple queries like:

- How do I use Let's Chat?
- How are you?
- Hello!
- Bye!

The more you train the Bot and the more questions you put in its knowledge base, the better it will be, so let's get started. First of all, we need to create a page that can be accessed anonymously, as this is **frequently asked questions (FAQ**), and hence the user should not be required to be logged in to the system to access this page. To do so, let's create a new controller called `FaqController` in our `LetsChat.csproj`. It will be a very simple class with just one action called `Index`, which will display the FAQ page. The code is as follows:

```
[AllowAnonymous]
public class FaqController : Controller
{
    // GET: Faq
    public ActionResult Index()
    {
        return this.View();
```

```
        }
    }
```

Notice that we have used the `[AllowAnonymous]` attribute, so that this controller can be accessed even if the user is not logged in. The corresponding `.cshtml` is also very simple. In the solution explore, right-click on the **Views** folder under the `LetsChat` project and create a folder named `Faq` and then add an `Index.cshtml` file in that folder. The markup of the `Index.cshtml` would look like this:

```
@{
    ViewData["Title"] = "Let's Chat";
    ViewData["UserName"] = "Guest";
    if(User.Identity.IsAuthenticated)
    {
        ViewData["UserName"] = User.Identity.Name;
    }
}
<h1>
  Hello @ViewData["UserName"]! Welcome to FAQ page of Let's Chat
</h1>
<br />
```

Nothing much here apart from the welcome message. The message displays the username if the user is authenticated, else it displays `Guest`. Now, we need to integrate the Chatbot stuff in this page. To do so, let's browse to `http://qnamaker.ai`. This is Microsoft's QnA (as in questions and answers) maker site which a free, easy-to-use, REST API and web-based service that trains **artificial intelligence (AI)** to respond to user questions in a more natural, conversational way. Compatible across development platforms, hosting services, and channels, QnA Maker is the only question and answer service with a graphical user interface—meaning you don't need to be a developer to train, manage, and use it for a wide range of solutions. And that is what makes it incredibly easy to use. You would need to log in to this site with your Microsoft account (`@microsoft/@live/@outlook`).

If you don't have one, you should create one and log in. On the very first login, the site would display a dialog seeking permission to access your email address and profile information. Click **Yes** and grant permission:

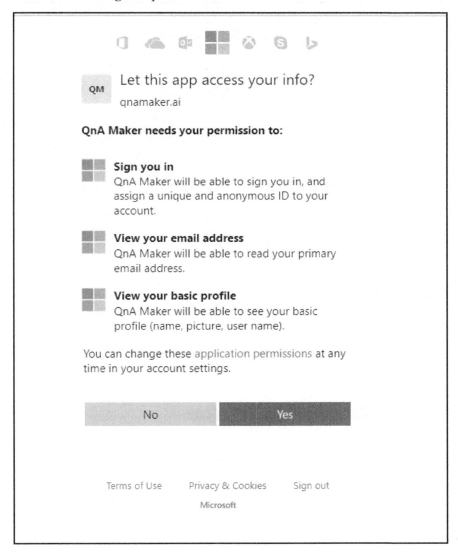

You would then be presented with the service terms. Accept that as well. Then navigate to the **Create New Service** tab. A form will appear as shown here:

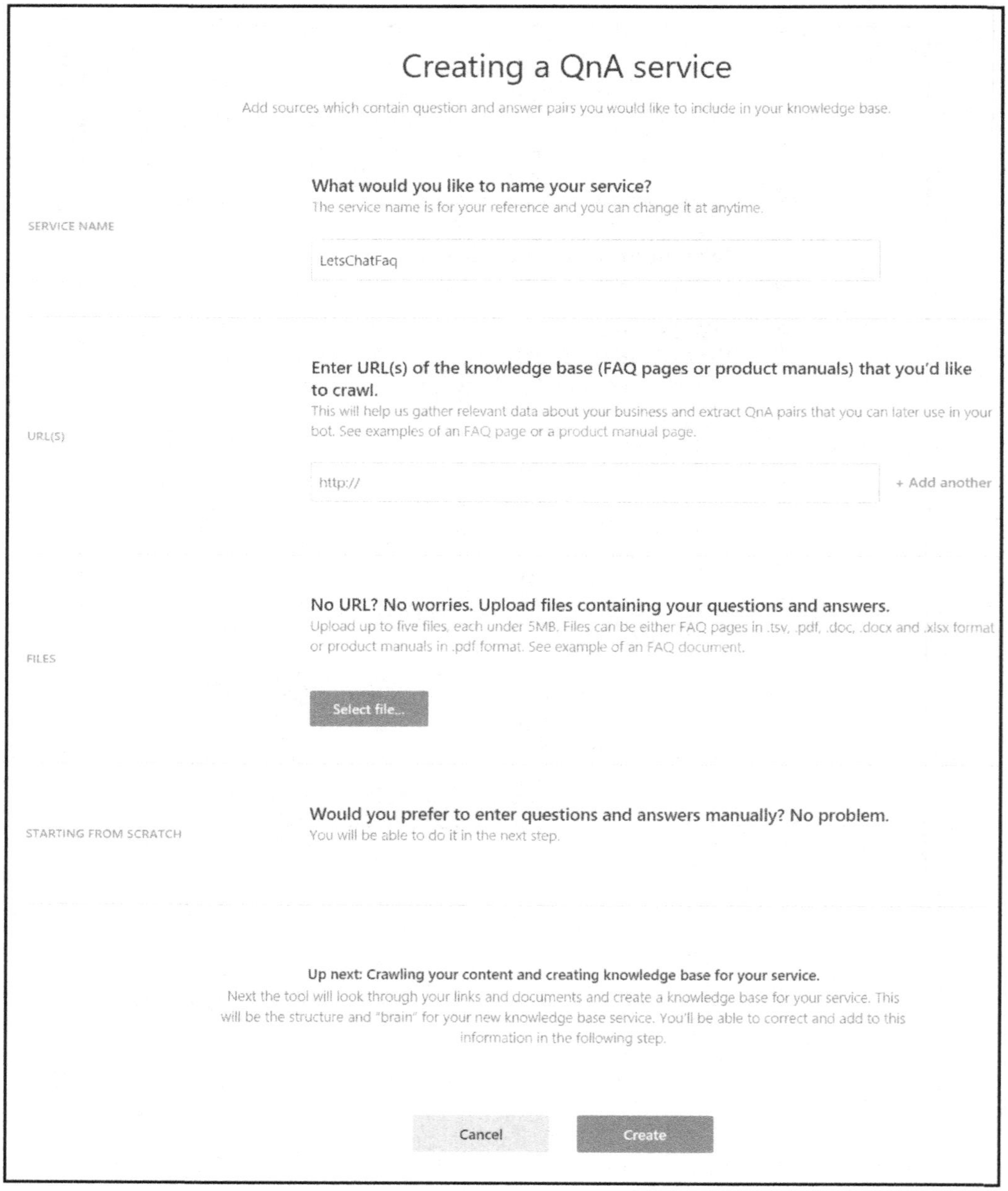

Creating a QnA service

Add sources which contain question and answer pairs you would like to include in your knowledge base.

SERVICE NAME

What would you like to name your service?
The service name is for your reference and you can change it at anytime.

LetsChatFaq

URL(S)

Enter URL(s) of the knowledge base (FAQ pages or product manuals) that you'd like to crawl.
This will help us gather relevant data about your business and extract QnA pairs that you can later use in your bot. See examples of an FAQ page or a product manual page.

http://   + Add another

FILES

No URL? No worries. Upload files containing your questions and answers.
Upload up to five files, each under 5MB. Files can be either FAQ pages in .tsv, .pdf, .doc, .docx and .xlsx format or product manuals in .pdf format. See example of an FAQ document.

Select file...

STARTING FROM SCRATCH

Would you prefer to enter questions and answers manually? No problem.
You will be able to do it in the next step.

Up next: Crawling your content and creating knowledge base for your service.
Next the tool will look through your links and documents and create a knowledge base for your service. This will be the structure and "brain" for your new knowledge base service. You'll be able to correct and add to this information in the following step.

Cancel   Create

The form is easy to fill in and provides the option to extract the question/answer pairs from a site or `.tsv`, `.docx`, `.pdf`, and `.xlsx` files. We don't have questions handy and so we will type them; so do not bother about these fields. Just enter the service name and click the **Create** button. The service should be created successfully and the knowledge base screen should be displayed. We will enter probable questions and answers in this knowledge base. If the user types a question that resembles the question in the knowledge base, it will respond with the answer in the knowledge base. Hence, the more questions and answers we type, the better it will perform. So, enter all the questions and answers that you wish to enter, test it in the local Chatbot setup, and, once you are happy with it, click on **Publish**. This would publish the knowledge bank and share the sample URL to make the HTTP request. Note it down in a notepad. It contains the knowledge base identifier guide, hostname, and subscription key. With this, our questions and answers are ready and deployed. We need to display a chat interface, pass the user-entered text to this service, and display the response from this service to the user in the chat user interface. To do so, we will make use of the Microsoft Bot Builder SDK for .NET and follow these steps:

1. Download the `Bot Application` project template from `http://aka.ms/bf-bc-vstemplate`.

2. Download the `Bot Controller` item template from `http://aka.ms/bf-bc-vscontrollertemplate`.

3. Download the `Bot Dialog` item template from `http://aka.ms/bf-bc-vsdialogtemplate`.

4. Next, identify the project template and item template directory for Visual Studio 2017. The project template directory is located at `%USERPROFILE%\Documents\Visual Studio 2017\Templates\ProjectTemplates\Visual C#\` and the item template directory is located at `%USERPROFILE%\Documents\Visual Studio 2017\Templates\ItemTemplates\Visual C#\`.

5. Copy the `Bot Application` project template to the project template directory.

6. Copy the `Bot Controller` ZIP and `Bot Dialog` ZIP to the item template directory.

7. In the solution explorer of the `LetsChat` project, right-click on the solution and add a new project. Under **Visual C#**, we should now start seeing a `Bot Application` template as shown here:

8. Name the project `FaqBot` and click **OK**.

9. A new project will be created in the solution, which looks similar to the MVC project template. Build the project, so that all the dependencies are resolved and packages are restored. If you run the project, it is already a working Bot, which can be tested by the Microsoft Bot Framework emulator. Download the BotFramework-Emulator setup executable from `https://github.com/Microsoft/BotFramework-Emulator/releases/`.

10. Let's run the Bot project by hitting *F5*. It will display a page pointing to the default URL of `http://localhost:3979`. Now, open the Bot framework emulator and navigate to the preceding URL and append `api/messages`; to it, that is, browse to `http://localhost:3979/api/messages` and click **Connect**. On successful connection to the Bot, a chat-like interface will be displayed in which you can type the message. The following screenshot displays this step:

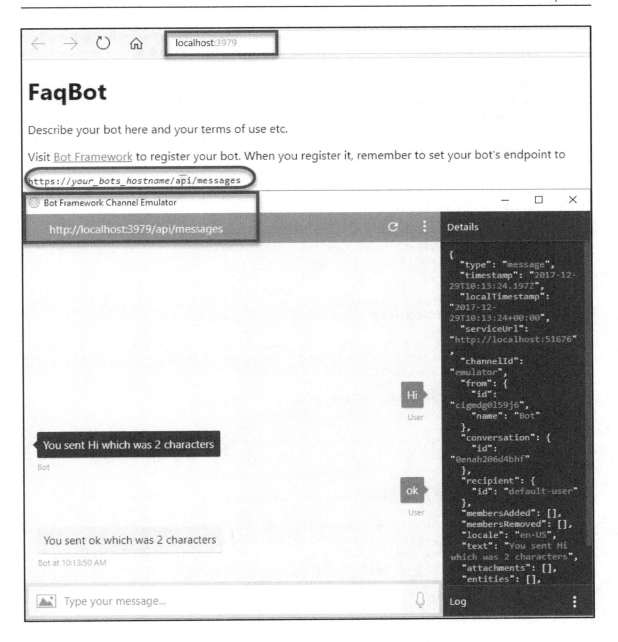

We have a working Bot in place which just returns the text along with its length. We need to modify this Bot, to pass the user input to our QnA Maker service and display the response returned from our service. To do so, we will need to check the code of `MessagesController` in the `Controllers` folder. We notice that it has just one method called `Post`, which checks the activity type, does specific processing for the activity type, creates a response, and returns it. The calculation happens in the `Dialogs.RootDialog` class, which is where we need to make the modification to wire up our QnA service. The modified code is shown here:

```
private static string knowledgeBaseId =
ConfigurationManager.AppSettings["KnowledgeBaseId"]; //// Knowledge
base id of QnA Service.

 private static string qnamakerSubscriptionKey =
 ConfigurationManager.AppSettings["SubscriptionKey"];
////Subscription
 key.

 private static string hostUrl =
 ConfigurationManager.AppSettings["HostUrl"];


 private async Task MessageReceivedAsync(IDialogContext context,
 IAwaitable<object> result)
 {
     var activity = await result as Activity;
     // return our reply to the user
     await
     context.PostAsync(this.GetAnswerFromService(activity.Text));
     context.Wait(MessageReceivedAsync);
 }

 private string GetAnswerFromService(string inputText)
 {
     //// Build the QnA Service URI
     Uri qnamakerUriBase = new Uri(hostUrl);
     var builder = new
UriBuilder($"{qnamakerUriBase}/knowledgebases
     /{knowledgeBaseId}/generateAnswer");
     var postBody = $"{{\"question\": \"{inputText}\"}}";
     //Add the subscription key header
     using (WebClient client = new WebClient())
     {
         client.Headers.Add("Ocp-Apim-Subscription-Key",
         qnamakerSubscriptionKey);
         client.Headers.Add("Content-Type", "application/json");
```

```
            try
            {
                var response = client.UploadString(builder.Uri,
                postBody);
                var json = JsonConvert.DeserializeObject<QnAResult>
                (response);
                return json?.answers?.FirstOrDefault().answer;
            }
            catch (Exception ex)
            {
                return ex.Message;
            }
        }
    }
```

The code is pretty straightforward. First, we add the QnA Maker service subscription key, host URL, and knowledge base ID in the appSettings section of Web.config. Next, we read these app settings into static variables so that they are available always. Next, we modify the MessageReceivedAsync method of the dialog to pass the user input to the QnA service and return the response of the service back to the user. The QnAResult class can be seen from the source code.

11. This can be tested in the emulator by typing in any of the questions that we have stored in our knowledge base, and we will get the appropriate response, as shown next:

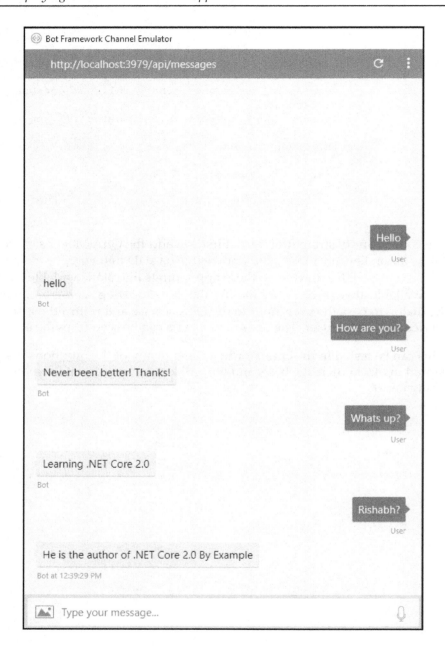

Deploying it in our Let's Chat application would need a basic knowledge of Azure, which we have not touched on yet. We will continue deploying and integrating this Chatbot in our Let's Chat application later in `Chapter 10`, *Functional Programming with F#*, when we discuss and learn Azure fundamentals and will be deploying ASP.NET Core 2.0 applications in the cloud.

This concludes our awareness discussion on developing a basic Chatbot using the Microsoft Bot Framework, the QnA Maker service, and ASP.NET Core 2.0. The Bot can be deployed in Azure and can be integrated to work with a variety of channels such as Skype, Facebook, web chat, and so on. With this, we conclude our chapter as well. In the next chapter, we would look into a new term that has sprung up over the last few years called microservices, with respect to ASP.NET Core 2.0.

Summary

In this chapter, we learnt about Razor syntax, Views, Razor pages, and Tag Helpers. We then coded the Chat hub module of our Let's Chat application. We also learnt the importance of testing and how we can write unit tests using Moq and xUnit. We saw a new productivity-enhancing feature introduced in Visual Studio 2017 Enterprise edition called Live Unit Testing and how it helps us write better-quality code. We also learnt about containers and how we can deploy our application in Docker from Visual Studio itself. We concluded the chapter by learning about developing a FAQ Bot using the Microsoft Bot Framework and ASP.NET Core 2.0. We have not deployed our application in the cloud yet, which we will do in `Chapter 10`, *Functional Programming with F#*. In the next couple of chapters, we will delve into the new world of microservices.

7
To the Cloud

So far we have learned and explored the fundamentals of ASP.NET Core 2.0 by developing applications that ran locally in our machines. The real value of these apps can be realized only when these apps are deployed and available on the internet, so that they can be accessed from virtually anywhere and everywhere on the planet. To do so, we need to learn to deploy our ASP.NET Core 2.0 apps in the cloud, Microsoft Azure. An obvious question that comes to mind is *Why should I care about the cloud?* In this chapter, we will answer this question and get introduced to Microsoft Azure, our cloud platform, and learn its basics. So far, we deliberately developed applications that did not do any data persistence and hence did not use a relational database. We will also learn to develop an end-to-end application that uses a relational database for data persistence and learn about Entity Framework Core in the process. We will grasp these concepts by developing a simple movie booking web app and then deploy this web app on Azure. Finally, we will integrate the Chatbot that we developed earlier in the book with our movie booking site. We have a lot of ground to cover, so let's get into the cloud!

We will cover the following topics in this chapter:

- Introduction to the cloud
- Types of cloud
- Getting started with Azure

Introduction to the cloud

For the cloud, we're all in.

– Steve Ballmer

At our core, Microsoft is the productivity and platform company for the mobile-first and cloud-first world.

– Satya Nadella

These two quotes from the former and current Microsoft CEO highlight the importance of the cloud. The cloud has been one of the hottest buzzwords over the last few years but you shouldn't be surprised to know that we have been using the cloud for a decade, maybe more, without realizing it. Gmail, Facebook, Skype, Dropbox, OneDrive, and so on are all examples of cloud solutions that we use almost everyday.

Cloud computing is an **information technology (IT)** paradigm that enables ubiquitous access to shared pools of configurable system resources and higher-level services that can be rapidly provisioned with minimal management effort, often over the internet. Cloud computing relies on the sharing of resources to achieve coherence and economy of scale, similar to a utility. Clouds enable organizations to focus on their core businesses instead of expending resources on computer infrastructure and maintenance. Cloud computing allows enterprises to get their applications up and running faster, with improved manageability and less maintenance, and it enables IT teams to more rapidly adjust resources to meet fluctuating and unpredictable business demand.

The fundamental idea behind the cloud is that we can access all the information over the internet without worrying about detailed information about the infrastructure needed to enable it.

The cloud provides businesses and organizations with:

- **Flexibility**: Based on the business requirements, such as enhancing a basic plan to a premium plan, we can scale the number of servers up or down. Imagine a cake business web app. During the Christmas holiday season, the demand for cakes and thus traffic to the website increases manyfold. So to serve this increased load, the number of servers can be increased during the holiday season, and during a lean phase, it can be decreased. This flexibility is key in today's economy where businesses have to save and excel in every little margin.almost instantly by the consumer as and when needed without any human

- **On-demand self-service**: The services can be provisioned or decommissioned almost instantly by the consumer as and when needed without any human intervention.
- **Security**: Security is paramount. Rest assured that your data is more secure in the cloud than in the desktop located at your desk or the laptop that you carry. A lost/stolen laptop is a frequently encountered issue. More than financial cost, loss of sensitive data is exorbitantly costly, not just financially but also regarding reputation and trust. The cloud gives you better security when this happens. As the data is stored in the cloud, you can access it no matter what happens to your machine. You can even remotely wipe out data from your machine, if it falls into the wrong hands.
- **Cost**: Using the cloud saves on maintenance costs and the high cost of hardware. No more servers, software, and update fees. You simply *pay as you go* and enjoy a subscription. You also save on the cost of people to procure the hardware, maintain it, and update it.
- **Disaster recovery**: A robust disaster recovery plan in needed for any large or small enterprise as one disaster can put you out of business. The cloud lets you do it easier than ever.
- **Automatic updates**: Since all the servers are off-premise on the cloud, you don't have to worry about wasting time maintaining the system yourself. The cloud provider takes care of maintenance for you and rolls out regular software updates. This keeps you free to focus on the things that matter, such as growing your business.
- **Collaboration**:When your teams can access, edit, and share documents anytime from anywhere, they're able to do more things better collaboratively. Cloud-based workflow and file sharing apps help them make updates in real time and give them full visibility of their collaborations.
- **Work from home**: Why just home? Work from anywhere you have the internet. Yes, that's a reality with the cloud.

This and many more benefits make the cloud indispensable for any modern day IT professional. I would go one step ahead and say that:

If you are not in cloud, you are out of IT.

Next, let's have a look at different types of cloud.

Types of cloud

Broadly speaking, the cloud deployment model can be classified into:

- **Public cloud:** This is the most commonly used cloud deployment model. A public cloud is one in which the service provider makes resources such as services, applications, or storage available to the general public over the internet. Public cloud services may be *free* or offered on a *pay as you go* model. Some examples of public cloud services are Microsoft Azure, Amazon **Elastic Compute Cloud (EC2)**, IBM's Blue Cloud, Google App Engine, and so on.
- **Private cloud:** A private cloud offers similar advantages to a public cloud, but through a proprietary architecture. Unlike a public cloud, a private cloud is dedicated to a single organization. Since there is a lot of cost involved, only a large organization can invest in private clouds. Organizations with a lot of software developers are use cases for private clouds, as developers have frequent requests for new virtual machines. For example, the **State Bank of India (SBI)** has built a private cloud named **Meghdoot** which powers multiple business services.
- **Hybrid cloud:** This is a combination of public cloud services and private clouds. It is not necessary to have a private cloud in order to use a hybrid cloud. A hybrid cloud can also be a combination of virtualized, on-premise data centers and public cloud services. A hybrid cloud can also be seen as a bridge between the public and private clouds, which enables moving workloads between the earlier two deployments based on policy, costs, and so on. Most companies today operate using this deployment model. For example, Marriot and Dominos Pizza make use of hybrid clouds.

Cloud computing services can be categorized into three service delivery models:

- **Infrastructure as a Service (IaaS)**
- **Platform as a Service (PaaS)**
- **Software as a Service (SaaS)**

The following diagram should illustrates these service delivery models:

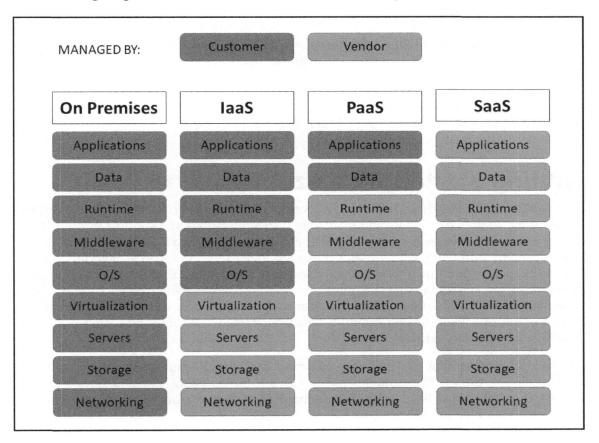

We can see that:

- In **On-Premises** deployment, the customer has to manage each and every thing from hardware to software; for example, any software deployed in the server hosted on company premises.
- In **IaaS**, all the required infrastructure is managed by the vendor. The customer just manages the operating system, software, runtime, and the application and its data; for example, Amazon EC2, Microsoft Azure, and Google Compute Engine.

- In **PaaS**, the infrastructure as well as the operating system and runtime is managed by the vendor. The customer just manages the applications and its data; for example, Google App Engine, Heroku, and Microsoft Azure.
- In **SaaS**, the entire infrastructure and software is managed by the vendor. The customer just consumes the software as a service; for example, Microsoft Office 365, Gmail, and OneDrive.

Now we are aware of the basics of the cloud, it's time to get started with the cloud platform that is the future and we all need to embrace, Microsoft Azure.

Getting started with Azure

Microsoft Azure (formerly called Windows Azure) is the cloud service created by Microsoft for building, testing, deploying, and managing web applications and services through a global network of Microsoft-managed data centers. It provides SaaS, PaaS, and IaaS, and supports many different programming languages, tools, and frameworks, including both Microsoft-specific and third-party software and systems. All the examples in this book are developed in a **virtual machine (VM)** hosted in Azure. Since we also needed a Linux VM to demonstrate ASP.NET Core 2.0 cross-platform support, the Linux VM is also created and hosted in Azure. This is the best example to demonstrate how flexible and easy it is for developers to embrace and use Azure.

An obvious question that may come to your mind is: why use Azure and not Amazon's AWS or Google Cloud? Fair enough, I am completely biased on this one and I strongly believe Microsoft Azure is way ahead of its competitors in numerous parameters. Some them are highlighted in the following list:

- **Security compliance and trust**: Azure has more comprehensive compliance coverage with more than 70 compliance offerings and is the first major cloud provider to contractually commit to the requirements of the **General Data Protection Regulation (GDPR)**. To protect your organization, Azure embeds security, privacy, and compliance into its development methodology and has been recognized as the most trusted cloud for US government institutions.
- **Global presence with most regions**: Azure has the largest number of regions in the world covered, with 42 announced Azure regions—more than any other cloud provider. You can choose the data center and region which is right for you and your customers, with the performance and support you need, where you need it.

- **Support for multiple development tools and language**: When Satya Nadella said *"Microsoft ♥ Linux"*, it gave a strong message to the world that Microsoft is actively listening to its customers and embracing open source at its core. The same strategy shows in the Microsoft cloud as well, which supports numerous tools, frameworks, and languages. Microsoft is the leading open source contributor on GitHub and actively supports multiple open source community projects.
- **Real hybrid cloud approach**: Azure offers hybrid consistency everywhere from application development, security, identity management, and data platforms. This helps reduce the risk and cost of the hybrid cloud environment.
- **Unmatched artificial intelligence**: It's never been easier to develop intelligent solutions that scale using Microsoft Cognitive services, bots, machine learning, and **Blockchain as a Service (BaaS)** capabilities that can be found only with Azure.
- **Big data with advanced analytics**: Azure Cosmos DB enables you to scale your application limitlessly with big data support. Then the advanced business analytic services provided by Azure make you go way higher than your competitors.
- **Manage and optimize cloud cost**: With free Azure cost management, it is easy to optimize cloud resources and budget them within your allocated funds.
- **IoT ready**: You can quickly develop the most common IoT scenarios, such as remote monitoring, using the pre-configured solutions in the Azure IoT suite.
- **Unmatched developer productivity**: Azure is developer-friendly, and as we will see in a short while, we can develop, deploy, and test our app in Azure from within Visual Studio or PowerShell.

A data center is a facility composed of networked computers and storage that businesses or other organizations use to organize, process, store, and disseminate large amounts of data. A business typically relies heavily upon the applications, services, and data contained within a data center, making it a focal point and critical asset for everyday operations.

Azure is an expanding network of data centers around the world. These data centers form **regions**. This provides us with the flexibility to use the region of our choice to deploy the resources/applications for the best performance. The following screenshot showing the Microsoft Azure website (https://azure.microsoft.com/en-us/) illustrates these different regions on the world map. We can see multiple regions in the United States, UK, Europe, India, and Japan. When we deploy an application, we need to select a region for the deployment. I might select a specific region to keep the application geographically close to me or my customers. I live in India, so I might use the West or Central or South India region for my development purposes. I can also deploy to multiple regions if I wanted some redundancy. The takeaway from this diagram is that Microsoft Azure is running millions of computer servers, physical machines that are spread around these regions around the world, and Microsoft ensures that these machines are up and running, healthy, and physically secure. We just need to leverage a portion of this enormous computing power to do our work:

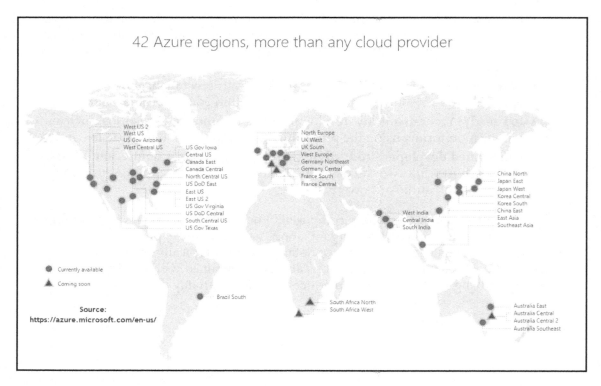

Now that we have the fundamental concepts of the cloud (and Microsoft Azure) in place, let's get started using the Azure platform.

First of all, you will need to register your account with Azure. To do so, go to `https://portal.azure.com/` and register with any of your Microsoft accounts, such as Hotmail, MSN, Outlook, or Live. At the time of writing this chapter, Azure offered the following great and free benefits when creating an account. These may vary by the time you read the book:

- 12 months' free access to popular products. You also get 25 always free products.
- A $200 credit to use on any Azure products for 30 days.
- Azure uses credit card information only for identity verification and you are not charged until you change your subscription to a *pay as you go* subscription. If you work in a large enterprise or a Microsoft partner, or a BizSpark program or MSDN subscriber, you already get a subscription to Azure cloud resources.

Once you are registered, you will see a nice dashboard. This is the Azure management portal. The dashboard user interface keeps getting better and is updated from time to time, so by the time you read this chapter, the user interface may be different from what it is right now. The important thing to notice is that there is a left panel which lists all of the Azure services that you can use. First-time users should take the guided tour of Azure to get themselves familiar with the user interface as it is very rich in features. Let's have a quick look at the user interface. The following screenshot illustrates the Azure dashboard after you log in. We have marked the user interface with numbers so that we can see each of these items in reasonable depth:

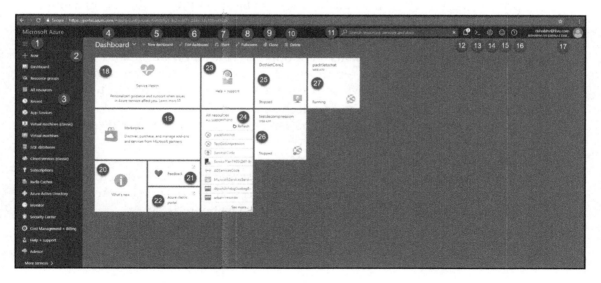

Let's have a look at the different components:

1. **Hamburger button**: Shows the hamburger menu on the left panel. This has the standard hamburger button behavior. When expanded, it shows the icon as well as a description of the various services that Azure provides. On collapse, it increases the real estate for the right column (where the **Dashboard** is showing up) as only icons are displayed in the collapsed left panel.

2. **New**: Creates a new resource. On clicking, displays the resource that needs to be created from the Marketplace. You can also use this to view the wide variety of services in Azure Marketplace.

3. **Left panel hub displaying favorite Azure services**: All your favorite or commonly used services/resources that Azure offers are displayed in this area that we call a hub. This is the place to go when you want to create or manage the resources that you own in Azure. Don't get confused with the word resource; just like a software developer is referred to as a resource when managers talk, everything that we can create from virtual machines to web apps, Redis Cache, and so on, are generally called resource. Well, there are so many Azure resources that not all of them can fit in the hub, so what can be shown are shown and the rest are shown under the item **More Services**.

4. **Dashboard on right panel**: In the screenshot, this is displaying the Azure **Dashboard** from all the subscriptions. We can have two types of dashboard: private and shared. Shared dashboards can be shared with other users, while private is as the name suggests. The intent of the dashboard is to have quick access to the resources you use, so that you can view and manage them quickly.

5. **New dashboard**: This presents an option to create a new dashboard where you can customize the tiles for resources to be shown in the way you want them to show up. You can pin, move, or resize the resource tiles the way you want.

6. **Edit dashboard**: Enables you to edit the dashboard. You can remove a tile from the dashboard, or add a new one, or maybe just drag and change its position. You can make a tile smaller or larger as per your preference.

7. **Share**: Enables you to share the dashboard with other users. You can share the dashboard by publishing it as an Azure resource. Azure **Role-Based Access Control (RBAC)** will determine who has access to the dashboard. Access to individual tiles can differ from access to the dashboard itself.

8. **Fullscreen**: Displays the portal full-screen.

9. **Clone**: Clones the dashboard.

10. **Delete**: Deletes the dashboard.

11. **Search**: To search the resource/services you are looking for.

12. **Notifications**: Clicking on this bell-like icon displays notifications and status updates, such as billing updates, resource start/stop/error notifications, and other information.

13. **Cloud Shell**: Using this command prompt-like icon, you can select bash or PowerShell. You can change shells any time through the environment selector in the Cloud Shell toolbar. The most recently used environment will be the default for your next session.

14. **Settings**: The gear icon represent settings in the current portal. It allows you to customize the portal settings, themes, language, and so on.

15. **Feedback**: To share the feedback from the Azure portal with the Microsoft Azure product team.

16. **Help**: To get help and support. You can create or track a support ticket and monitor the health of your Azure services and resources. You can also check the keyboard shortcuts, with a guided tour here.

17. **Account information**: Switch directories, change your password, view permissions, submit an idea, or view your bill.

18. **Service Health**: Personalized guidance and support when issues in Azure services affect you.

19. **Marketplace**: Discover, purchase, and manage add-ons and services from Microsoft partners.

20. **What's new**: Keeps you updated with the latest and greatest information on Azure.

21. **Feedback**: Same as *Step 15*.

22. **Azure classic portal**: To view the old classic Azure portal, for old users of Azure who are comfortable with the old portal.

23. **Help + support**: Same as *Step 16*.

24. **All resources**: Displays all resources and services from the subscription that you are using.

Though we have discussed and defined tiles here, please note that since the dashboard is customizable, you can choose to have a tile or remove it altogether. So, a few of the tiles may show / not show in your dashboard. The intent here is to make you aware of the portal. Also there are tiles numbered **25**, **26**, and **27** in the screenshot, which I have pinned after creating these resources (actually, Azure pins resource to the **Dashboard** as soon as you create it based on a setting). These tiles display the resources/services that I am using and their status. In the screenshot, **25** is a tile named **DotNetCore2**. It is a virtual machine and it has stopped. **26** shows a web app named **testdecompression** which is stopped as well. **27** is a web app named **packtletschat**, which is up and running. Hopefully, this discussion has got you started with the Azure management portal. Next we will create a virtual machine and web app in Azure and then see how we can deploy our ASP.NET Core 2.0 apps published in Azure.

Creating a VM in Azure

In this section, we will learn to create a VM in Azure. Developers need VMs all the time. If you are wondering what I mean, just imagine that you wanted to try out out some new version of a tool or software that is not yet production-ready and you do not wish to try it out on your own laptop due to probable instability issues this new untested software may cause. I always do so, whenever I am trying out nightly builds of products or getting hands-on with any new product. Azure provides you with great flexibility and choice. There are numerous choices and configurations available to select the operating system that you want and the size that you require. We, being passionate .NET developers, may want a VM which has the great Visual Studio 2017 installed, so that we can start developing as soon as we provision the VM. To this end, we will learn to create a VM in Azure. To do so, let's perform the following steps:

1. On the left panel (hub) of the Azure management portal, click on **Virtual machines**. Ensure you click on **Virtual machines** and not **Virtual machines (classic)**. We will discuss the difference between classic and the resource manager later in this section.

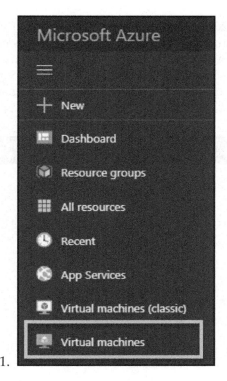

1.

You will see a **Virtual machines** screen, which lists all the virtual machines that you have as well as providing the user interface to **Add** a virtual machine, **Start**, **Stop**, **Delete**, and **Restart** a virtual machine, as shown in the following screenshot:

2. Click on the **Add** button. This will open a new fly-out on the right side, displaying a number of virtual machine images to choose from. This fly-out is what we call a blade. You can have Red Hat Linux, Windows Server, Ubuntu, or anything else based on your requirements. Since we need a Windows 10 machine with Visual Studio 2017 Community Edition installed, let's search for Visual Studio 2017. This shows the following list of results:

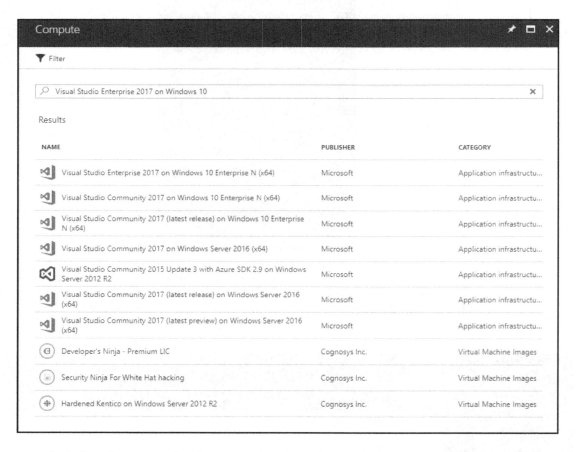

3. Select the image that best suits your needs. On doing so, a new blade will appear displaying the details of the virtual machine image, its publisher, useful links, last updated date, its desktop screenshot, deployment model, and so on. Always select the deployment model as **Resource Manager** as it gives you the ability to automate with PowerShell, unlike **Classic**. This blade can be seen in the following screenshot:

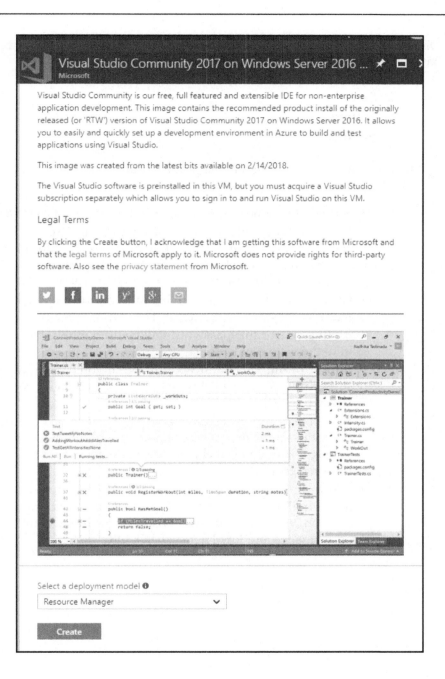

4. On clicking the **Create** button, the following screen will display, which has four basic steps to create a virtual machine:
    1. **Basics**
    2. **Size**
    3. **Settings**
    4. **Summary**

The **Basics** section gathers fundamental information about the virtual machine to be created, such as:

- **Name**: The name of the virtual machine, which has to be unique.
- **VM disk type**: This can be **solid-state drive** (**SSD**), which offers consistent, low-latency performance and is ideal for production use or standard disks (HDD) that are backed by magnetic drives and are preferred for applications where data is accessed infrequently.
- **User name**: The username to log in to the virtual machine.
- **Password**, **Confirm password**: These should be the same as the user name and this password will be used with the username to log in to the virtual machine.
- **Subscription:** This is auto-populated. If you have numerous subscriptions, you can choose the one with which you wish to create the virtual machine.
- **Resource group**: A resource group is a collection of resources that share the same life cycle, permissions, and policies. For better management, you can choose to **Create new** or reuse an existing resource group.
- **Location**: The Azure data center that you wish to use for creating the virtual machine. Based on your location or your customer's location, you may want to choose the closest location for performance and low latency. Click **OK**:

5. In the **Size** section, choose the size that suits your needs. Azure lists recommended sizes in the blade, but if it doesn't fit your requirements, click on **View all** and you will see a lot more configurations to choose from. You can also customize the supported hard disk type, minimum CPU, and memory by moving the slider bars against these parameters. Azure lists CPUs, memory, number of data disks, disk size, and other included features with an important parameter for the cost in local currency that you would need to shell out per month to use it, so use this wisely. Once you nail down on size, click **Select**:

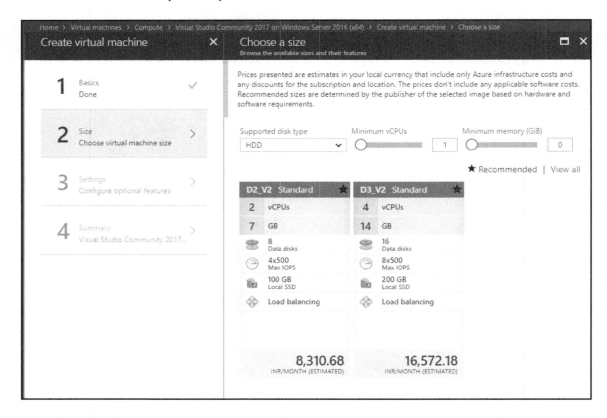

6. The **Settings** section includes important yet auto-populated settings for the VM. Some important ones are discussed here:

- **Availability set**: Azure has an availability SLA of 99.95%. For high availability of the virtual machine, it is recommended to have redundancy and group two or more VMs in an availability set. The advantage is that in the event of planned or unplanned maintenance, at least one virtual machine will be available, meeting the Azure availability SLA of 99.95%. This setting cannot be changed after the virtual machine is created. In our case, we do not need this, so we will go with the default value of **None**.

- **Use managed disk**: This feature may not be available in all the regions. When this is set to **Yes**, Azure automatically manages the availability of the disks to provide data redundancy and fault tolerance.

- **Auto-shutdown**: This feature is very important, at least financially. While your virtual machine is running, every minute, so keep it switched on only when you need it to keep your bills affordable. If you enable auto-shutdown, you can configure the VM to shut down daily at a specified time. For example, if the VM is being used only during office hours, it makes perfect sense to shut it down out of office hours and save on money. The **Settings** blade is shown in the following screenshot:

7. Click **OK**. A **Summary** page with all the settings will be displayed in the **Summary** blade along with terms of use. If you agree to it, click **Create** and your virtual machine will start to be created. You will be taken to your **Dashboard** page, which will now has a new tile added with the name of your virtual machine and it will show the status of this resource. Within a matter of a few minutes your virtual machine will be provisioned. Once it is provisioned, you will get a notification stating that the virtual machine is successfully deployed and the dashboard tile of the virtual machine will display the state as **Running**.

8. Click on the tile of the virtual machine that we have created. It will take us to the **Overview** blade of the virtual machine, as shown in the following screenshot:

You will see the following options:

- **Connect**: On clicking **Connect**, the **Remote Desktop Protocol (RDP)** file will be downloaded. Clicking on this downloaded RDP will enable remote desktop connection to the virtual machine, after providing the username and password that you used while creating the virtual machine.
- **Start**: Starts the virtual machine, if it's not started. The button will be enabled only if virtual machine is not running.
- **Restart**: Restarts the virtual machine.
- **Stop**: Stops the virtual machine and deallocates it.
- **Capture**: This can be used to create a virtual machine image. We generally use it if we need a base image with additional configuration.
- **Move**: To move the virtual machine to another resource group or subscription.
- **Delete**: To delete the virtual machine.
- **Refresh**: To refresh the status of the virtual machine.

Azure has great documentation and cool training videos. They also have getting started guides and architecture recommendations to create and use Azure resources. You can find the documentation, the SDK, on the Azure site at https://docs.microsoft.com/en-us/azure/. Training, webinars, events, code samples, videos, whitepapers, and case studies can be found at https://azure.microsoft.com/en-us/resources/.

With this, we have created our very first virtual machine on the cloud (Azure) and we can use it as well by clicking the remote desktop file that we downloaded. On clicking the .rdp file, it will prompt for the username and password in the standard way as any other remote desktop connection does. It's just that this virtual machine is hosted in the cloud, in Azure. Once you are logged in, you can use it the way you want. Remember, once the virtual machine is started, irrespective of whether you use it or not, it starts costing you. So, if you wish to be cost-efficient, ensure you turn it off when you are not using it and start it when you do. This concludes our discussion on virtual machines. Next, we will see how we can use PowerShell to automate resource creation and management in Azure.

Automating using PowerShell

In this section, we will learn to automate resource creation and management in Azure using PowerShell. The user interface route to creating resources in Azure is very effective and easy. You may be wondering: Do you have to log in to the Azure portal to do every single thing? No. Everything that you can set and do in the Azure portal can also be automated by writing a program, or by writing a script. Also, being a developer, I prefer my code to do the work rather than going to the portal and doing operations manually. The code can also help us do the automation, so preventing the need for human intervention. There are SDKs available for many languages, from C#, to JavaScript, to Ruby, and so on. We will look at how to start and stop the virtual machine that we just created using PowerShell by performing the following steps:

1. Go to the URL at https://azure.microsoft.com/en-us/downloads/. This is the central place where you can get SDKs and command-line tools. On this page, we can see there are SDKs for .NET developers, Java developers, Node.js, and so on. If we scroll down a little, we can see **command-line tools**. Click on the **Windows install** link under **PowerShell**. It will download the installer executable:

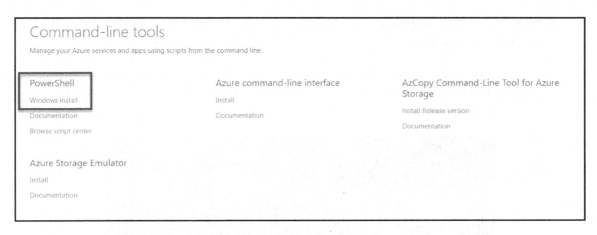

2. Run the executable once the download is complete, following the installation instructions. Now open PowerShell ISE. It should be installed already. If not, you can also use PowerShell by searching for Windows Powershell on your Windows 10 machine. The first thing that we need to do is associate our PowerShell session with the Azure account. We can do that with the `Login-AzureRmAccount` command. PowerShell has tab completion, so after typing a few chars in your tab, it will try to complete the command. When you press **Enter**, you'll be given an interface where you need to log in with your Microsoft account, as shown in the following screenshot:

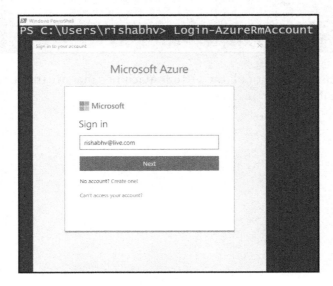

3. Enter your username and password. If you have two-factor authentication enabled, you may need to enter code as well. Type the `Get-AzureRmSubscription` command. This will show the list of all the subscriptions displaying the subscription name, subscription ID, tenant ID, and state; that is, whether it is enabled or inactive. The PowerShell cmdlet has `AzureRm` in the name, `Rm` being resource manager:

```
PS C:\Users\rishabhv> Get-AzureRmSubscription

Name       : Visual Studio Ultimate with MSDN
Id         : 9b9bd9d1-6058-4257-933c-a5ef7740573f
TenantId   : 0d75d140-f6b1-42df-a62a-587e1cdbbb73
State      : Enabled
```

4. Next, we check `Get-AzureRmContext`. This cmdlet gives the current context, as shown in the following screenshot:

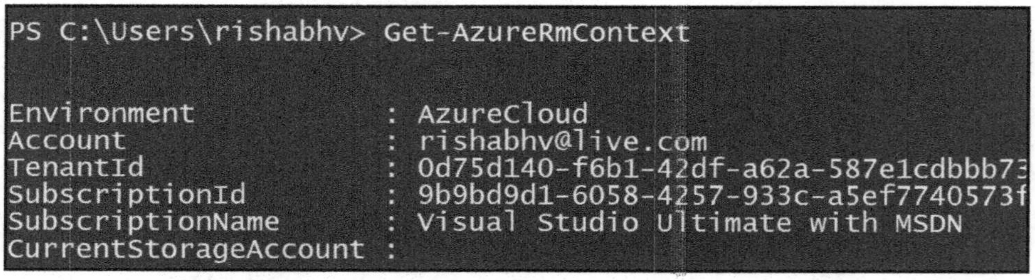

```
PS C:\Users\rishabhv> Get-AzureRmContext

Environment           : AzureCloud
Account               : rishabhv@live.com
TenantId              : 0d75d140-f6b1-42df-a62a-587e1cdbbb73
SubscriptionId        : 9b9bd9d1-6058-4257-933c-a5ef7740573f
SubscriptionName      : Visual Studio Ultimate with MSDN
CurrentStorageAccount :
```

5. Now, let us get a list of all the virtual machines that are in the subscription. We can get that with `Get-AzureRmVM`:

```
PS C:\Users\rishabhv> Get-AzureRmVM

ResourceGroupName         Name    Location            VmSize  OsType              NIC ProvisioningState
-----------------         ----    --------            ------  ------              --- -----------------
DOTNETCORE2          DotNetCore2 WestIndia Standard_DS2_v2 Windows dotnetcore2736          Succeeded
```

6. To start the virtual machine, we will use the cmdlet `Start-AzureRmVM`, passing `Name` and `ResourceGroupName` as parameters, as shown in the following screenshot. The command will take a while to start the virtual machine, as can be seen from the `StartTime` and `EndTime` values:

```
PS C:\Users\rishabhv> Start-AzureRmVM -Name DotNetCore2 -ResourceGroupName DotNetCore2

OperationId :
Status      : Succeeded
StartTime   : 1/11/2018 11:22:30 PM
EndTime     : 1/11/2018 11:23:15 PM
Error       :
```

7. To stop the virtual machine, we can use the cmdlet `Stop-AzureRmVM`, passing `Name` and `ResourceGroupName` as parameters with the `Force` flag . The `Force` parameter is used just to make it non-interactive; otherwise, there will be a prompt for confirmation. Like the `Start-AzureRmVM` command, this command also takes a while, as shown in the following screenshot:

```
PS C:\Users\rishabhv> Stop-AzureRmVM -Name DotNetCore2 -ResourceGroupName DotNetCore2 -Force

OperationId :
Status      : Succeeded
StartTime   : 1/11/2018 11:24:24 PM
EndTime     : 1/11/2018 11:27:26 PM
Error       :
```

We saw how easy it is to manage a virtual machine from PowerShell. Managing it from the portal is easier, as it is just a click of a button, but the intent here is to demonstrate the flexibility provided by Azure. We can also execute these PowerShell commands in the Cloud Shell that we saw earlier in this chapter; that is, we execute the commands directly in the shell opened in a browser on the Azure portal. This needs additional storage and hence cost. This is a very basic getting-started discussion on Azure automation using PowerShell. There is an ocean of information to be learned and grasped. An enthusiastic learner should go through the documentation to enhance their knowledge and get a handle on the subject from the official Microsoft Azure documentation at `https://docs.microsoft.com/en-us/powershell/azure/overview?view=azurermps-5.1.1`. There are books and sample modules as well, built by the Microsoft and the Azure community for a variety of scenarios, that the reader can leverage to learn, understand, and experiment. These can be seen at `https://docs.microsoft.com/en-us/azure/automation/automation-runbook-gallery`.

Next, we will learn to publish a web app in Azure, which is the most commonly used operation.

Publishing a web app in Azure

In this section, we will learn to publish a web app in Azure. As discussed in the previous two sections, we can create a resource from the Azure portal or we can write code on top of the SDK of our preferred language; for example, C#, PowerShell, and so on. As a developer working on Microsoft technologies, most of my productive work time is spent on Microsoft Visual Studio, so I would like to publish the web app on Azure. This is the most common scenario that we perform as, after developing the web app, it should be hosted in the cloud for it to be available for a larger audience and more users. If we look at the Azure portal, we will see a service called **App Services** in the left panel or hub. Let's discuss App Services first.

Azure App Services

Azure App Services is the solution if we want to build an application or an API that runs on a platform in the cloud. App Services supports a wide variety of technologies and application types from traditional web applications, such as a blog, or an e-commerce site, or a **content management system** (**CMS**). We can write the application in ASP.NET, Node.js or PHP, for that matter, many other frameworks and languages. If we just want to build a service/API and serve data, modern-day **Single-Page Applications** (**SPA**), or a logic app, App Services supports all of these. The process that we used to create the virtual machines in the last section on the Azure portal can be used to create an App Service as well. With virtual machines, we selected the operating system that we wanted. With App Services, we can go with a pre-configured App Service. For example, if we wanted to set up a WordPress blog, we could select the **WordPress entry** and click **Create**, and, with a little more configuration, we would have a WordPress site up and running. The name of the App Service that we want to create should be unique on `azurewebsites.net`, where the app will eventually be hosted. Next, we have to select a resource group. We can use an existing resource group or create a new resource group. Since it's a logical container for the resources, I prefer having separate resource groups, so once I am done with that resource, I can get rid of the entire resource in one go. The next thing we are asked by the Azure portal is to choose an App Service Plan. If we have to draw an analogy, think of it as something very similar to size when we created a virtual machine. The concept of the App Service Plan is very important. Every **web application** we will create will be placed into a **single App Service** dedicated to that application. And then every **App Service** maps to a single **App Service Plan**. A plan describes the performance characteristics of the machine that will host the App Service. Behind the scenes, the App Service Plan uses a virtual machine, but the virtual machine is abstracted away by Azure. We don't need to worry about managing the virtual machine as Azure takes care of it and abstracts this away from the end user. We can simply use the App Service Plan to describe how many CPUs and how much memory we need; Azure takes care of the rest. One important point to note about the App Service Plan is that we can deploy multiple App Services into Azure and have them all mapped to the same App Service Plan. Select an existing App Service Plan or a new App Service Plan, based on your web app needs. If you need to serve a lot of users, if there are going to be a lot of users using your web app, then we can select a bigger service plan from the portal which can serve a higher number of requests, we can reuse an existing service plan (if we have one already), or we can use a free or less costly plan. After completing all the configurations, we are good to click on **Create**. Since all this is very similar to virtual machine creation, we are not delving much into the details. Within a few minutes, the App Service should be up and running. Now that we have our App Service created, we can publish our web app to this created App Service.

Publishing the web app

Let's publish an ASP.NET Core 2.0 web app in Azure using Visual Studio:

1. Create a new ASP.NET Core 2.0 project in Visual Studio or use one of the existing applications that we have created thus far in the book. We will use one of the web apps that we developed in the book thus far for illustration purposes.

2. Right-click the project. On the context menu, click **Publish**:

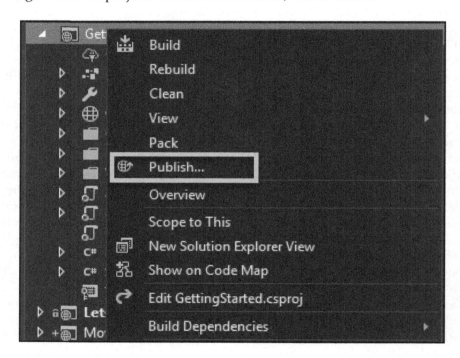

3. This will display a nice-looking user interface, presenting us with three options. We can publish on:

- **Microsoft Azure App Service**: The container for the web app.
- **IIS, FTP**: For deploying on IIS or FTP on a virtual machine.
- **Folder**: To publish the app in the local filesystem.
- **Import profile:** To import a publish profile from the Azure portal and publish the app. We will see this later in the chapter.
- **Microsoft Azure Virtual Machines:** To publish the app in a virtual machine hosted in Azure.

We will select the **Microsoft Azure App Service**. That gives us two options: either to select an existing App Service or create a new one. We can use either of the options. This is to illustrate that we can create a brand new App Service directly from within Visual Studio or use an existing App Service that you created. Click on the **Publish** button and we will get a series of dialogs. If you are not logged in with your Azure subscription credentials, you will need to do so.

4. You will notice that on the top right, it shows my Microsoft account with which I am logged in. I need to enter an **App Name** that is unique. **Subscription** will be auto-populated. But, if you have multiple subscriptions, you must choose the subscription that you wish to use. Both **Resource Group** and **App Service Plan** can be either created brand new or chosen from an existing one. Here, in the screenshot, I have chosen an already existing one. Click **Create**. It will show a **Summary** screen:

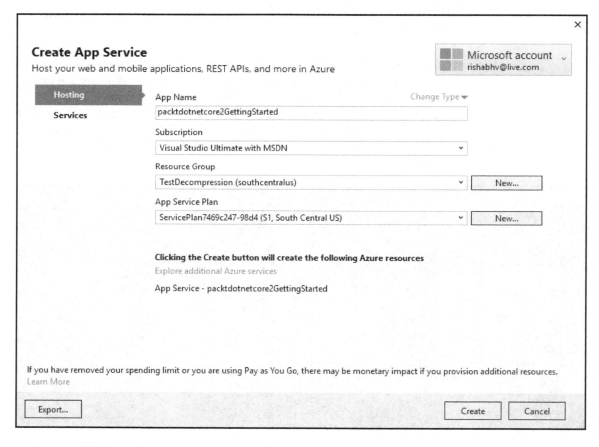

5. Click on **Publish** and the app will be published on Azure. Visual Studio saves the publish settings file for the project. This can take a while the first time we publish because Visual Studio has to push up all the assemblies and artifacts that are needed for the App Service. But once it's published into Azure, and we just make a change to something like a Razor view file or script file and publish the next time, all Visual Studio needs to do is upload just the few changed files.

6. After some time, upon successful publishing, the deployed application will open in the browser, as shown in the following screenshot:

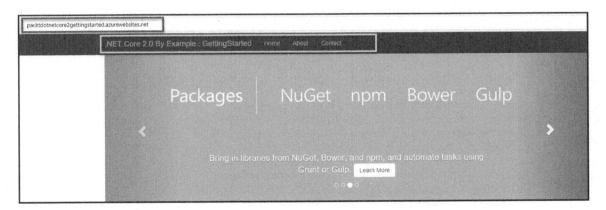

Behind the scenes a publishing profile is created by Visual Studio, so let's have a quick look at it.

Publishing profiles

Upon publishing, Visual Studio will create a publishing profile. It's basically a folder containing files created in the project, and can be seen in the **Properties** node of the project, as shown in the following screenshot:

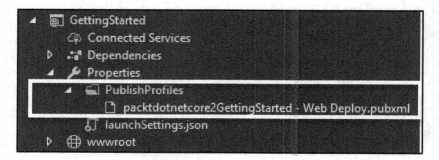

We can have multiple profiles and these profiles will be stored in the `PublishProfiles` folder with the file extension `.pubxml`, as these are XML files. `.pubxml` files contain information such as the type of build ; for example, the release/debug build. It has URLs and a username that are part of the deployment credentials, as shown in the following code:

```xml
<?xml version="1.0" encoding="utf-8"?>
<!--
This file is used by the publish/package process of your Web project. You
can customize the behavior of this process
by editing this MSBuild file. In order to learn more about this please
visit https://go.microsoft.com/fwlink/?LinkID=208121.
-->
<Project ToolsVersion="4.0"
xmlns="http://schemas.microsoft.com/developer/msbuild/2003">
  <PropertyGroup>
    <WebPublishMethod>MSDeploy</WebPublishMethod>
    <ResourceId>/subscriptions/9b9dd9d2-6058-4257-933c-
    a5ef7740573f/resourcegroups/TestDecompression
    /providers/Microsoft.Web/sites/
    packtdotnetcore2GettingStarted</ResourceId>
    <ResourceGroup>TestDecompression</ResourceGroup>
    <PublishProvider>AzureWebSite</PublishProvider>
    <LastUsedBuildConfiguration>Release</LastUsedBuildConfiguration>
    <LastUsedPlatform>Any CPU</LastUsedPlatform>
    <SiteUrlToLaunchAfterPublish>http://packtdotnetcore2gettingstarted
    .azurewebsites.net</SiteUrlToLaunchAfterPublish>
    <LaunchSiteAfterPublish>True</LaunchSiteAfterPublish>
    <ExcludeApp_Data>False</ExcludeApp_Data>
    <ProjectGuid>a1a01377-c3df-4586-9838-10c733becf91</ProjectGuid>
```

```
<MSDeployServiceURL>packtdotnetcore2gettingstarted
.scm.azurewebsites.net:443</MSDeployServiceURL>
<DeployIisAppPath>packtdotnetcore2GettingStarted</DeployIisAppPath>
<RemoteSitePhysicalPath />
<SkipExtraFilesOnServer>True</SkipExtraFilesOnServer>
<MSDeployPublishMethod>WMSVC</MSDeployPublishMethod>
<EnableMSDeployBackup>True</EnableMSDeployBackup>
<UserName>$packtdotnetcore2GettingStarted</UserName>
<_SavePWD>True</_SavePWD>
<_DestinationType>AzureWebSite</_DestinationType>
</PropertyGroup>
</Project>
```

The file doesn't contain a password. So it can be checked in the source control without worrying about compromising security. The deployment password by default is placed into a different file that is not part of the project but is in the same folder:

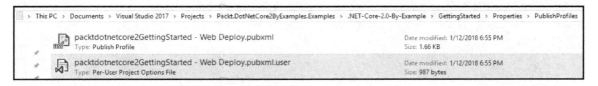

It is the `pubxml.user` file. The file does not contain the password in plain text. It's encrypted with a logged-in user-specific key, so if the file is copied and pasted and used by another user, the password will not decrypt correctly (as the key is user-specific, it will not match), hence the password will not work for them. So the obvious question that comes to mind is: What if I miss the password or delete the `pubxml.user` file and want to publish the app? We can do so by performing the following steps:

1. Go to the Azure portal, and the **Overview** blade of the App Service that we wish to publish to. Click on **Get publish profile** to download the publish profile, as shown in the following screenshot:

2. In Visual Studio, right-click on the project and click **Publish**; select **Import profile** and click **OK**:

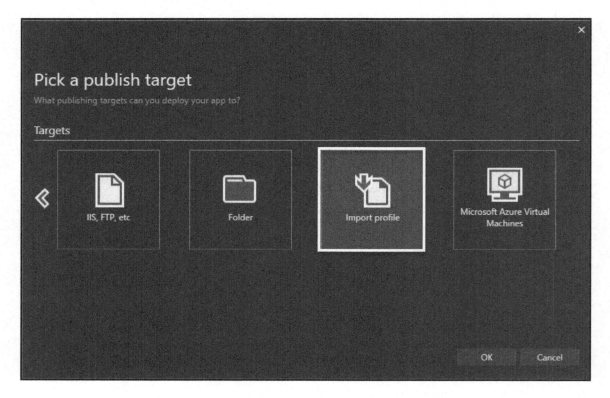

3. Click **Publish** and the web app will be published.

Next, let's have a look at a few of the commonly used features of Azure that every .NET developer must be conversant with.

App Service features

If we look at the App Service items that we created, we will notice a plethora of things. To describe them in detail would need a chapter of its own, so we will quickly look at few of the most common and important ones from a .NET developer perspective:

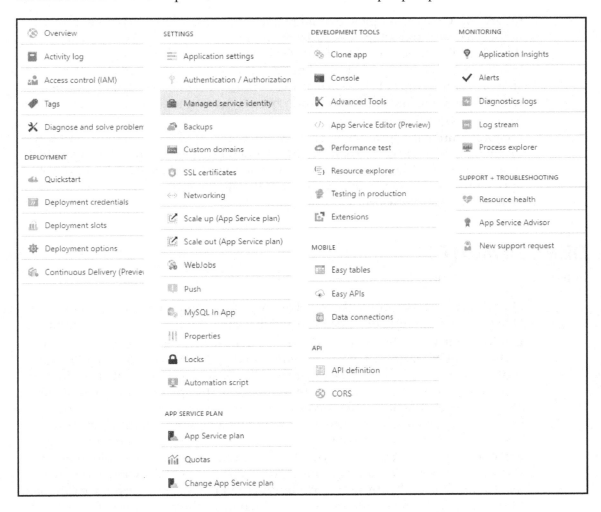

As we can see, there are subsections for **DEPLOYMENT, SETTINGS, APP SERVICE PLAN, DEVELOPMENT TOOLS, MOBILE, API, MONITORING, SUPPORT + TROUBLESHOOTING**. Let us discuss each of these sections so that we know everything Azure has to offer and we can then leverage it as and when needed. The most basic and most frequently used ones are:

- **Overview**: Gives a complete overall picture of the App Service. We can browse the service, and start/stop/restart/delete the service from here. We can also download the publish profile of the service and reset the publish profile to invalidate previously downloaded publish profiles. The charts display the statistics of the App Service, such as the number of HTTP 5xx or server errors with the timeline, data in and out, number of requests, and average response time to serve a request.
- **Diagnose and solve problems**: This provides an easy way to diagnose and solve problems with web apps. There are pre-defined categories of problem available which you can select and get a diagnosis using the Azure Health Checkup web app, which gives an in-depth overview of the app health based on requests, CPU usage, and memory usage.

DEPLOYMENT

In this category, the options are:

- **Quickstart**: Provides guidance to get you up and running with app deployment. Quickstart has handy guidance for ASP.NET, Java, Node.js, PHP, and Python.
- **Deployment slots**: Deployment slots let us deploy different versions of web apps to different URLs. We can test a certain version and then swap the content and configuration between slots. Deployment slots enable us to validate that the app is working properly in Azure, before we promote the app into production. This also eliminates downtime, and gives the new deployment a chance to warm up before customers use it. We can have more than one slot with the right App Service Plan. For example, we might want one slot for testing, one for staging, and one for production. And once it has been validated that the deployment into staging is working, we can swap the slots; that is, we can take what is tested in the staging slot, and with a click of a button (or a PowerShell script), we can make the staging deployment into the new production. In the worst case, if something goes wrong it's very easy to swap these back and take the last working production deployment and put it into production again.

- **Deployment options**: To configure the source control of your choice for deployment. **Visual Studio Team Services (VSTS)**, OneDrive, Git, Bitbucket, and Dropbox are supported.
- **Continuous Delivery**: This is currently in preview at the time of writing this chapter. Continuous delivery in Visual Studio Team Services simplifies setting up a robust deployment pipeline. The pipeline builds, runs load tests, and deploys to the staging slot and then to production.

SETTINGS

Here the options are as follows:

- **Application settings**: The place where we can define and overwrite application settings and connection strings. We will see this in action in the next chapter, when we build our movie booking web app. This is also the place where we will enable WebSockets for our SignalR-based applications and convert the application to always-on; otherwise, the web application gets unloaded if it remains idle. Remote debugging is also enabled and disabled from this blade.
- **Authentication / Authorization**: To enable/disable authentication.
- **Backups**: Configures backups to create restorable archive copies of web app content, configurations, and databases.
- **Custom domains**: This is the place to configure and manage custom hostnames assigned to the web app. For example, my blog site is rishabhverma.net. If I want to link this domain with the web app, this is where I need to make the configuration. I can also enable an HTTPS-only flag here, so that all the traffic for HTTP is redirected to HTTPS, making my app more secure.
- **Scale up**: To serve the increased/decreased load or demands of the web app, we need a higher/lower configuration of the App Service Plan and this is the blade to use for this purpose.
- **Scale out**: In this blade, we can enable autoscaling, which will automatically scale the app, if the load increases based on the configured rule. We can also choose the instance count of the machines hosting the App Service in this blade.
- **Automation script**: In this blade, we can automate deploying resources with Azure Resource Manager templates in a single, coordinated operation. We can also define resources and configurable input parameters and deploy with script or code.

We have discussed the App Service Plan in some length, so as an exercise readers are expected to understand and learn the details of the App Service Plan, as that is directly linked to the performance and cost of the web app that you host in Azure.

DEVELOPMENT TOOLS

Let's have a look at the options:

- **Advanced Tools**: Advanced Tools (Kudu) provides a collection of developer-oriented tools and extensibility points for the App Service. This will be one of the most frequently used blades, once we deploy our app in Azure. I would highly encourage readers to read the Kudu wiki at `https://github.com/projectkudu/kudu/wiki` as it gives detailed information about Kudu.
- **Performance test**: In this blade, we can perform the load testing of our App Service by simulating the virtual load of any number of users and the duration that we want to test against by specifying the number of users and test duration. We can specify either an API endpoint URL or a Visual Studio Web Test to run for performance testing.
- **Extensions**: Extensions add functionality to the App Service, such as the image optimizer for an image upload application, and so on.

API

Here are the options:

- **API definition**: API definition lets us configure the location of the Swagger 2.0 metadata describing the API exposed through the App Service. This makes it easy for others to discover and consume the API.
- **CORS**: **Cross-Origin Resource Sharing (CORS)** allows JavaScript code running in a browser on an external host to interact with the App Service backend. We can specify the origins that should be allowed to make cross-origin calls.

MONITORING

Let's have a look at the available options:

- **Application Insights:** It helps us detect and diagnose quality issues in web apps and web services, and helps us understand what users are actually using in the App Service. This is of tremendous importance to analyze the performance and error characteristics of the App Service. We will make use of application insights while building our movie booking app in the next chapter.
- **Alerts**: This is one of the superb features of Azure. If we want to know when our web app is performing poorly or there is a high CPU or memory usage due to load, we can configure rule-based email alerts in this blade and we will be notified by email if the rule criteria are met. Then with the help of other diagnostics we can figure out and fix the issue.
- **Diagnostic logs**: In this blade, we can enable/disable application logging in a filesystem or blob. We can also enable/disable detailed error messages and failed request tracing. One thing to notice here is that filesystem logging is automatically disabled after 12 hours to keep the logs from bloating the filesystem, whereas blob logging will keep on going indefinitely.
- **Process explorer**: To monitor/kill the processes running the App Service and monitor their memory and CPU usages.

SUPPORT + TROUBLESHOOTING

The options are:

- **Resource health:** Resource health watches resource and tells us if they're running as expected and if not, what actions can be taken.
- **App Service Advisor:** App Service Advisor provides insights for improving the app experience on the App Service platform.

Visual Studio provides very rich extensibility support. There are numerous extensions for Azure as well. One great extension for Azure is Cloud Explorer, which should already be available with Visual Studio 2017. If not, I highly recommend you try it out. To search, download, and install any available Visual Studio extensions, click **Tools | Extensions and Updates**. Then search `Cloud Explorer` after clicking **Online** on the left panel of the window. Cloud explorer can be opened by clicking on **View | Cloud Explorer.** Cloud Explorer can be thought of as a minified version of the Azure management portal, which can be used from within Visual Studio IDE. We can start/stop a VM or App Service, profile the App Service, download the publish profile and logs, attach the debugger to Azure, and much more from this extension. The following screenshot displays the Cloud Explorer extension:

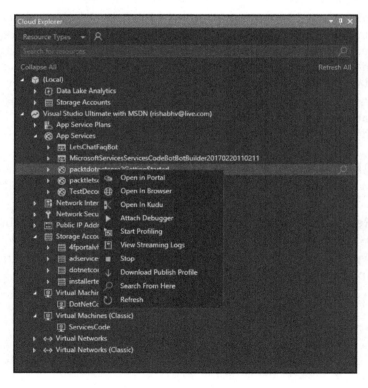

And this concludes our discussion of Azure. Next we will discuss cloud storage and Azure functions that provide cheap serverless computing.

Cloud storage

We are all aware of SQL Server (if not, do not worry). Azure SQL is just SQL Server deployed on Azure. We will not be discussing Azure SQL in this section as we will be using Azure SQL in the next chapter and hence will be discussing it at length then. We will check out the storage accounts. Storage accounts can store hundreds of terabytes (roughly speaking 1 Terabyte = 1,000 Gigabytes) of data. We will discuss how to use Azure storage as a place to keep uploaded files for our web application and how we can enable users to download files from storage by creating and handing out what's known as a **shared access signature** (**SAS**). So, lets get started.

In the Azure portal, click on **New** and select **Storage** and then click **Storage account - blob, file, table, queue**, as shown in the following screenshot:

There is also a link to a **Quickstart tutorial**, which I would highly recommend as it has great getting-started videos and tutorials from the leading tech evangelists to get you up and running with Azure storage. On clicking **Storage account - blob, file, table, queue**, a new blade named **Create storage account** will display, as shown in the following screenshot:

In the blade, enter the required fields:

- **Name:** This should comprise 3-24 characters in lowercase or numeric text that should be unique across all Azure storage, as it is exposed on **.core.windows.net**.
- **Deployment model**: This should be kept as **Resource manager**.
- **Account kind**: This can be a general storage V1 or V2 or dedicated blob storage. We will keep it as general storage.
- **Performance**: This can be chosen as **Premium** or **Standard** as required.
- **Secure transfer required**: This should be **Enabled** for any serious web app.
- **Resource group**: This can be created new or reused.
- **Location**: Select the location which is nearest to your business requirement.

You can choose to pin the storage account to the dashboard by checking the **Pin to dashboard** checkbox. Click **Create**. After a while, the storage account will be created. Once the storage account is created, click on the pinned tile on the dashboard and it will take you to the storage account overview blade, which summarizes the storage account details. The important thing to note is in the middle of the blade and lists the different types of storage, as shown in the following screenshot:

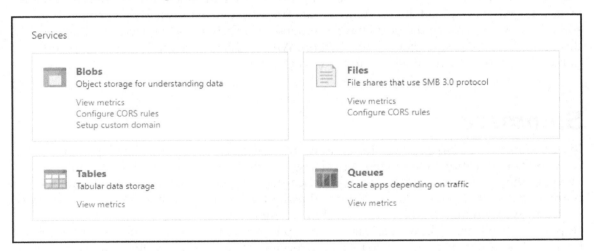

So we can use four types of storage with the storage account. Let's briefly discuss these:

- **Blob storage**: Blob is an abbreviation of **Binary large object**. We can store any type of file in blob storage.
- **Table storage**: Table storage is a no-SQL database and is similar to a document DB but instead of storing documents, table storage is optimized for storing key value pairs. Table storage is really cheap and it's a good place to store large volumes of data.
- **File storage**: File storage allows us to set up **Server Message Block** (SMB 3.0 protocol) file shares in the cloud. This storage is preferred generally when we have an existing application that needs to be migrated to Azure and the application already uses file shares.
- **Queue storage**: Queues allow us to store and retrieve messages. And they are an important technology to have if we want to build reliable high-scale websites because they allow us to put a buffer between an application and the backend services that it uses.

Blobs and queues are more frequently used and we shall be using blob storage in our next chapter when we develop our movie booking site, so we will conclude our brief discussion of storage. How to upload and download data from storage using an SAS token is something we will see in the next chapter in detail. This brings us to the end of this discussion and chapter on cloud introduction. We should now be ready to develop and deploy in Azure, which we will do in the next chapter.

Summary

In this chapter, we learned what the cloud is and why the modern-day developer should be conversant with cloud technologies. We also got started with Azure, and made ourselves aware of the Azure management portal. We learned to create a virtual machine from the portal and saw that this could be automated using PowerShell or other languages by using the SDK. We then managed a virtual machine using PowerShell and saw how to start and stop it. We also learned how to create a web app in Azure from Visual Studio 2017 itself and learned about publish profiles. We took an overview of App Services, and a quick look at Azure storage. Now that we have a grasp of the fundamentals, we will develop a movie booking application and deploy it in Azure in the next chapter.

8
Movie Booking Web App

So far, we have been exploring the features and fundamentals of ASP.NET Core 2.0. The applications we have developed are good examples to learn the concepts but do not make use of data persistence. In this chapter, we will learn to do read, write, update, and delete data operations, making use of Entity Framework Core. We will also learn how to deploy a web app in Azure and monitor its health. We will demonstrate this by developing a simple movie booking web app, where a user can book a ticket for a movie. So, in this chapter, we will cover the following topics:

- Introducing Entity Framework and Entity Framework Core
- Getting started with Entity Framework Core
- Movie booking app requirements
- Designing the movie booking app
- Coding the movie booking app
- Deploying the movie booking app
- Monitoring the movie booking app

Let's start with an introduction to Entity Framework.

Introducing Entity Framework

So what is **Entity Framework** (EF)? Is it some other fancy framework that I need to learn? If these thoughts are coming to mind, get rid of them, as EF is just a set of .NET APIs for accessing data. EF is the official data access tool from Microsoft. Like most Microsoft products, it originated from Microsoft Research, and later it was adopted by the ADO.NET team as the next innovation in Microsoft's data access technology. EF has evolved over time. It had a sluggish start in 2008 when developers found it hard to digest a new way of accessing data. But with EF4 (yes, the second version of EF was 4, as it was aligned with .NET 4), it had become the norm to use EF for data accessing with .NET. Continuing the journey, it became open source in version EF6 and moved to CodePlex (http://www. codeplex.com). This opened up new avenues for EF. As it became open source, the community could make contributions as well. Now that CodePlex is archived, EF6 has moved to GitHub and is actively being developed.

EF is also referred to as an ORM. What is an ORM? An **ORM** stands for **object-relational mapping,** which broadly means mapping objects to relational tables. An ORM refers to the technique for converting data between two incompatible type systems. For example, let us consider a C# **plain old CLR object (POCO)** of a Person class. An instance of the Person class has the Name, Id, and Age properties of string, int and int types, respectively. In the SQL database, this data would be persisted in a table named Person with the columns Name, Id, Age, and so on. An ORM maps the Person POCO to the Person database table. The primary intent of an ORM is to try and shield the developer from having to write optimized SQL code for this inter-conversion. An ORMs are designed to reduce the friction between how data is structured in a relational database and how the classes are defined. Without an ORM, we typically need to write a lot of code to transform database results into instances of the classes. An ORM allows us to express our queries using our classes, and then an ORM builds and executes the relevant SQL for us, as well as materializing objects from the data that came back from the database. What I say here is an oversimplification and there's a lot more to an ORMs and to Entity Framework than this. Entity Framework can really enhance developer productivity and we will see this while developing the movie booking app. EF has a dedicated team at Microsoft. It has been around for almost a decade now. Rather than writing the relevant SQL to target whatever relational database you're working with, Entity Framework uses the **Language-Integrated Query (LINQ)** syntax that's part of the .NET framework. LINQ to Entities allows developers to use a consistent and strongly-typed query language irrespective of what database they're targeting. Additionally, LINQ to Objects is used for querying other elements of .NET, even InMemory objects, so developers benefit from their knowledge of LINQ.

Since we are working with .NET Core and want to make a cross-platform app, we cannot use Entity Framework, as it's not compatible with ASP.NET Core. Don't worry! We have solutions. Either we can compile our project against the full .NET Framework or we can use the latest and greatest version of Entity Framework called Entity Framework Core, which is a lightweight and cross-platform version of Entity Framework, rewritten from scratch to support a variety of platforms. Let's discuss Entity Framework Core.

Presenting Entity Framework Core

EF Core was released in June 2016 after more than 2 years of dedicated effort and following numerous alpha, beta, and even a few release candidate versions. It was originally named Entity Framework 7, but later its name was changed to Entity Framework Core. So what exactly is Entity Framework Core? The official Microsoft documentation (`https://docs.microsoft.com/en-us/ef/core/`) describes Entity Framework Core as a lightweight and extensible version of Entity Framework. In other words, this is not simply an update from EF6; it's a brand new Entity Framework altogether. EF6 is still actively supported and will continue to have tweaks and fixes made to it, though for many reasons, all of the true innovation has gone into Entity Framework Core. Apart from new features that the team wanted to add to Entity Framework, there are also some critical and comprehensive themes for developing EF Core which align with ASP.NET Core and the underlying .NET Core. The idea behind developing EF Core is that it should be built from lightweight composable APIs; that is, it should be able to run on different operating systems that can host native implementations of the CoreCLR and, equally important, use modern software practices in the design, coding, and delivery of Entity Framework Core. Like EF6, EF Core is open source and available on GitHub. The source code of EF Core can be seen at `https://github.com/aspnet/EntityFrameworkCore`. The EF team has a road map for the features that they are prioritizing and the order in which they will be shipped in the upcoming releases. The road map for EF Core can be seen at `https://github.com/aspnet/EntityFrameworkCore/wiki/roadmap`.

EF Core runs on .NET Core, and .NET Core runs in a lot of places, such as Windows and Linux-based systems, as we have seen in earlier chapters. It runs inside the full .NET Framework, so any version that is 4.5.1 or newer. .NET Core itself can run on the CoreCLR; that's the runtime. CoreCLR can run natively, not only on Windows, but also on Macintosh and Linux. EF Core can also be used with the **Universal Windows Platform (UWP)** for Windows 10, so it runs on any device or PC that can run on Windows 10. So one may be tempted to think, should I use EF Core anywhere and everywhere, just because it is supported? The answer is *no*. This is a really important point to keep in mind. EF Core is a brand new set of APIs, and so it doesn't have all of the features that you might be used to with EF 6, and while some of those features will be coming in future versions of EF Core, there are a few that will never be part of EF Core, so it's important to understand this, and hence you may not want to start every single new project with EF Core. Before using EF Core, ensure that EF Core has all the features that you need. For a comprehensive list of features that are available in EF and EF Core and for a comparison, I would highly recommend that you visit the official Microsoft documentation describing the feature comparison between EF and EF Core in depth at `https://docs.microsoft.com/en-us/ef/efcore-and-ef6/features`.

For the sake of completeness, the subset of the feature comparison containing the important features are listed in the following table:

Name of feature	EF6	EF Core
Entity Data Model Extension (EDMX) designer support	Yes	No
Entity Data Model Wizard (for database first approach)	Yes	No
Automatic migration	Yes	No
Lazy loading of data	Yes	No
Stored procedure mapping with DbContext	Yes	No
Batch `Insert`, `Update`, `Delete` operations	No	Yes
In-memory provider for testing	No	Yes
Support for **Inversion of Control (IoC)**	No	Yes
Field mapping	No	Yes
DbContext pooling	No	Yes

If you are overwhelmed with this comparison and feel out of place with the listed features, do not worry. EF is indeed a huge topic to learn. However, we will learn to use it from scratch to have the basic fundamentals in place. To do so, we will learn to create a simple data access console application. Once we know how to use EF Core, we can then use it in our movie booking app.

Getting started with Entity Framework Core

In this section, we will create a simple console application to perform CRUD operations using Entity Framework Core. The intent is to get started with EF Core and understand how to use it. Before we dive into coding, let us see the two development approaches that EF Core supports:

- Code-first
- Database-first

These two paradigms have been supported for a very long time and therefore we will just look at them at a very high level. EF Core mainly targets the code-first approach and has limited support for the database-first approach, as there is no support for the visual designer or wizard for the database model out of the box. However, there are third-party tools and extensions that support this. The list of third-party tools and extensions can be seen at `https://docs.microsoft.com/en-us/ef/core/extensions/`.

In the code-first approach, we first write the code; that is, we first create the domain model classes and then, using these classes, EF Core APIs create the database and tables, using migration based on the convention and configuration provided. We will look at conventions and configurations a little later in this section. The following diagram illustrates the code-first approach:

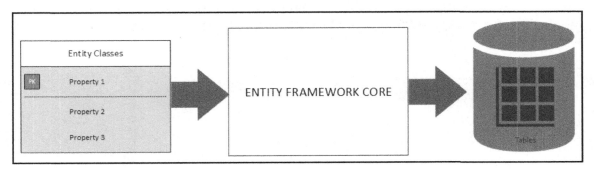

In the database-first approach, as the name suggests, we have an existing database or we create a database first and then use EF Core APIs to create the domain and context classes. As mentioned, currently EF Core has limited support for it due to a lack of tooling. So, our preference will be for the code-first approach throughout our examples. The reader can discover the third-party tools mentioned previously to learn more about the EF Core database-first approach as well. The following image illustrates the database-first approach:

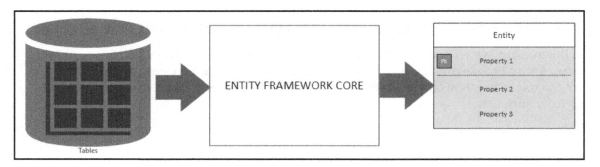

 We will refer to properties as scalar properties and navigation properties. Although it's an old concept, it's worth revisiting it again to gain a better understanding. A property can contain primitive data (such as a string, an integer, or a Boolean value), or structured data (such as a complex type). Properties that are of a primitive type are also called **scalar** properties. The complex properties or properties of another non-simple type are referred to as **complex** or **navigation** properties.

Now that we understand the approaches and know that we will be using the code-first approach, let's dive into coding our getting started with EF Core console app. Before we do so, we need to have SQL Express installed in our development machine. If SQL Express is not installed, download the SQL Express 2017 edition from `https://www.microsoft.com/en-IN/sql-server/sql-server-downloads` and run the setup wizard. We will do the **Basic** installation of SQL Express 2017 for our learning purposes, as shown in the following screenshot:

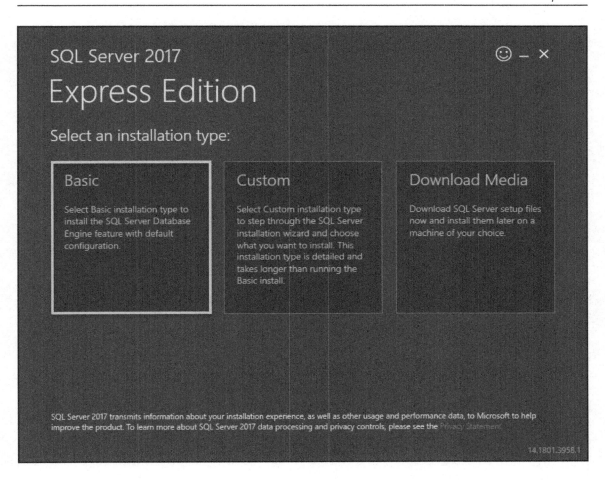

Our objective is to learn how to use EF Core and so we will not do anything fancy in our console app. We will just do simple **Create Read Update Delete (CRUD)** operations of a simple class called `Person`, as defined here:

```
public class Person
{
    public int Id { get; set; }
    public string Name { get; set; }
    public bool Gender { get; set; }
    public DateTime DateOfBirth { get; set; }
    public int Age
    {
        get
        {
            var age = DateTime.Now.Year - this.DateOfBirth.Year;
```

```
                    if (DateTime.Now.DayOfYear <
                    this.DateOfBirth.DayOfYear)
                    {
                        age = age - 1;
                    }

                    return age;
                }
            }
        }
```

As we can see in the preceding code, the class has simple properties. To perform the CRUD operations on this class, let's create a console app by performing the following steps:

1. Create a new .NET Core console project named GettingStartedWithEFCore, as shown in the following screenshot:

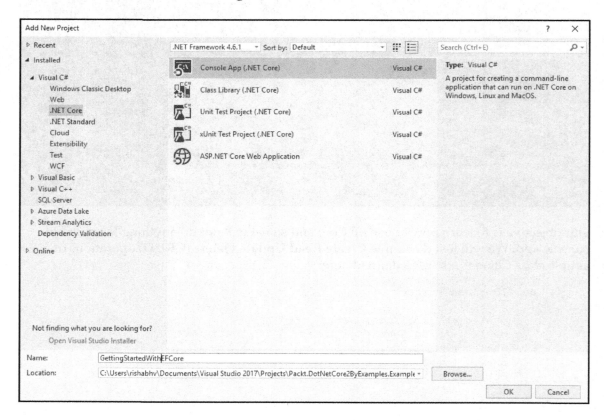

2. Create a new folder named `Models` in the project node and add the `Person` class to this newly created folder. This will be our model entity class, which we will use for CRUD operations.

3. Next, we need to install the EF Core package. Before we do that, it's important to know that EF Core provides support for a variety of databases. A few of the important ones are:

   - SQL Server
   - SQLite
   - InMemory (for testing)

   The complete and comprehensive list can be seen at `https://docs.microsoft.com/en-us/ef/core/providers/`. We will be working with SQL Server on Windows for our learning purposes, so let's install the SQL Server package for Entity Framework Core. To do so, let's install the `Microsoft.EntityFrameworkCore.SqlServer` package from the **NuGet Package Manager** in Visual Studio 2017. Right-click on the project. Select **Manage Nuget Packages** and then search for `Microsoft.EntityFrameworkCore.SqlServer`. Select the matching result and click **Install**:

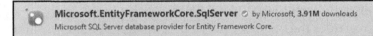

Microsoft.EntityFrameworkCore.SqlServer ⊘ by Microsoft, 3.91M downloads   v2.0.1
Microsoft SQL Server database provider for Entity Framework Core.

4. Next, we will create a class called `Context`, as shown here:

```
public class Context : DbContext
{
    public DbSet<Person&gt; Persons { get; set; }

    protected override void OnConfiguring(DbContextOptionsBuilder
    optionsBuilder)
    {
        //// Get the connection string from configuration
        optionsBuilder.UseSqlServer(@"Server=.\SQLEXPRESS
        ;Database=PersonDatabase;Trusted_Connection=True;");
    }

    protected override void OnModelCreating(ModelBuilder
    modelBuilder)
    {
        modelBuilder.Entity<Person&gt;
        ().Property(nameof(Person.Name)).IsRequired();
```

```
        }
    }
```

The class looks quite simple, but it has the following subtle and important things to make note of:

- The `Context` class derives from `DbContext`, which resides in the `Microsoft.EntityFrameworkCore` namespace. `DbContext` is an integral part of EF Core and if you have worked with EF, you will already be aware of it. An instance of `DbContext` represents a session with the database and can be used to query and save instances of your entities. `DbContext` is a combination of the Unit Of Work and Repository Patterns. Typically, you create a class that derives from `DbContext` and contains `Microsoft.EntityFrameworkCore.DbSet` properties for each entity in the model.
- If properties have a `public` setter, they are automatically initialized when the instance of the derived context is created.
- It contains a property named `Persons` (plural of the model class `Person`) of type `DbSet<Person&gt;`. This will map to the `Persons` table in the underlying database.
- The class overrides the `OnConfiguring` method of `DbContext` and specifies the connection string to be used with the SQL Server database. The connection string should be read from the configuration file, `appSettings.json`, but for the sake of brevity and simplicity, it's hardcoded in the preceding code. The `OnConfiguring` method allows us to select and configure the data source to be used with a context using `DbContextOptionsBuilder`. Let's look at the connection string. `Server=` specifies the server. It can be `.\SQLEXPRESS`, `.\SQLSERVER`, `.\LOCALDB`, or any other instance name based on the installation you have done. `Database=` specifies the database name that will be created. `Trusted_Connection=True` specifies that we are using integrated security or Windows authentication. An enthusiastic reader should read the official Microsoft Entity framework documentation on configuring the context at `https://docs.microsoft.com/en-us/ef/core/miscellaneous/configuring-dbcontext`.

- The `OnModelCreating` method allows us to configure the model using the `ModelBuilder` Fluent API. This is the most powerful method of configuration and allows configuration to be specified without modifying the entity classes. The Fluent API configuration has the highest precedence and will override conventions and data annotations. The preceding code has same effect as the following data annotation has on the `Name` property in the `Person` class:

```
[Required]
public string Name { get; set; }
```

5. The preceding point highlights the flexibility and configuration that EF Core brings to the table. EF Core uses a combination of conventions, attributes, and Fluent API statements to build a database model at runtime. All we have to do is to perform actions on the model classes using a combination of these and they will automatically be translated to appropriate changes in the database. Before we conclude this point, let's have a quick look at each of the different ways to configure a database model:

    - **EF Core conventions**: The conventions in EF Core are comprehensive. They are the default rules by which EF Core builds a database model based on classes. A few of the simpler yet important default conventions are listed here:

        - EF Core creates database tables for all `DbSet<TEntity&gt;` properties in a `Context` class with the same name as that of the property. In the preceding example, the table name would be `Persons` based on this convention.

        - EF Core creates tables for entities that are not included as `DbSet` properties but are reachable through reference properties in the other `DbSet` entities. If the `Person` class had a complex/navigation property, EF Core would have created a table for it as well.

        - EF Core creates columns for all the scalar read-write properties of a class with the same name as the property by default. It uses the reference and collection properties for building relationships among corresponding tables in the database. In the preceding example, the scalar properties of `Person` correspond to a column in the `Persons` table.

- EF Core assumes a property named ID or one that is suffixed with ID as a primary key. If the property is an integer type or Guid type, then EF Core also assumes it to be IDENTITY and automatically assigns a value when inserting the data. This is precisely what we will make use of in our example while inserting or creating a new Person.
- EF Core maps the data type of a database column based on the data type of the property defined in the C# class. A few of the mappings between the C# data type to the SQL Server column data type are listed in the following table:

C# data type	SQL server data type
int	int
string	nvarchar(Max)
decimal	decimal(18,2)
float	real
byte[]	varbinary(Max)
datetime	datetime
bool	bit
byte	tinyint
short	smallint
long	bigint
double	float

There are many other conventions, and we can define custom conventions as well. For more details, please read the official Microsoft documentation at https://docs.microsoft.com/en-us/ef/core/modeling/.

- **Attributes**: Conventions are often not enough to map the class to database objects. In such scenarios, we can use attributes called data annotation attributes to get the desired results. The `[Required]` attribute that we have just seen is an example of a data annotation attribute.
- **Fluent API**: This is the most powerful way of configuring the model and can be used in addition to or in place of attributes. The code written in the `OnModelConfiguring` method is an example of a Fluent API statement.

6. If we check now, there is no `PersonDatabase` database. So, we need to create the database from the model by adding a migration. EF Core includes different migration commands to create or update the database based on the model. To do so in Visual Studio 2017, go to **Tools** | **Nuget Package Manager** | **Package Manager Console**, as shown in the following screenshot:

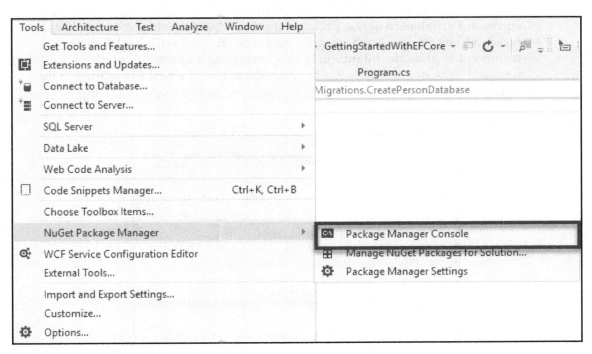

This will open the **Package Manager Console** window. Select the Default Project as `GettingStartedWithEFCore` and type the following command:

```
add-migration CreatePersonDatabase
```

If you are not using Visual Studio 2017 and you are dependent on .NET Core CLI tooling, you can use the following command:

```
dotnet ef migrations add CreatePersonDatabase
```

7. We have not installed the `Microsoft.EntityFrameworkCore.Design` package, so it will give an error:

```
Your startup project 'GettingStartedWithEFCore' doesn't reference
Microsoft.EntityFrameworkCore.Design. This package is required for
the Entity Framework Core Tools to work. Ensure your startup
project is correct, install the package, and try again.
```

So let's first go to the **NuGet Package Manager** and install this package. After successful installation of this package, if we run the preceding command again, we should be able to run the migrations successfully. It will also tell us the command to undo the migration by displaying the message `To undo this action, use Remove-Migration`. We should see the new files added in the **Solution Explorer** in the `Migrations` folder, as shown in the following screenshot:

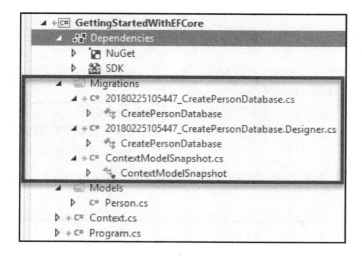

8. Although we have migrations applied, we have still not created a database. To create the database, we need to run the following commands.

In Visual Studio 2017:

```
update-database -verbose
```

In .NET Core CLI:

```
dotnet ef database update
```

If all goes well, we should have the database created with the `Persons` table (property of type `DbSet<Person&gt;`) in the database. Let's validate the table and database by using **SQL Server Management Studio** (**SSMS**). If SSMS is not installed in your machine, you can also use Visual Studio 2017 to view the database and table.

9. Let's check the created database. In Visual Studio 2017, click on the **View** menu and select **Server Explorer**, as shown in the following screenshot:

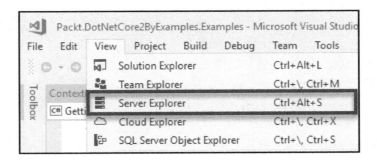

10. In **Server Explorer**, right-click on **Data Connections** and then select **Add Connection**. The **Add Connection** dialog will show up. Enter `.\SQLEXPRESS` in the **Server name** (since we installed SQL EXPRESS 2017) and select `PersonDatabase` as the database, as shown in the following screenshot:

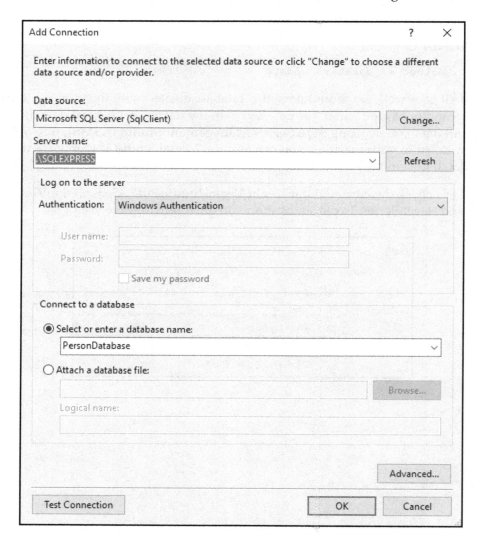

11. On clicking **OK**, we will see the database named `PersonDatabase` and if we expand the tables, we can see the `Persons` table as well as the `_EFMigrationsHistory` table. Notice that the properties in the `Person` class that had setters are the only properties that get transformed into table columns in the `Persons` table. Notice that the `Age` property is read-only in the class we created and therefore we do not see an age column in the database table, as shown in the following screenshot:

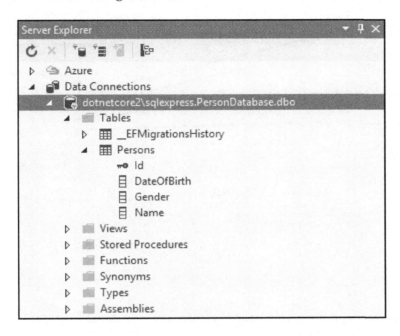

This is the first migration to create a database. Whenever we add or update the model classes or configurations, we need to sync the database with the model using the `add-migration` and `update-database` commands. With this, we have our model class ready and the corresponding database created. The following image summarizes how the properties have been mapped from the C# class to the database table columns:

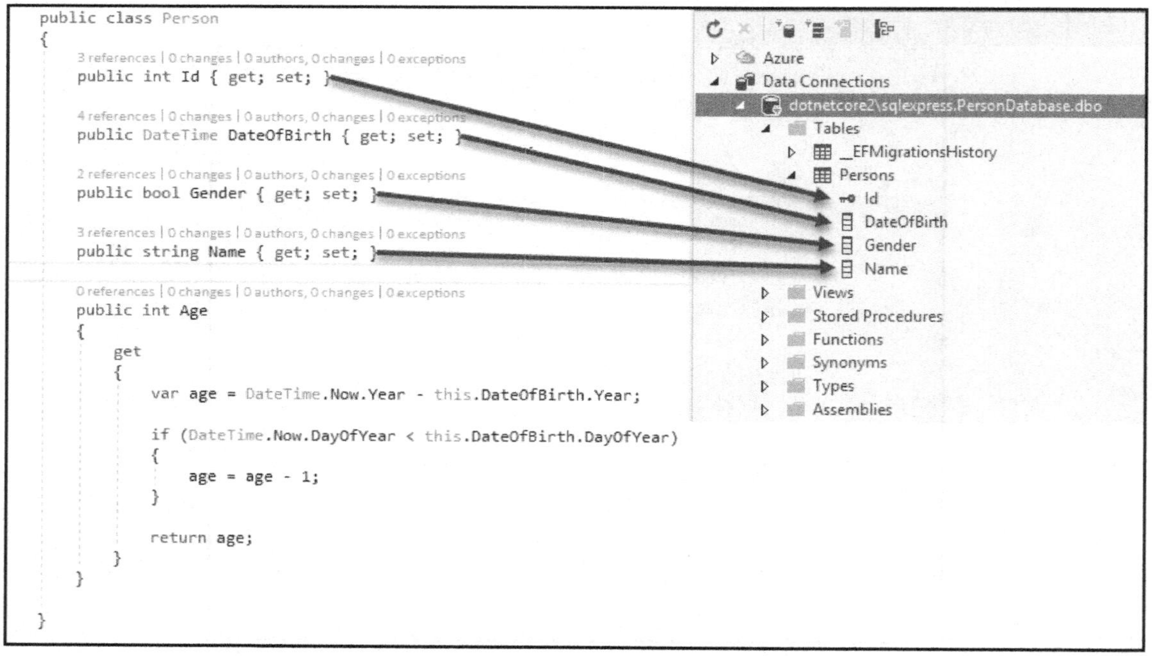

Now, we will use the `Context` class to perform CRUD operations.

12. Let's go back to our `Main.cs` and write the following code. The code is well commented, so please go through the comments to understand the flow:

```
class Program
{
    static void Main(string[] args)
    {
        Console.WriteLine("Getting started with EF Core");
        Console.WriteLine("We will do CRUD operations on Person
        class.");
        //// Lets create an instance of Person class.
```

```
Person person = new Person()
{
    Name = "Rishabh Verma",
    Gender = true, //// For demo true= Male, false =
    Female. Prefer enum in real cases.
    DateOfBirth = new DateTime(2000, 10, 23)
};

using (var context = new Context())
{
    //// Context has strongly typed property named Persons
        which referes to Persons table.
    //// It has methods Add, Find, Update, Remove to
        perform CRUD among many others.
    //// Use AddRange to add multiple persons in once.
    //// Complete set of APIs can be seen by using F12 on
        the Persons property below in Visual Studio IDE.
    var personData = context.Persons.Add(person);
    //// Though we have done Add, nothing has actually
        happened in database. All changes are in context
        only.
    //// We need to call save changes, to persist these
        changes in the database.
    context.SaveChanges();

    //// Notice above that Id is Primary Key (PK) and hence
        has not been specified in the person object passed
        to context.
    //// So, to know the created Id, we can use the below
        Id
    int createdId = personData.Entity.Id;
    //// If all goes well, person data should be persisted
        in the database.
    //// Use proper exception handling to discover
        unhandled exception if any. Not showing here for
        simplicity and brevity. createdId variable would
        now hold the id of created person.

    //// READ BEGINS
    Person readData = context.Persons.Where(j =&gt; j.Id ==
    createdId).FirstOrDefault();
    //// We have the data of person where Id == createdId,
        i.e. details of Rishabh Verma.
    //// Lets update the person data all together just for
        demonstarting update functionality.
    //// UPDATE BEGINS
    person.Name = "Neha Shrivastava";
    person.Gender = false;
```

```
        person.DateOfBirth = new DateTime(2000, 6, 15);
        person.Id = createdId; //// For update cases, we need
        this to be specified.

        //// Update the person in context.
        context.Persons.Update(person);
        //// Save the updates.
        context.SaveChanges();

        //// DELETE the person object.
        context.Remove(readData);
        context.SaveChanges();
    }

    Console.WriteLine("All done. Please press Enter key to
    exit...");
    Console.ReadLine();
    }
}
```

With this, we have completed our sample app to get started with EF Core. I hope this simple example will set you up to start using EF Core with confidence and encourage you to start exploring it further. The detailed features of EF Core can be learned from the official Microsoft documentation available at `https://docs.microsoft.com/en-us/ef/core/`. Now that we have an understanding of EF Core, we are ready to use it in our movie booking app. Let's check out the requirements for the movie booking app.

Movie booking app requirements

In this section, we will discuss the requirements for developing our movie booking web app in ASP.NET Core 2.0. To keep things simple and understandable, we will create a single-screen cinema hall and not a multiplex. The requirements for our sample movie booking app are as follows.

As a user or a movie buff, I should be able to:

1. See the list of movies showing in the cinema hall with timings
2. See the short description and star cast of the movie before booking
3. Select seats from the available seats
4. Book the selected seats
5. Optionally log in to the seat with Facebook/Google credentials or continue as a guest.

Now that we have the requirement specifications in place, let's see the activity flow of the app and come up with a flowchart. The following is the rough flowchart of the app workflow:

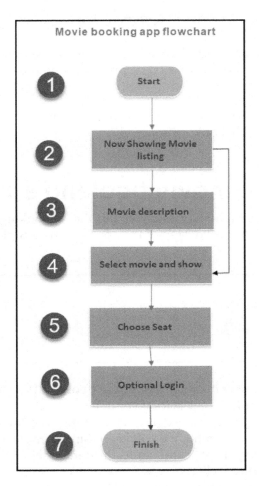

Let's discuss this flowchart in detail:

1. **Start**: This is the start of the flow. The user browses the movie booking app.
2. **Now Showing Movie Listing**: The user can see the the list of movies with timings that are shown in the cinema hall.
3. **Movie description**: The user can optionally check out the movie description by clicking on the selected movie in the list.

4. **Select movie and show**: The user can select an available show.

5. **Choose Seat**: The user can choose a seat from the available seats for the chosen show.

6. **Optional Login**: The user can optionally log in to the web app or continue as a guest.

7. **Finish**: We will not be implementing a payment interface, as we only intend to learn ASP.NET Core and EF Core. Upon choosing the seat and navigating ahead, we finish the flow.

Now that we have an understanding of the requirements and a fair idea of what we wish to achieve, let's design the movie booking app.

Designing the movie booking app

In this section, we will do a high-level design of our movie booking web app using ASP.NET Core 2.0. The high-level design of the app is pretty simple, as shown in the following diagram:

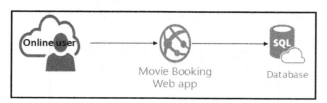

We can see that an **Online user** browses the **Movie Booking Web app**, which is an Azure web app. Ideally, there should be a service layer in between the **Movie Booking Web app** and the **Database**, to allow for a neat, extensible, modular, and layered architecture. However, for the purpose of learning, we will keep things simple and eliminate the service layer for now. The web app gets data and stores the data in the SQL Azure database. If you are worrying about the Azure web app or SQL Azure, stop doing so. We will develop the app locally development machine and deploy it in Azure, and at that time we will take care of the Azure web app and SQL Azure.

Based on the requirements, we need to design the following:

1. A user interface of the movie booking web app.
2. A page to list all the movies currently being shown. We will need to design the database model to show the list of the movies currently being shown.
3. A page to display the details of the selected movie.

4. A page to display the available seats to choose from.
5. A login/authentication module using Facebook or Gmail.

For *Steps 2* to *4*, we need to do database modeling. We will use SQL Express on Windows and use EF Core, which we discussed earlier. Let's do the class design to fulfill the requirements and create the database following the code-first approach. A movie booking system is a complicated and time-consuming system to make. However, what we will make here is a very simple and limited version of a movie booking system, so that we can focus on learning fundamentals rather than on the design of the system. From the requirements, it is clear that we need to have a `Movie` class to contain the movie information and an `Auditorium` class where the movie will be shown. The information about which movie is being shown in the auditorium should be stored in a `Show` class. The auditorium has seats, so we will need a `Seat` class so that the user can choose a seat and book it using a `Booking` class to get a ticket through the `Ticket` class. It's worth reiterating that this is a an over-simplistic design to enable an easy grasp of the system the actual system; may be more complex. The following diagram shows how our classes will be designed as per the preceding analysis:

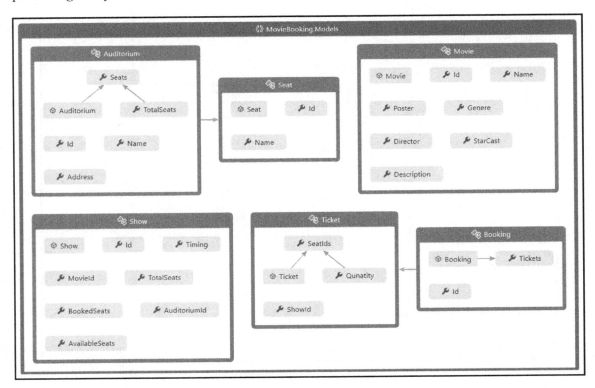

Since we are using EF Core, our database model will be a replica of these classes, as we saw in the earlier section on getting started with EF Core. Once we are done with these, we will have to develop a simple application that will just do CRUD operations. Now that we have a high-level architecture and class diagrams in place, let's start the coding of the web app.

Coding the movie booking app

In this section, we will code the movie booking app, according to the requirements and design we put together in the preceding sections. We will be using the EF Core code-first approach with SQL Express. To make the coding easy to understand, we will code in a step-by-step manner. The steps are as follows:

1. Create a new ASP.NET Core 2.0 MVC app named `MovieBooking`, as we did in the *Creating a simple running code* section of `Chapter 1`, *Getting Started*.

2. If you wish to add authentication in your web app, you can click on the **Change Authentication** button at the time of selecting the template, as shown in the following screenshot:

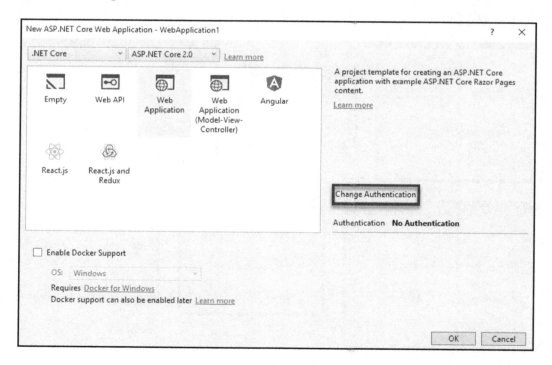

A new dialog will display, as shown in the following screenshot, which will offer multiple authentication options to us, as we discussed in `Chapter 3`, *Building Our First .NET Core Game – Tic-Tac-Toe*. To keep things simple, you can select **Individual User Accounts** and then choose **Store user accounts in-app**. This will do all the boilerplate code needed to enable the app-level user registration, sign-in, and sign-out functionality. Since we have already seen how to use OpenID Connect using the Facebook authentication provider in the Let's Chat web application, we will not go deep into this part and we encourage the reader to reuse the same code and explore and extend it further.

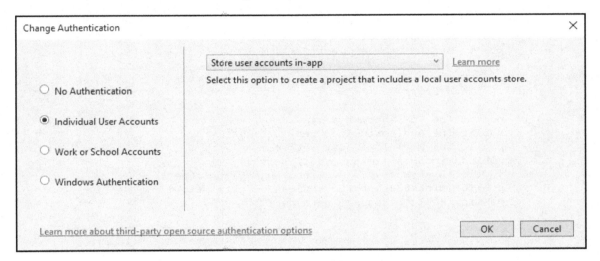

3. Next, we will add the `Models` folder in the project and add the classes for `Auditorium`, `Movie`, `Show`, `Seat`, `Booking`, and `Ticket` that we designed in the preceding section.

4. The code for the classes is listed next. Since the properties are self-explanatory by virtue of their naming, comments are not explicitly added, to maintain brevity:

```
public class Auditorium
{
    public int Id { get; set; }
    public string Name { get; set; }
    public string Address { get; set; }
    public virtual IList<Seat&gt; Seats { get; set; }
    public int TotalSeats =&gt; this.Seats == null ? 0 :
    this.Seats.Count;
}
```

```
public class Seat
{
    public int Id { get; set; }
    public string Name { get; set; }
}

public class Movie
{
    public int Id { get; set; }
    public string Name { get; set; }
    public string Poster { get; set; }
    public string Description { get; set; }
    public string Cast { get; set; }
    public string Director { get; set; }
    public string Genere { get; set; }
}

public class Show
{
    public int Id { get; set; }
    public int AuditoriumId { get; set; }
    public int MovieId { get; set; }
    public TimeSpan Timing { get; set; }
    public IList<Seat&gt; AvailableSeats { get; set; }
    public IList<Seat&gt; BookedSeats { get; set; }
    public int TotalSeats { get; set; }
}

public class Ticket
{
    public int ShowId { get; set; }
    public List<int&gt; SeatIds { get; set; }
    public int Qunatity =&gt; this.SeatIds == null ? 0 :
    this.SeatIds.Count;
}

public class Booking
{
    public int Id { get; set; }
    public IList<Ticket&gt; Tickets { get; set;}
}
```

With this, the models are ready.

5. Next, we need to install EF Core packages to make use of all the EF Core benefits, so let's install the `Microsoft.EntityFrameworkCore.SqlServer` and `Microsoft.EntityFrameworkCore.Design` NuGet packages in our project from the **NuGet Package Manager**. We have already done this while making the `GettingStartedWithEFCore` app.

6. Now, we need to create the context class to create the database based on this model. We will create the model named `MovieBookingContext`, as shown in the following code:

```
public class MovieBookingContext : DbContext
{
    public DbSet<Auditorium&gt; Auditoriums { get; set; }
    public DbSet<Movie&gt; Movies { get; set; }
    public DbSet<Show&gt; Shows { get; set; }
    public DbSet<Booking&gt; Bookings { get; set; }
    public DbSet<Ticket&gt; Tickets { get; set; }
    public
    MovieBookingContext(DbContextOptions<MovieBookingContext&gt;
    options) : base(options)
    {
    }
}
```

7. Notice that `MovieBookingContext` doesn't have the `OnConfiguring` method call that we used to configure the SQL database in our last EF Core sample. This is to show a different way of configuring the database. We will read the connection string from the `appsettings.json` configuration file, which has the following configuration entry:

```
"ConnectionStrings": {
    "DefaultConnection":
"Server=.\\SQLEXPRESS;Database=MovieBookingDemo;Trusted_Connection=
True;"
    },
```

8. Next, we will configure the database through the context by reading the configuration in the `ConfigureServices` method of `Startup.cs`, as shown in the following code:

```
public void ConfigureServices(IServiceCollection services)
{
    services.AddDbContext<MovieBookingContext&gt;(options =&gt;
    options.UseSqlServer(Configuration.GetConnectionString
    ("DefaultConnection")));
    services.AddMvc();
}
```

9. After developing the context, we need to create the database. To do so, we we need to run the following commands in order. The first command will add the migration and the second command will actually create the database:

```
add-migration CreateMovieBookingDemo
update-database -verbose
```

10. Now we have the database, but we do not have the necessary data in the tables to list the movie information. To do so, we can either write a script, a small EF Core-based program, or enter it manually in the table. Since this is SQL stuff, we will not go into great detail, but an aware reader should be able to insert this data in the corresponding tables correctly.

11. Next, we need to create controllers and views for the screens and wire up the data access layer. At the outset, the user should be able to see the list of shows in the home screen, so we will develop the home screen first. To do so, we will reuse the `Index` action of `HomeController.cs` as it is and modify the `Index` view to display the user interface, as shown in the following screenshot:

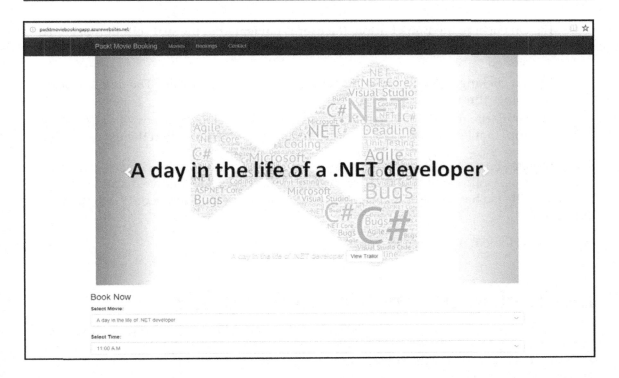

There is nothing fancy here. The user interface has an image carousel, which displays the posters of the movies and the quick booking section, which lists the movies and show times. Just replace the URLs of the default carousel (which comes out of the box in the default template) with the image URLs of movie posters by searching them online through Bing.

12. To show the list of movies, we need an API returning the list of movies called as `GetMovies` API. Recall that we have added the movie data in the database already, so we have movies to be fetched. On selecting a movie, we need to fetch the available show times for the movie, so we need another API to fetch the show time based on the movie called `GetShowTimesForMovie` API. We have seen how to create APIs using the `Context` object in the *Getting started with Entity Framework Core* section. We then wire up the APIs to the controller to populate data in the view.

13. On clicking the **Book** button, the user is navigated to the seat selection page. To display the seats, we again need an API to get the available seats for a show named `GetAvailableSeatsForShow` API.

14. On clicking a movie, we can view the selected movie details. The data for this comes through the `GetMovieDetails` API.

15. Similarly, the UI and corresponding APIs are developed, as now it's just a simple app, that fetches the data from the database and displays it in the user interface.

The complete source code can be seen at `https://github.com/PacktPublishing/.NET-Core-2.0-By-Example`, which lists all the APIs and the view code that we discussed previously. It also has a script, that can be executed to insert the sample data into the application.

We will next look at deploying this app.

Deploying the movie booking app

We have already deployed one of our sample web apps in Azure and this is no different. The assumption here is that the reader already has an Azure subscription and is logged in with the email ID used for the subscription. If this is not the case, please go through the previous chapters where we have discussed Azure subscription at length. Let's have a look at steps to deploy our movie booking app on the cloud:

1. In the Visual Studio **Solution Explorer** window, right-click on the `MovieBooking` project and then click **Publish**. It will open a **Publish** dialog.

2. Select **Create New** and then click **OK**. It will open the **Create App Service** dialog. Enter the required fields, as shown in the following screenshot:

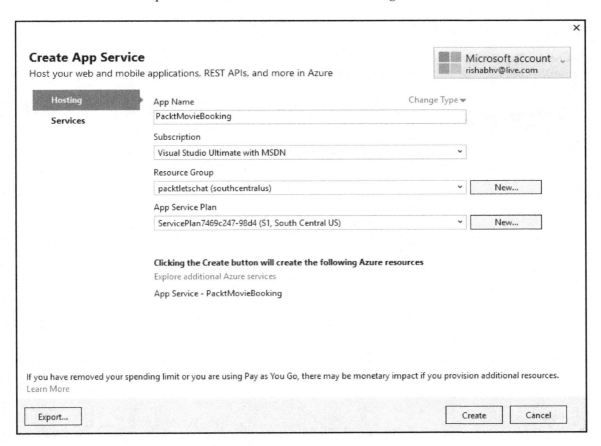

3. After filling in all the required input, click on **Services** on the left panel. It will display the following dialog:

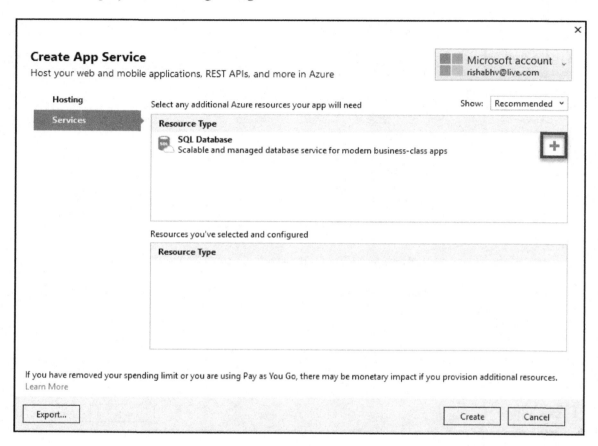

4. We need a database for our app to function and the dialog shows the **SQL Database** as the additional Azure resource that we need to deploy. Click on the **+** icon on the right-hand side. It will open a new dialog **Configure SQL Database**, as shown in the following screenshot:

5. Enter the required details. Make a note of the username and password as well as the database name and connection string name, as these will be used in the code. Click **OK** and then click **Create**. This will create the publish profile and deploy the app.

6. However, we need to ensure that our database gets created, our intended connection string is used, and migrations are applied. To do so, in the **Publish** window, click on the **Settings** link, as shown in the following screenshot:

7. The **Publish** dialog will open. On the **Settings** tab, ensure that for **DefaultConnection**, under the **Databases** section, the **Use this connection string at runtime** checkbox is checked, as shown in the following screenshot:

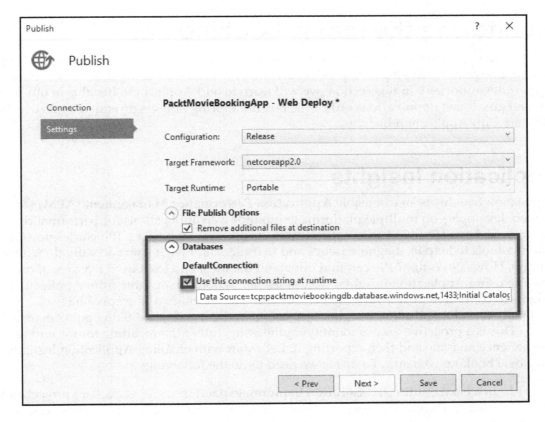

8. If you deploy for the first time, you may also see **Entity Framework Migrations**, just like the **Databases** section shown in the preceding screenshot. If so, please check **Apply this migration on publish**. Since I have already applied the migrations, I don't have it in in preceding screenshot.

9. Click **Save** and then click **Publish**. This will publish the web app as well as the database and migrations.

With this, our web app is deployed and after successful deployment, the app will automatically be launched in the browser. The sample app can be seen at `http://packtmoviebookingapp.azurewebsites.net/`.

Monitoring the movie booking app

Coding and deploying an app is fine, but it's equally important to ensure that the app keeps running fine once it's deployed in production and end users start using it. So monitoring an app is quite important. In this section, we will learn to add Application Insights in our web app and also touch upon various out-of-the box monitoring options provided by Azure. We will start with Application Insights.

Application Insights

Application Insights is an extensible **Application Performance Management (APM)** service for web developers on multiple platforms to monitor web applications for performance, usability, and availability. It automatically detects performance issues. It includes powerful analytics tools to help us diagnose issues and to understand what users actually do with our app. How cool is that? We can find out about the most and least used features of our web app using Application Insights. We can use the actionable insights from Application Insights to continuously improve the performance and usability of the app. I have personally found Application Insights very useful in diagnosing and fixing performance issues. This is a proactive way of identifying the issue, rather than waiting for the end user to experience an issue and then reporting it. Let's start with enabling Application Insights in our movie booking web app. To do so, we need to do the following:

1. In Visual Studio 2017 **Solution Explorer**, expand the `MovieBooking` project and click on **Connected Services**. This will display the **Connected Services** page, as shown in the following screenshot:

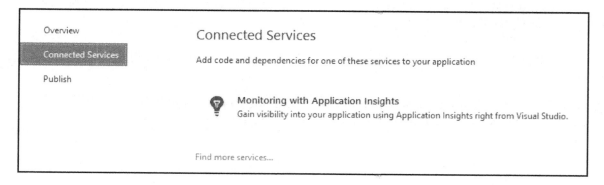

2. Click on **Monitoring with Application Insights**. This will open the **Application Insights** configuration screen, as shown in the following screenshot:

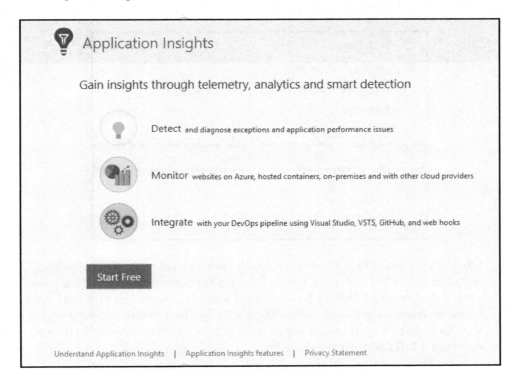

This same screen can be reached by right-clicking on the MovieBooking project in **Solution Explorer** and then clicking **Add | Application Insights Telemetry**, as shown in the following screenshot:

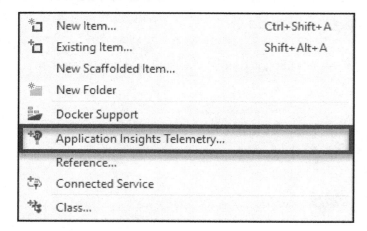

3. Click on the **Start Free** button. This will take us to the registration screen, shown in the following screenshot. Choose the **Subscription** and **Resource** based on your requirements. Here, I have created a new resource but you may want to reuse an existing resource. We will go with the free variant, so choose the option in which Application Insights will remain free and halt data collection after the quota of **1 GB / Month** is exhausted:

Register your app with Application Insights

Account

Microsoft account
rishabhv@live.com

Subscription

Visual Studio Ultimate with MSDN

Resource

MovieBooking (New resource)

Configure settings...

Base Monthly Price	Free
Included Data	1 GB / Month
Additional Data	$2.30 per GB*
Data retention (raw and aggregated data)	90 days

*Pricing is subject to change. Visit our pricing page for most recent pricing details.

○ Allow Application Insights to collect data beyond 1GB/Month.

◉ Application Insights will remain free and halt data collection after 1GB/Month.

Register

Getting started will...

Add the AI SDK to your project   Send data to Azure   Automatically track exceptions   Automatically send publish annotations

Or just add the SDK to try local only mode

4. Click on **Register**. This may take a while and hence show a progress bar, shown in the following screenshot. Look at the screenshot and we can see how powerful Application Insights is. It has **Smart Detection**, **App Map**, **Analytics**, and **CodeLens**, among other great features:

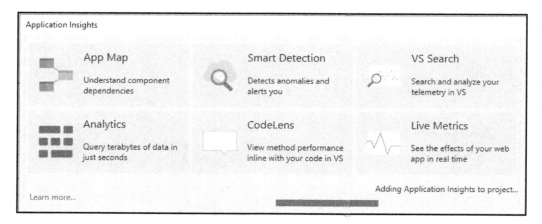

5. Once the configuration is done, the progress bar will disappear. Application Insights telemetry should now be enabled in the selected project. The configuration will add the instrumentation key in `appsettings.json` as well and so, after successfully enabling Application Insights, you may get a prompt that the file has been modified. This is fine and expected, so click **OK**:

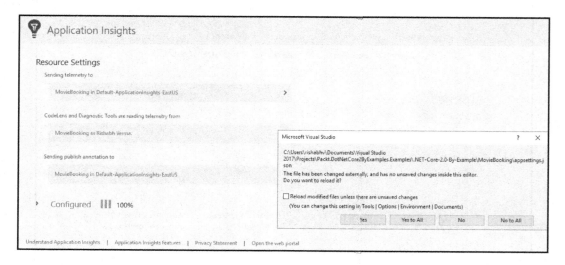

We are now ready to monitor the web app after publishing it to remain in sync with the instrumentation key changes and Application Insight SDK changes that we have just done. With this, we are done with setting up Application Insights. Now, we will see how we can monitor the web app and leverage the benefits of Application Insights. We can see the telemetry data of our local debugging setup in Visual Studio itself, while the Azure portal is where we can see the insights of our deployed application.

In the Visual Studio **Solution Explorer**, we will now have the `Application Insights` folder inside **Connected Services** for our movie booking project, as shown in the following screenshot:

Right-click on the **Application Insights** folder and we will get a number of options. A few of the important ones are shown in the following screenshot:

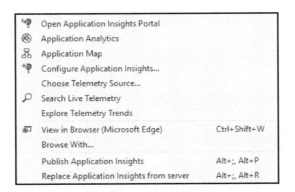

Here are the explanations of these options:

- **Open Application Insights Portal**: This will directly open Application Insights in the Azure web portal.
- **Application Analytics**: This will open the application analytics portal, where we can perform detailed analytics and filtering of data.
- **Application Map**: This will open the application map for the project in the Azure portal. The application map helps us to spot performance bottlenecks or failure hotspots across all components of the distributed application.

- **Configure Application Insights**: This can be used to configure Application Insights.
- **Choose Telemetry Source**: This configures the app that will be used as the telemetry source. By default, the current web app will be the telemetry source.
- **Search Live Telemetry**: This searches the data in the telemetry from Visual Studio or in the Azure web portal. Using this, we can also see debug telemetry data from the Visual Studio debugging.

To conclude this discussion, let us see the Application Insights data that was collected while I wrote this section. The following screenshot shows what it looks like for the movie booking app that we developed:

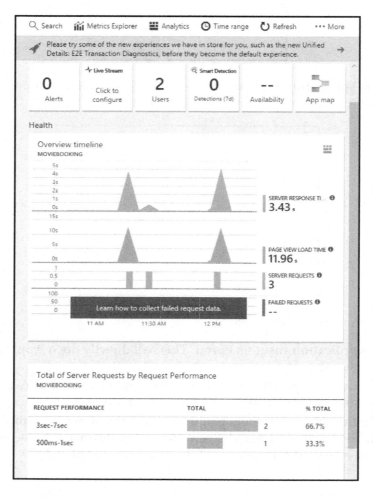

Application Insights is a huge topic and one section of a chapter doesn't do justice to this great and important feature. For a thorough and detailed coverage Application Insights, I would highly recommend readers to read the wonderful documentation on Application Insights at `https://docs.microsoft.com/en-us/azure/application-insights/`.

In this section, we have looked at Application Insights, which is a great monitoring tool in the developer's repertoire. However, Azure has much more to offer in terms of monitoring options and we will explore these in the next chapter, where I will also discuss how to use Application Insights telemetry data to investigate issues. With this note, we conclude this chapter.

Summary

In this chapter, we learned about Entity Framework and Entity Framework Core, and understood the features of each and the differences between the two. We also learned that we should use EF Core only if EF cannot be used or there is a pressing cross-platform requirement to use EF Core. We learned how to do CRUD operations using EF Core by creating a simple app. We then developed a simple movie booking app and learned how to deploy it using Visual Studio. We also saw how we can monitor our web app by enabling Application Insights. So far, we have only seen monolithic apps where all the APIs reside in one web app. If that one web app goes down, our entire app can come to a standstill. There is a way to circumvent this by deploying the app in smaller, independent modules, called microservices. In the next chapter, we will explore microservices.

Microservices with .NET Core

9

Over the last few years, a paradigm shift has happened in the way applications are designed, in the form of suites of smaller and independently deployable services, also known as **microservice architecture** or just **microservices**. The intent is to develop simpler and independent services, to release them quickly, and to release them often and ensure that if one service is down then other services are not impacted, making the app more robust, reliable, and highly scalable. In the spirit of this new philosophy, and keeping up with the latest and greatest in the technology space, we will cover the following topics in this chapter:

- Introduction to microservices
- Handy things to know
- Blazor—a new experiment from the ASP.NET team
- What's coming in .NET Core 2.1

We have a lot to cover, so let's start with microservices.

Introduction to microservices

To better understand and appreciate the microservice architecture, we first need to see what a service is and how the traditional service monolithic architecture has limitations that can be overcome by microservices. Once we have this context set up, we will define microservices.

A traditional service

When we create any server-side enterprise app, it must support a variety of different clients, including desktop and mobile browsers, mobile apps, and so on. We may also expose APIs, so that third parties can consume them and integrate with our system. Like third parties, we may also need to integrate our application with other applications through APIs. The app would handle the requests by executing business logic, then performing read-write operations by accessing a database and/or other data providers and systems, and return an HTML/JSON/XML response. What I have described here is a typical enterprise application. We have different logical modules in the application to fulfill the business requirements. These modules are what we can refer to as services.

In essence, a service is just a software component that provides functionality to other pieces of software within your system. A service should be well defined, self contained, and should not depend on the context or state of other services. The other pieces of software could be anything—a website, a web app, a mobile app, a desktop app, or even another service. If I were to give an example, take any e-commerce website of your choice. The website displays the products and the deals. To display products and deals, it talks to a service. The service is actually responsible for the creation,update, deletion, and retrieval of data from the database, so the service provides functionality to the website.

The communication between the different software components and the service normally happens over a network using some kind of communication protocol. For example, your Facebook mobile app communicates to a service through the internet. A system which uses a service or multiple services in this fashion has what's called a **service-oriented architecture**, abbreviated as **SOA**. The idea behind SOA is to use a thick server rather than a thick client. This way, many clients can have the same functionality. In future, we can have newer or different types of clients connecting to the same service, reusing this functionality. As a software architecture, SOA has been very successful. A few of the benefits and features of SOA are:

- It allows the application to scale up when demand increases, by enabling us to have a copy of the service on multiple servers. When the burst of traffic comes in, a load balancer will redirect requests to a specific instance of the service. We can have multiple instances of a service.
- It allows reusability of functionality. For instance, in a shopping web app, the function to create an order could be the same functionality, which is triggered by a mobile app on our service. So, it's the same code creating an order for both the website and the mobile app.

- It allows standardized contracts or interface-based development. When a client application calls a service, it actually invokes a method in the service. The signature of the method typically doesn't change when the service implementation changes, so we can upgrade our service without having to upgrade our clients, as long as the contract and the signature of the method doesn't change. This way, we do not have to upgrade the clients when the service is upgraded.
- It is stateless. When a request comes from a client to a service, that instance of the service does not have to remember the previous request from that specific client. It has all the information from the request that it needs in order to retrieve all the data associated with the previous request within the service, so a service does not have to remember the previous call the client has made to that particular instance of the service and no context needs to be maintained. It's stateless, therefore any instance of the service can honor any income request from a client, because it does not have to remember any previous interaction with any other instance of a service.
- It is simple to develop, deploy, and scale the application.

We should now have a fair idea of the SOA that we may have been using without knowing what it is for years. Traditional services, which may be using SOA, have typically been deployed as a monolith. Monolith consists of two words, mono and lith. Mono means single and lith means stone. However, in a software dictionary, monolithic architecture refers to applications that are deployed as a single unit. An important consideration when developing an application is how easy it is to learn and modify, and how quickly new developers can become productive on the application. These desired features give rise to an architecture that is simple and easily understandable. Another desired aspect is that it should be easy to deploy. Keeping all these things in mind, the architecture would be a layered application that has a user interface layer which communicates to a service layer, which does the data manipulation on the data provider. A typical layered application architecture would look as shown here:

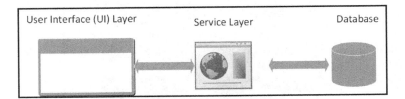

The application is deployed as a single monolithic application and we can run multiple instances of the application behind a load balancer in order to scale and improve availability.

Over time, as the number of users of the application grows and new enhancements are added to the application, the code base grows at a rapid pace and it becomes difficult to understand and modify the code. So, the developers become less productive, especially the new ones. Since it is complex to understand and modify the code base, the bug count in the application increases, which degrades the quality of the application. As the code base grows, the IDE (such as Visual Studio) becomes overloaded and hence slower, making developers less productive. A large monolithic application is also an obstacle to continuous deployment. In order to update/deploy one component, the entire application needs to be deployed, which results in down time. A monolithic application is also an obstacle to scaling development. Once the application gets to a certain size, it's useful to divide up the engineering organization into teams that focus on specific functional areas. The trouble with a monolithic application is that it prevents the teams from working independently, as the code and functionality is coupled in a single monolith. Monolithic architecture forces us to be married to a technology stack. So if we have used a Java stack, we need to be with Java as long as the application lasts, even if there are better tools and technology innovations in other stacks.

The monolithic architecture of an e-commerce website is shown here:

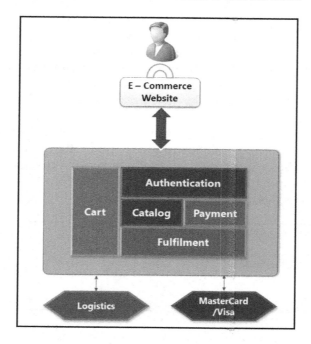

Due to these limitations, monolithic architecture, which has been around for a quite a while, has started to lose popularity over the years. Data speaks for itself. So, if we look at the Google trend report for SOA over the last five years, it is a graph of losing interest over time. It can be seen at `https://trends.google.com/trends/explore?date=today%205-yq=SOA`:

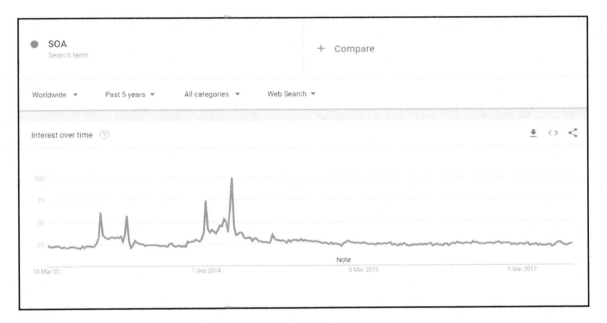

Unfortunate but true, as it happens everywhere else, a loss for one is a gain for another. The decline of SOA has seen the rise of microservices. If we look at the Google trend report for microservices over the same period of the last five years, we see a graph of increasing interest over time, as shown here. This can be seen at `https://trends.google.com/trends/explore?date=today%205-yq=Microservice`:

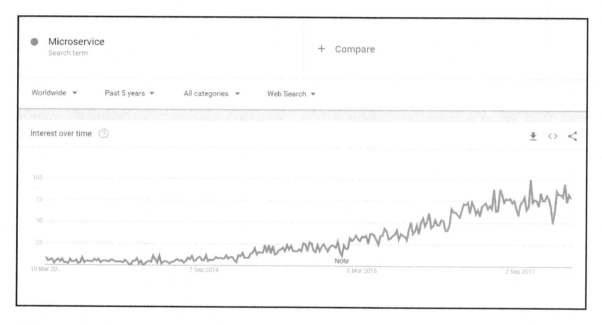

This is not just because it is trending, but because major large enterprises such as Netflix, Amazon, eBay, and so on have talked about the way they scaled and eased out the continuous delivery of their services using microservice architecture, so microservice architecture design doesn't seems to be a buzz to ignore. This architectural framework is one of the core selling points for emerging start-ups, such as Docker, which at the time of writing is valued at about $1 billion while still in funding.

Let's have a look at microservices.

Microservices

Microservices, also known as the **microservice architecture**, is an architectural style that structures an application as a collection of loosely coupled independent services that implement business capabilities. The microservice architecture enables the continuous delivery and deployment of large, complex applications. It also enables an organization to evolve its technology stack. The microservice architecture is basically an improved version of SOA, and therefore it shares all the key characteristics of SOA, such as scalability, re-usability, standardized contracts in interfaces for backwards compatibility, and the idea of having a stateless service that we discussed previously. Microservice capabilities are expressed formally with business-oriented APIs. In short, the microservice architectural style defines a setup where application components are standalone applications of their own. These independent application components talk to each other either using **Remote Method Invocation** (**RMI**), RESTful web services or push messaging. Each microservice owns its related domain data model and domain logic, based on different data storage technologies and different programming languages.

Because of the name, you may ask what the size of a microservice should be. When developing microservices, size is not a critical factor to consider. The imperative point is to make loosely coupled services, so that we have autonomy of development, and deployment and scaling for each service. Obviously, we should strive to make them as small as possible, as long as we don't have an excessive number of direct dependencies upon other microservices.

The following image shows a typical microservice architecture of an e-commerce website:

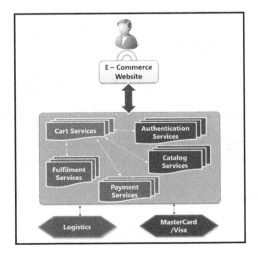

We can see that, compared to the monolithic architecture, this has a lot more modularity and autonomy and the services communicate with other microservices. Think of a situation where, due to some unavoidable issue, **Payment Services** goes down, maybe due to bad code being checked in. The users of the site would still be able to view and update the cart. Only the payment functionality would be down and the rest of the services would keep serving the users. Now, think about a monolithic architecture where there is no independence of module and this sort of bad code issue happens. The chances of failure in such cases would be higher in monolithic architecture and we may even have a situation where a number of features stop working due to dependency.

The following image presents a good comparison between monolithic and microservice architectures:

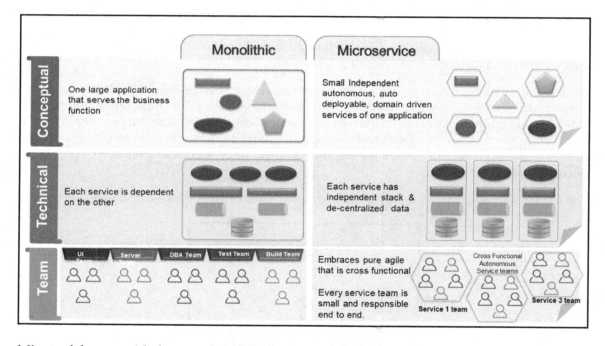

Microsoft has provided a sample reference app and architecture guidance for microservices with ASP.NET Core. The sample is available on GitHub at `https://github.com/dotnet-architecture/eShopOnContainers`.

To get a reasonable understanding and hands-on experience in the development of microservices, it is recommended that the reader has a good look at the repository. What we have discussed is the tip of the iceberg and just an introduction to microservices. We will conclude this discussion with the reference links to microservices, so that enthusiastic readers can gain more insights into this new paradigm:

- **.NET application architecture**: `https://www.microsoft.com/net/learn/architecture`
- **News on .NET architecture**: `https://github.com/dotnet-architecture/News`
- **Martin Fowler on microservices**: `http://martinfowler.com/articles/microservices.html`
- **Microservice architecture pattern**: `http://microservices.io/patterns/microservices.html`

In the next section, we will be discussing tips and tricks that I found really helpful while doing development, debugging, and monitoring the ASP.NET Core 2.0 web apps.

Handy things to know

It's important for us to understand that there are fundamental architecture differences between ASP.NET and ASP.NET Core. A few of the important ones are listed here:

- An important difference between ASP.NET and ASP.NET Core is that ASP.NET Core doesn't have a request queue, unlike ASP.NET. The `RequestQueue` class which resides in the `System.Web` namespace is designed to prevent thread pool starvation in ASP.NET. This no longer exists in ASP.NET Core, so as you can rightly guess, there can be thread pool starvation if we do not write proper code. Just so that we are on the same page, starvation describes a situation where a thread is unable to gain regular access to shared resources and is unable to make progress. This happens when shared resources are made unavailable for long periods by greedy long running threads. For example, suppose an object provides a synchronized method that often takes a long time to return. If one thread invokes this method frequently, other threads that also need frequent synchronized access to the same object will often be blocked.

- AppDomain is another area where ASP.NET Core is different to ASP.NET. Running many instances of AppDomain require runtime support and are generally quite expensive. ASP.NET Core doesn't use AppDomain. There is a single process and a single AppDomain, if that makes things easier to comprehend.

- ASP.NET Core doesn't have SyncronizationContext. If you don't know SyncronizationContext, don't worry. We are discussing it right now. C# 5 came with two new keywords, async and await, which provide a new and easier asynchronous programming experience. The approach to use is simple. Have the async keyword in the method definition. Change the return type of the method from T to Task<T> or Task, if it doesn't return anything (I would not recommend using void, unless it's an event handler method). It is also a good practice to use the async suffix in the method name, so that it is easy to identify that the method is asynchronous. You would also need to use at least one await statement in the method. Under the hood, the compiler translates the async method into a state machine and virtually converts it into a method that is invoked multiple times, once at the actual method invocation that proceeds till the statement containing the await keyword and then returns. When the statement containing the await keyword is executed, the method is invoked again from there and executes the remainder of the statements, in the same fashion. The following code lists a sample async method leveraging the async and await keywords:

```
public async Task<Stream> GetFileContentAsync()
{
    using(var httpClient = new HttpClient())
    {
        var stream = await
        httpClient.GetStreamAsync(
        "http://localhost:9596/api/Files/1");
        return stream;
    }
}
```

An important feature of the `async` and `await` keywords is support for `SyncronizationContext`. `SyncronizationContext` has been inside the framework since .NET 2.0 and is not something newly added to the framework. As discussed previously, when we `await` on an `async` method, the compiler hooks up the continuation, if there is any, and the resulting code is aware of the context. So, if the `SyncronizationContext` is available, the `await` expression will capture it and use it to invoke the continuation, very similar to the `ContinueWith` method offered in the **Task Parallel Library (TPL)**. `SyncronizationContext` should be used with utmost care and if we consume the method in blocking fashion, it may lead to deadlock. For example, in a non-ASP.NET Core environment, if we wait on a `Task` using the `Wait` method or using the `Result` property, we block the main thread. When eventually the task completes inside that method in the thread pool, it will invoke the continuation to post back to the main thread. But since we have blocked the main thread and the task is waiting for the main thread, we will have deadlock. As a precaution, library writers are advised to use `ConfigureAwait(false)` while invoking `async` APIs, to avoid deadlock. Now that we know `SyncronizationContext`, remember that ASP.NET Core doesn't have it! So `ConfigureAwait(false)` doesn't do anything in ASP.NET Core. But that doesn't mean threads can't get blocked in ASP.NET Core. Bad code can still do wonders.

- While ASP.NET works on top of `System.Web`, has a rather tight integration with **Internet Information Server (IIS)**, and runs inside the IIS process (`w3wp.exe`), ASP.NET Core runs outside of the IIS process. The **ASP.NET Core Module (ANCM)** enables the ASP.NET Core apps to run behind IIS in a reverse proxy configuration, which we saw in an earlier chapter. Just to refresh our memories, the work of the proxy or forward proxy is to send a request to the server on behalf of a client, while that of the reverse proxy is to receive the request on behalf of a server. The following image is the high-level architecture of ASP.NET Core. Notice that the center box containing ANCM is the only module that runs inside of `w3wp.exe`. The **Kestrel** server and the **App Code** runs inside `dotnet.exe`. Contrast it with traditional ASP.NET, which runs inside `w3wp.exe`:

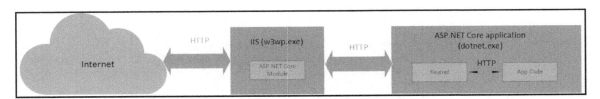

General tips

Now that we know the differences, let's move on to some tips and tricks that are based on top of these architectural differences and more:

- Recently, I was working on the performance optimization of the ASP.NET Core app. We had used in-memory caching with a cache get timeout of five seconds. You would expect that any data from in-memory caching would be retrieved in a matter of milliseconds as it is an in-process cache and this was generally true. However, under load we figured out that data was not getting picked up from the cache. Once we added logging, we figured out that the Get operation in cache was timing out. Yes, even with a five-second value, we had a timeout while fetching data from the cache. On investigation, we figured out that we had thread starvation in the app. As discussed previously, there is no RequestQueue class in ASP.NET Core for avoiding this, so here are some tips to avoid thread starvation:
    - Always prefer to use async all the way, that is, all the APIs must be async.
    - Avoid blocking APIs in your ASP.NET Core application as much as possible. So, **DON'T USE**:
        - Task.Wait()
        - Task.Result
        - Thread.Sleep
        - GetAwaiter().GetResult().
    - Avoid sync over async as they are essentially blocking async methods.
    - Avoid async over sync as they have scalability issues.
    - Log thread pool stats in the application code. This helps identify thread starvation. Here is the sample code that can be used for logging thread stats. It gives stats for both iopc and worker threads:

```
private static int GetThreadPoolStats(out string iocp, out
string worker)
{
    int maxIoThreads, maxWorkerThreads;
    ThreadPool.GetMaxThreads(out maxWorkerThreads, out
maxIoThreads);

    int freeIoThreads, freeWorkerThreads;
    ThreadPool.GetAvailableThreads(out freeWorkerThreads,
```

```
out freeIoThreads);

int minIoThreads, minWorkerThreads;
ThreadPool.GetMinThreads(out minWorkerThreads, out
minIoThreads);

int busyIoThreads = maxIoThreads - freeIoThreads;
int busyWorkerThreads = maxWorkerThreads -
freeWorkerThreads;
iocp = $"(Busy={busyIoThreads},
Free={freeIoThreads},Min=
{minIoThreads},Max={maxIoThreads})";
worker = $"(Busy={busyWorkerThreads},Free=
{freeWorkerThreads},Min={minWorkerThreads},Max=
{maxWorkerThreads})";
return busyWorkerThreads;
}
```

- Use tools such as `https://github.com/benaadams/Ben.BlockingDetector` to diagnose blocking.
- Set minimum threads using `ThreadPool.SetMinThreads` to keep you safe from starvation. The number of minimum threads depends on what your app does and you may have to fine-tune it based on your testing. Note that `ThreadPool` can quickly (read instantly) span the threads up to the minimum number of thread pool threads specified. After that, if more threads are needed, they are throttled by 500 ms and this can cause delays or timeouts in service, which are hard to comprehend in production environments.
- You may also want to read about this issue here: `https://github.com/aspnet/KestrelHttpServer/issues/2104`.

- The concept of `AppDomain` no longer exists in ASP.NET Core, so for code isolation, Microsoft recommends processes and/or containers. For dynamic loading of assemblies, the recommendation is to use the `AssemblyLoadContext` class.
- Since there is no `SyncronizationContext` in ASP.NET Core, thankfully there shouldn't be any deadlocks in ASP.NET Core if you block a task through `Task.Wait` or `Task.Result`. However, this should not be taken as a license to use blocking. We must always strive for `async` all the way.

- As discussed previously, `ConfigureAwait (false)` has no effect in ASP.NET Core, so the following two code snippets work the same way:

```
var stream = await
httpClient.GetStreamAsync("http://localhost:9596/api/Files/1");
var stream = await
httpClient.GetStreamAsync("http://localhost:9596/api/Files/1").Conf
igureAwait(false);
```

- Task continuations in ASP.NET Core are queued to `ThreadPool` and hence can run in parallel. Don't be surprised if your `task.ContinueWith(x=>SomeFunction())` stops working in ASP.NET Core.

- `HttpContext` is not thread safe. Accessing it in parallel may lead to unreliable data and issues.

- Use Swagger for API testing and documentation. Swagger makes it incredibly easy to document and test your APIs. I highly recommend you make use of Swagger for the documentation of APIs. There are other tools such as Postman and Fiddler that can be used for testing the APIs but Swagger does a great job at it as well. Performing a basic API test is as simple as reading this link: `https://swagger.io/blog/how-to-perform-a-basic-api-test/`. Read the steps for using Swagger to generate documentation at `https://docs.microsoft.com/en-us/aspnet/core/tutorials/web-api-help-pages-using-swagger?tabs=visual-studio`.

- The `InMemory` provider of Ef Core is very useful when you want to test components using something that approximates connecting to the real database, without the overhead of actual database operation. Please see this link for the step-by-step approach: `https://docs.microsoft.com/en-us/ef/core/miscellaneous/testing/in-memory`.

- ANCM is designed in such a way that if your first request takes a lot of time, it will disconnect the client and close the process.

- Security is one of the most important but often overlooked aspects in the development of web apps. Security is such a vast topic to cover that it is beyond the scope of this book, but I would highly recommend developers thoroughly go through the security documentation of ASP.NET Core at `https://docs.microsoft.com/en-us/aspnet/core/security/` and inculcate their learning in day-to-day development activities.

- At times, we may have an issue even while starting the app, due to an incorrect code. Though the console logger logs the output in the console window that appears briefly at the startup, as soon as the console vanishes (which happens pretty quickly), we have no means to know what happened or what prevented the app from being started. In such situations, generally the ASP.NET Core module configuration can help us unearth the root cause of the issue. The configuration is done in the `aspNetCore` section of the `system.webserver` node present in the `web.config` file, which is located at the root of the web app. We can enable the output logging and specify the log file path. So, in such cases, the detailed error message will be logged, and we will be able to identify the cause of the issue. The following entry from `web.config` illustrates this:

```
<aspNetCore processPath=".\PacktLetsChat.exe"
stdoutLogEnabled="true"                      stdoutLogFile=".\logs" />
</system.webServer>
```

When the app is deployed in Azure, the `stdoutLogFile` path is modified to direct the app to the `LogFiles` folder of the app.

In this section, we discussed a few points relating to the usage of ASP.NET Core. In the next section, we will discuss a few tips on performance.

Performance tips

ASP.NET Core is one of the fastest platforms on the fundamentals of web request routing, as per benchmarks. Read the complete story at `https://www.techempower.com/blog/2016/11/16/framework-benchmarks-round-13/`. In this section, we will discuss the points we can use to achieve better performance in our ASP.NET Core apps:

- It might sound repetitive, but please use `async` all the way. This is key to the performance of an ASP.NET Core app.

- Test, test, and test! Perform load testing of your app early and often to find the issues early in development. Our team, in fact, came up with a radical idea to identify performance bottlenecks. The idea is to write middleware, that calculates the response time of the API, and if the response time is higher than the threshold, throw an exception, so the developer has to fix it. I would not recommend going this drastic but the intent is to identify the performance issues early in the game. If your app is deployed in Azure, you can do the performance testing in the Azure portal itself, using the following simple steps (here I am assuming there is no authentication header needed, otherwise we can write Visual Studio performance tests as well):

  1. In the Azure portal, navigate to the App Service that we wish to performance test.
  2. On the left panel of the App Service, there is an item called **Performance test**. Click on it. It will open the **Performance test** blade.
  3. Enter the required fields for user load and duration. Each of the fields has a help tool tip so it should be easy to identify the purpose of each field.
  4. Configure the test to use either a manual URL or a Visual Studio web test. If you select manual test, you will need to specify the URL that needs to be load tested. If of a Visual Studio web test, you will need to upload the Visual Studio web test file.
  5. Click **Done** and then click **Run test**.
  6. The performance test will run and display the run stats, such as successful requests, failed requests with errors, memory and CPU usage, and so on:

- Use caching to store static, less frequently changing and frequently accessed data. If you are building an enterprise application, consider leveraging the Azure Redis cache for fast data access.
- Use the garbage collector in server garbage collection mode. This will ensure that your memory footprint doesn't increase over time. This can be done by the following configuration in the `web.config` file, or add an `app.config` file with the following code:

```
<configuration>
  <runtime>
    <gcServer enabled="true"/>
  </runtime>
</configuration>
```

You can read more about the `gcServer` element at `https://docs.`
`microsoft.com/en-us/dotnet/framework/configure-apps/file-schema/`
`runtime/gcserver-element`.

- If you make use of web APIs in your application, use `HttpClient` to make the API calls. Remember to create the `HttpClient` instance only once and reuse it multiple times, that is, create a singleton instance of `HttpClient` and don't create it every time. In terms of Dependency Injection, use it as singleton and not as transient or scoped.
- While developing the API, follow these rules:
    - **Bring only the data that you need**: For the purpose of code re-usability, I have seen teams using a single API that returns a plethora of data, even though only a part of it is needed. For a small number of users, it may not perform badly, but as the user load increases, this will start causing performance bottlenecks, so be very miserly with the data that your service returns.
    - **Choice of serializer**: A considerable amount of time is spent by a service API in serializing the data and then sending it as a response. The client then gets the response and deserializes it back which again takes time. It is worth investing in a serializer that does the job faster, to provide better response time performance. There are a number of serializers at the developer's disposal such as JSON, BSON, MessagePack, Protocol Buffers, and so on. We recently changed JSON to MessagePack and found massive performance gains, as a MessagePack payload is about 66% of JSON and about three times as fast.

- **Compression:** Think of compressing the data sent from the service API to the client. This will be beneficial to mobile users, as well as to whoever may be using your app on a flaky and low bandwidth network, so less data to load would make apps faster. Also, by compressing the payload, we make our application scalable as the bandwidth available to us is limited. There are numerous ways of doing it. Of course, HttpClient has support for GZip compression so we can leverage it. Equally important is the fact that we can choose what properties to serialize. So, if your entity has ten properties and you need only two properties, then it makes perfect sense to serialize only those two properties and ignore the remaining eight properties, to reduce the payload. This is well supported in JSON and we made extensive use of it, and in a few cases came down from 32 MB data to less than 1 MB data. Imagine if this API is called by hundreds of users!

- Make good use of bundling and minification, as discussed in an earlier chapter.
- Response caching reduces the number of requests a client or proxy makes to a web server. Response caching also reduces the amount of work the web server performs to generate a response, hence improving the performance. Please make a note that response caching is not supported for ASP.NET Core Razor pages, but support is expected to come in ASP.NET Core 2.1.
- While using parallelism or multiple threads to write data, make use of concurrent collections. In fact, if you think you may have multiple threads modifying a collection, it's always safe to use concurrent collections, with little overhead.
- Avoid API or database calls inside a loop. In the case of APIs, try to create an API that takes the collection as input and processes that to return a consolidated but trimmed set of required data. In the case of a database, create a stored procedure that accepts a user-defined table as a parameter and returns the data in one go. This will make the application less chatty.
- Do not perform string concatenation inside loops. Use StringBuilder if you need to concatenate strings inside loops.

- Visual Studio has great support for profiling your application to identify high CPU issues, so do make good use of the Visual Studio profiler while in the development phase. It's very simple to use, as illustrated in these steps:
    1. Ensure that the app that you wish to profile is up and running in the machine.
    2. Open Visual Studio and in the quick launch, search for **Performance Explorer**. Alternatively, you can navigate through **Debug | Profiler | Performance Explorer | Attach/Detach,** as shown here:

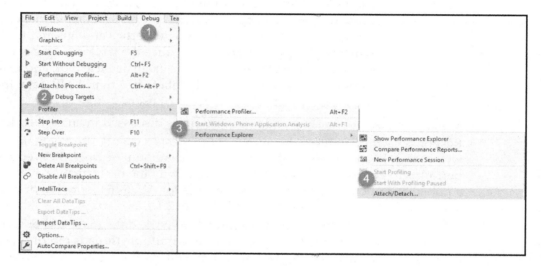

    3. It will open a dialog, displaying the list of running processes. Select the process that you wish to profile and click **Attach.**
    4. The profiling will start. Now is the time to reproduce your high CPU issue and once it is reproduced, stop the profiling. It will generate a detailed profiling report. We will see what the profile report looks like a little later when we discuss profiling in Azure.

- Profile your memory to identify whether there is a memory leak. Always remember, that if your memory percentage remains constant or keeps increasing over a period of time, there may be a memory leak. Memory leak can be described as a situation where a program holds on to the memory even if that memory is discarded and no longer needed. Due to bad coding, the developer code can prevent the **Garbage Collector (GC)** from reclaiming the memory, and hence, used memory keeps increasing over a period of time, resulting in performance issues or failures. Apart from Visual Studio, there are many good profiling tools that can be used such as dotTrace, MemProfiler, ANTS Memory Profiler, PerfView, to name a few. One of the common causes of memory leak in the ASP.NET Core applications that I have encountered is wrong Dependency Injection. So, if an object needs to be scoped or transient and you register it as a singleton, we may be injecting memory leak if it's not meant to be a singleton. Static objects and dictionaries are another common cause of memory leak, so please think multiple times before marking an object as static.

- ASP.NET Core has support for analyzers. Code analysis, as the name suggests, is the analysis of the code to identify potential code issues, such as improper coding, noncompliance to standards, security violations, and design problems. Code analysis can be static or dynamic. In static, the analysis is done without actually running the code. StyleCop, FxCop are few of the most well-known and frequently used code analyzers. Make use of analyzers to identify code issues early. A few of the great ones are `Microsoft.CodeAnalysis`, `SonarAnalyzer.Csharp`, `FxCop analyzer`, `Roslynator.Analyzers`, and `Stylecop analyzer`, to name a few. These are also simple to use—right-click on the project and select **Nuget Package Manager**. Search for the analyzer of your choice and install it. Build your project and observe the warnings and errors in the error window. This will help you nail a variety of issues, such as possible performance bottlenecks, security vulnerabilities, as well as not following best practices.

Read this excellent MSDN blog post on performance improvements in ASP.NET Core: `https://blogs.msdn.microsoft.com/dotnet/2017/06/07/performance-improvements-in-net-core/`.
Also, read the official performance documentation of ASP.NET Core at `https://docs.microsoft.com/en-us/aspnet/core/performance/`.

Next, we will look at a few of the cool and handy features of Azure that can help us be more productive.

Azure tips

Azure has a plethora of features and most of them remain unexplored or unused by a number of developers, though they are extremely useful and provide value. A few of the important ones I came across are listed here:

- **Azure in your pocket**: We will start with a cheesy one. Yes, Azure in your pocket. Now Azure is available as a mobile app, and you can virtually carry your Azure subscription wherever you go. You can keep track of your Azure resources on the go and stay connected—anytime, anywhere. The following image shows a glimpse of the Azure mobile app:

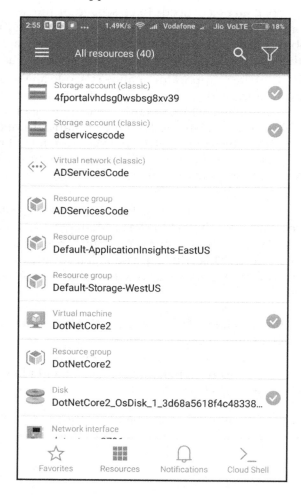

- **Advisor**: In the left panel of the Azure portal, there is an item called **Advisor**. Although it's free, it's a relatively lesser-used and talked about feature of Azure. It's completely free and it provides real-time advisory services on your Azure resources, based on how they are used. Just click on the **Advisor** and it will give security, performance, cost, and availability recommendations. The recommendations can also be downloaded in CSV or PDF format. Here is the teaser of Azure Advisor:

- **Security Center**: Just like **Advisor**, there is a **Security Center** option in the left panel. This is a great and free feature of Azure. It does threat detection all the Azure resources in your subscription and gives pointed recommendations. It also lets you know of any security incidents that occurred with your resources and threat assessment reports. There is a paid plan which has advanced threat detection but the free option is a good starting point. The following image shows the **Security Center**:

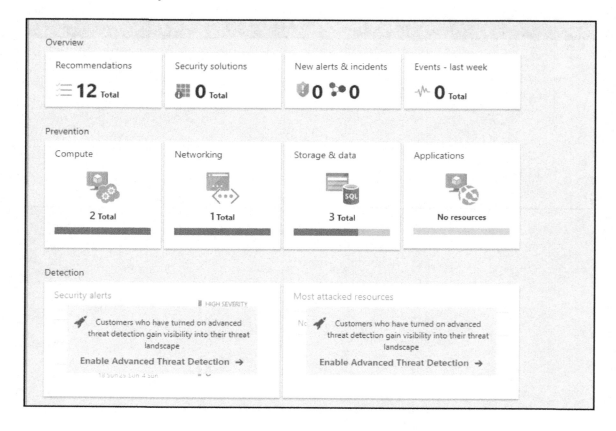

- **Activity logs**: When I have worked in a team that is working on Azure, there have been instances where I am working on the web app and some other team member accidentally changes the configuration, or maybe restarts or deletes a resource, and I have no clue what happened. I have myself been the culprit, modifying the configuration while the performance test was running, which restarted the web app. Azure has a solution for these kinds of situations as well. Every action that a user does is logged in the activity log of the resource you are working with. So, next time you encounter something like this, just go and see the activity log, as shown here. In the Azure portal, go to the resource you wish to see the activity log of. On the left panel of the resource, click on **Activity Log**. You can also apply filters and choose the time duration for which you wish to see the activity log:

- **Diagnostic logging**: If you are running into issues in the app deployed in Azure and do not know what's going on, enable logging and Application Insights in your app. We looked at Application Insights earlier. Logging can give us details such as failed request tracing and detailed error logs. You will see two options for Application Logging—**Blob** and **Filesystem**. As the name suggests, logs are stored in blob and filesystem. Filesystem logging is enabled only for 12 hours, as there is a risk of logs eating up memory. The following image shows the diagnostic logging configuration:

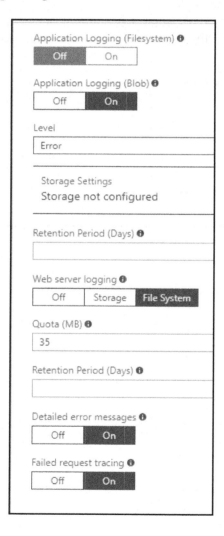

- **Diagnosing and solving issues**: This is another cool feature in Azure. If you run into issues or suspect something is going wrong in your App Service, Azure provides very good diagnoses and a fix for the issues. It is able to clearly identify whether the issue is due to a platform or application code issue. It diagnoses a variety of problem categories such as web app down, slow web app, high CPU usage, high memory usage, web app restarted, TCP connections. It has a chat interface making it easier to use. Just click on one of the problem categories and it will do the analysis on the app for the last 24 hours and share the graph and findings, which makes it extremely easy to identify the issue. It will also give recommendations if you need to scale out your app. Also, you can do a health checkup of the resource on demand, which gives a single view for application errors, performance, CPU, and memory usage. This is definitely a very handy tool to use for diagnosis. Here is the screenshot for diagnosing and solving issues:

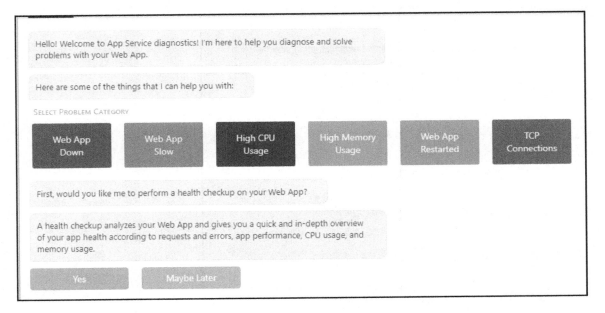

- **Diagnostics as a Service (DaaS)**: Yet another great troubleshooting tool for developers is DaaS. When you open the diagnose and solve issues blade for your App Service, there is a panel on the right displaying a number of links:

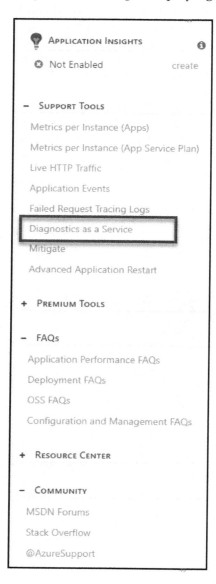

Each of them is a great diagnostic and support tool in itself, but we will focus on DaaS. I would highly recommend you explore each of these links. Coming back to DaaS, this is what it looks like:

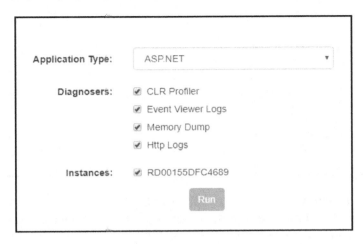

It has support for ASP.NET, PHP, and Java applications. We will select **ASP.NET** as our application type and when we do that, we will see ASP.NET-specific diagnosers such as **CLR Profiler**, **Event Viewer Logs**, **Memory Dump**, and **HTTP Logs**. Based on the diagnosis that we need to do, we can select appropriate options. I generally check everything whenever I am doing diagnosis. **Memory Dump** analysis can be great to identify memory leaks, but the dump needs to be taken when you observe constant high or increasing memory usage. Now, how to do it. Well, it's simple, you can see the memory and CPU usage of your App Service in the **Overview** blade of your App Service in the portal. Note that you would need at least two memory dumps to confirm a memory leak. Likewise, **CLR Profiler** can be used to find out what section of your code is doing the most work at the time of profiling, so it's important to profile when the time issue is occurring in your App Service. After selecting the options, click **Run**.

Azure will capture the data and then perform the analysis, and share the analysis report which you download and act upon, as shown in the following screenshot:

📅 2018-02-05 (04:23 AM)		
Diagnoser	Collection Status	Analysis Status
CLR Profiler	🗋 RD0003FF975239_w3wp_6348.diagsession	🗋 RD0003FF975239_w3wp_6348.html
Event Viewer Logs	🗋 eventlog.xml	🗋 EventLogAnalysisReport-eventlog-2018-2-5-4-25-31-79.html
Http Logs	❶	
Memory Dump	🗋	🗋

The **CLR Profiler** `.diagsession` file can be downloaded by clicking on the `.diagsession` file shown in the image under the **Collection Status** column, and opened in Visual Studio. It will give you the hot path as well as the code block and methods doing the most work during the profiling session. The **Memory Dump** can also be downloaded and you can do a memory dump analysis locally using Windbg or DebugDiag, as needed. Azure provides a DebugDiag analysis report which can be directly downloaded.

- **Azure Service Profiler**: Use Azure Service Profiler to identify high CPU issues. This has great support for ASP.NET Core 2.0. The setup details and value it provides can be seen at `https://www.azureserviceprofiler.com/`. On installing this Profiler for your web app, it will run as a web job and diagnose the issue by identifying the hot paths. It also summarizes performance data to find long-tail performance problems.

- **Profiling the app for high CPU**: With the detailed metrics on CPU and memory provided by Azure, we can easily identify whether the App Service is using high CPU. If it is, how do we figure out what is causing the app to use high CPU? Yes, profiling. Profiling is easy to do in Visual Studio and even in Azure. Even though DaaS does the profiling, I always see `w3wp.exe` getting profiled and not the actual application `.exe` that we have built. To profile our application code, we can do the following simple steps:
    1. In the Azure portal, select the App Service that you wish to profile (search for the App Service and click it).

2. In the left panel of the App Service, click on **Advanced Tools**. This will open the **Advanced Tools** blade. Click on the **Go** button in this blade. This will take you to the Kudu site of your App Service. There is a shortcut to reach here. If your App Service URL is `http://myappservice.azurewebsites.net`, then the corresponding Kudu site would be `http://myappservice.`**scm**`.azurewebsites.net`. Notice `scm` between `myappservice` and `azurewebsites.net`. You must have required access to the Kudu site, so not everyone can go to the Kudu site of any website:

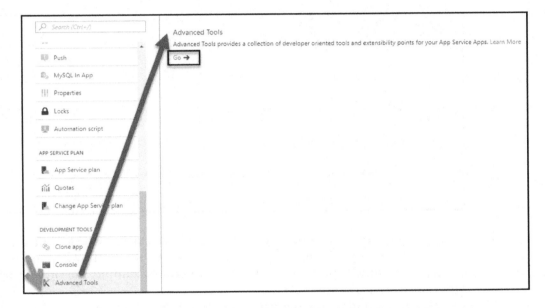

3. In the top bar, select **Process explorer.** This will open the **Process Explorer** as shown here:

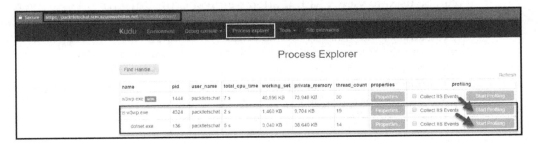

4. Click on the **Start Profiling** button of your application `.exe`, when you observe high CPU in the app. It will take a while to start profiling. Once the profiling is done, click on **Stop Profiling**. This will start generating the diagnostics and generate the `.diagsession` file, which you will be prompted to download.

5. Upon downloading the file, open it with Visual Studio. It will show the CPU graph. There will be a button called **Create detailed report**. Click on it and it will open a nice-looking report with hot paths, a summary, and will lead you to the code causing the high CPU, as shown here:

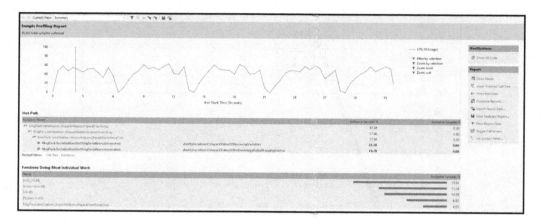

- **Support**: Now that we know the Kudu site, another diagnostic tool that may be useful is Azure App Service Support, which can be browsed by appending `/support` in the Kudu site URL. For the preceding example, the support site would be `http://myappservice.scm.azurewebsites.net/support`. As of writing this chapter, it is in a preview state. We can **Observe**, **Analyze**, and **Mitigate** the issues from here, as shown in the following screenshot. The **Observe** section can be used to view stats such as requests/second and errors/sec. The **Analyze** section can be used to view **FREB (Failed Request Error Buffering) Logs**, **Event Viewer** logs, and running **Diagnostics** to figure out CPU and memory issues. The **Mitigate** section has a switch to autoheal the app. Most memory and CPU issues are resolved upon restart and that is where the autoheal feature comes into the picture. If you have a scenario where you need to recycle the application automatically, after it has served, say, X number of requests in Y amount of time, you can consider autoheal as an option—X and Y can be configured by means of a rule:

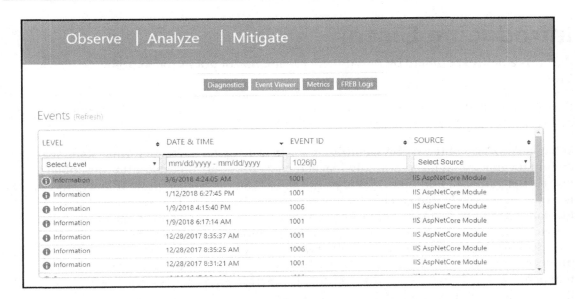

- **New support request**: If none of these options seem to have helped you identify the issue, which shouldn't happen often if done well, you can leverage the expertise of Azure support to help you with an issue, by creating a **New support request** in the left panel of your App Service, as shown here:

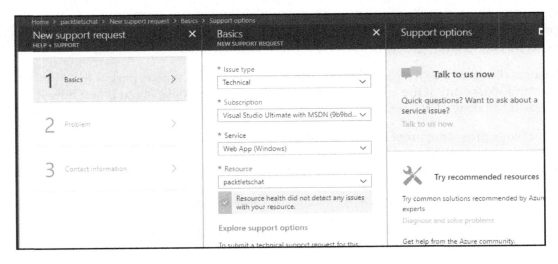

Next, let's have a quick look at a new experimental project of the ASP.NET team called Blazor.

Introducing Blazor

Blazor is a new experiment by the ASP.NET team. Blazor got its name from two words, Browser and Razor.

Blazor is an experimental web UI framework using C#, Razor, and HTML, running in the browser through WebAssembly.

What is WebAssembly? **WebAssembly** or **wasm** is an open, new-age format standard, with an initial version that has reportedly reached cross-browser consensus. It is described as *a new portable, size-and load-time-efficient format suitable for compilation to the Web.* WebAssembly is a new type of code that can be run in modern web browsers. It is a low-level assembly-like language with a compact binary format that runs with near-native performance and provides languages, such as C/C++, with a compilation target so that they can run on the web. It is also designed to run alongside JavaScript, allowing both to work together. It is a browser improvement. Since it is a binary format, we'll be able to compile binary bundles that compress to a smaller size than the text JavaScript. Smaller payloads means faster delivery and so it may run faster than JavaScript.

Blazor runs .NET code in the browser via a small, portable .NET runtime called **DotNetAnywhere** (**DNA**) compiled to WebAssembly. Essentially, Blazor makes life easier and happier for developers like me who are not great at JavaScript and want to write less of it. You can code your entire app in C#, Razor, and HTML, which runs inside the browser, without having to write a single line of JavaScript and it works just like any **Single-Page Application** (**SPA**). It gives all the benefits of a rich and modern platform while letting us use .NET end to end.

Blazor is developed as a personal project by Steve Sanderson, who is part of the ASP.NET team and works out of the UK. He has a detailed blog which talks about it and how it works. It can be read at http://blog.stevensanderson.com/2018/02/06/blazor-intro/.

Other blogs providing great insights into Blazor can be read at https://visualstudiomagazine.com./articles/2017/08/09/blazor.aspx and https://blogs.msdn.microsoft.com/webdev/2018/02/06/blazor-experimental-project/.

The demo of Blazor can be seen at https://blazor-demo.github.io/.

If this sounds exciting, there is even more exciting stuff in the upcoming 2.1 release of ASP.NET Core. Let's have a sneak peek at it.

What's coming in .NET Core 2.1

The preview version of .NET Core 2.1 is launched on February 27th 2018. We can start developing a .NET Core 2.1 application using Visual Studio 2017 15.6 Preview 6 or later, and also using Visual Studio Code. Let's see what is newly added to .NET Core 2.1.

- **Build performance:** In .NET Core 2.1, build time performance has improved. CLI tools and MSBuild have improved and are much faster than before.
- **Minor version roll forward:** We can run the .NET Core X.x application on later minor versions with the same major version range, such as .NET Core 2.1 applications on .NET Core 2.6. This roll forward feature is applicable to minor versions only, so 2.1 can't be automatically rolled forward to .NET Core 3.0, or any other major version. Roll forward behavior is only relevant when the expected .NET Core version is not present in the given environment. We can disable this feature using:
    - **Environment variable:**
      `DOTNET_ROLL_FORWARD_ON_NO_CANDIDATE_FX=0`
    - **runtimeconfig.json:** `rollForwardOnNoCandidateFx=0`
    - **CLI:** `roll-forward-on-no-candidate-fx=0`
- **Sockets performance and HTTP managed handler:** As part of the new version, socket performance has increased. Sockets are the basis of outgoing and incoming network communication. In .NET Core 2.0 ASP.NET, the Kestrel web server and `HttpClient` use native `Socket` not the .NET `Socket` class. There will be three significant performance improvements for sockets. It supports `Span<T>` and `Memory<T>` in `Socket` and `NetworkStream`. `SocketHttpHandler` performance has improved. A few benefits are:
    - Platform dependencies have been eliminated on libcurl (linux) and WinHTTP (Windows)—this simplifies both development, deployment, and servicing
    - Consistent behavior across all platforms and platform/dependency versions

- We can opt in to using the `SocketHTTPHandler` in one of the following ways with Preview 1:
  - **Environment variable:**
    `COMPlus_UseManagedHttpClientHandler=true`
  - **AppContext:**
    `System.Net.Http.UseManagedHttpClientHandl`
    `er=true`

- **Span<T>, Memory<T>:** New types are introduced for using arrays and for other types of memory, which is efficient and increases performance. Using `Span`, we can pass a subset of an array, for example 5 elements of a 100 element array, we can create a `Span<T>` which provides a virtual of that array, without time or space cost. Now, no need to make a copy of those five arrays. This is also `struct`, so no allocation cost. With slicing capabilities, it obviates the need for expensive copying and allocation in many cases, such as string manipulation buffer management and so on. Here is an example of creating `Span<T>` from an array:

```
var arrayExample= new byte[10];
Span<byte> bytes = arrayExample; // Implicit cast from T[] to
Span<T>
```

From there, we can easily and efficiently create a `Span` to represent/point to just a subset of this array, utilizing an overload of the span's `Slice` method. From there, you can index into the resulting span to write and read data in the relevant portion of the original array:

```
Span<byte> slicedBytes = bytes.Slice(start: 5, length: 2);
slicedBytes[0] = 42;
slicedBytes[1] = 43;
Assert.Equal(42, slicedBytes[0]);
Assert.Equal(43, slicedBytes[1]);
Assert.Equal(arrayExample [5], slicedBytes[0]);
Assert.Equal(arrayExample [6], slicedBytes[1]);
slicedBytes[2] = 44; // Throws IndexOutOfRangeException
bytes[2] = 45; // OK
Assert.Equal(arrayExample [2], bytes[2]);
Assert.Equal(45, arr[2]);
```

- **Windows Compatibility Pack:** When we port existing code from the .NET Framework to .NET Core, we can use the `new Windows Compatibility Pack`. It provides access additional 20,000 APIs, compared to what is available in .NET Core. This includes `System.Drawing`, EventLog, WMI, Performance Counters, and Windows Services. The following example illustrates accessing the Window registry with APIs provided by the Windows Compatibility Pack. The sample fetches the value of `TechnicalEditor` of book `NetCore2ByExample` from `CurrentUser` registry hive:

```
using (var userHiveRegKey =
Registry.CurrentUser.OpenSubKey(@"Software\Packt\Books\NetCore2ByEx
ample"))
        {
           var value = userHiveRegKey?.GetValue("TechnicalEditor");
        }
```

To learn more about .NET Core 2.1 features, please visit the following resources:

- `https://blogs.msdn.microsoft.com/webdev/2018/02/02/asp-net-core-2-1-roadmap/`
- `https://github.com/dotnet/core/blob/master/roadmap.md`

With this, we conclude the chapter.

Summary

In this chapter, we got an overview of microservice architecture how it is an extension of SOA and overcomes the limitations of traditional monolithic apps. We also learned the important architectural differences between ASP.NET and ASP.NET Core. We discussed a few tips to keep in mind while developing ASP.NET Core 2.0 applications, due to the architectural differences. We then discussed a few handy tips to improve the performance of ASP.NET Core apps. We discussed a few tips on Azure as well and then moved our discussion to the new experimental project of the ASP.NET Core team, called Blazor. We concluded the chapter with a discussion on the features that are coming in ASP.NET Core 2.1. In the next and final chapter of the book, we will discuss functional programming with F#.

10
Functional Programming with F#

In this chapter, we will learn how to build functional programs with F# that leverage .NET Core. We will also master data access layer implementation for microservices that use a SQL Server vNext database.

The topics to be covered in this chapter are:

- Introduction to functional programming
- Introduction to F#
- Data access layer with F#
- Querying SQL vNext with F#

Introduction to functional programming

We briefly discussed functional programming and F# in Chapter 1, *Getting Started*. In the F# primer section, we said that functional programming treats programs as mathematical expressions and evaluates expressions. It focuses on functions and constants, which don't change like variables and states. Functional programming solves complex problems with simple code; it is a very efficient programming technique for writing bug-free applications; for example, the null exception can be avoided using this technique.

Functional programming is language-agnostic, which means it is not language-specific. Functional programming focuses on a structured approach; it doesn't have multiple entry and exit points. It doesn't have goto statements, so it is easy to create small modules and create large modules using small blocks of structured code (or in other words sub-modules), which increases the re-usability of code. One function can be used as the input of another function and that function can output a new function.

Here are some rules which make it easy for us to understand functional programming:

- In functional programming, a function's output never gets affected by outside code changes and the function always gives the same result for the same parameters. This gives us confidence in the function's behavior that it will give the expected result in all the scenarios, and this is helpful for multithread or parallel programming.
- In functional programming, variables are immutable, which means we cannot modify a variable once it is initialized, so it is easy to determine the value of a variable at any given point at program runtime.
- Functional programming works on referential transparency, which means it doesn't use assignment statements in a function. For example, if a function is assigning a new value to a variable such as shown here:

```
Public int sum(x)
{
x = x + 20 ;
return x;
}
```

This is changing the value of x, but if we write it as shown here:

```
Public int sum(x)
{
return x + 20 ;
}
```

This is not changing the variable value and the function returns the same result.

- Functional programming uses recursion for looping. A recursive function calls itself and runs till the condition is satisfied.

Functional programming features

Let's discuss some functional programming features:

- Higher-order functions
- Purity
- Recursion
- Currying
- Closure
- Function composition

Higher-order functions (HOF)

One function can take an input argument as another function and it can return a function. This originated from calculus and is widely used in functional programming. Order can be determined by domain and range of order such as order 0 has no function data and order 1 has a domain and range of order 0, if order is higher than 1, it is called a higher-order function. For example, the ComplexCalc function takes another function as input and returns a different function as output:

```
open System
let sum y = x+x
let divide y = x/x
Let ComplexCalc func = (func 2)
Printfn(ComplexCalc sum) // 4
Printfn(ComplexCalc divide) //1
```

In the previous example, we created two functions, sum and divide. We pass these two functions as parameters to the ComplexCalc function, and it returns a value of 4 and 1, respectively.

Purity

In functional programming, a function is referred to as a pure function if all its input arguments are known and all its output results are also well known and declared; or we can say the input and output result has no side-effects. Now, you must be curious to know what the side-effect could be, let's discuss it.

Let's look at the following example:

```
Public int sum(int x)
{
return x+x;
}
```

In the previous example, the function sum takes an integer input and returns an integer value and predefined result. This kind of function is referred to as a pure function. Let's investigate the following example:

```
Public void verifyData()
{
  Employee emp = OrgQueue.getEmp();
  If(emp != null)
  {
    ProcessForm(emp);
  }
}
```

In the preceding example, the verifyData() function does not take any input parameter and does not return anything, but this function is internally calling the getEmp() function so verifyData() depends on the getEmp() function. If the output of getEmp() is not null, it calls another function, called ProcessForm() and we pass the getEmp() function output as input for ProcessForm(emp). In this example, both the functions, getEmp() and ProcessForm(), are unknown at the verifyData() function level call, also emp is a hidden value. This kind of program, which has hidden input and output, is treated as a side-effect of the program. We cannot understand what it does in such functions. This is different from encapsulation; encapsulation hides the complexity but in such function, the functionality is not clear and input and output are unreliable. These kinds of function are referred to as impure functions.

Let's look at the main concepts of pure functions:

- **Immutable data**: Functional programming works on immutable data, it removes the side-effect of variable state change and gives guarantee of an expected result.
- **Referential transparency**: Large modules can be replaced by small code blocks and reuse any existing modules. For example, if a = b*c and d = b*c*e then the value of d can be written as d = a*e.
- **Lazy evaluation**: Referential transparency and immutable data give us the flexibility to calculate the function at any given point of time and we will get the same result, because a variable will not change its state at any time.

Recursion

In functional programming, looping is performed by recursive functions. In F#, to make a function recursive, we need to use the `rec` keyword. By default, functions are not recursive in F#, we have to rectify this explicitly using the `rec` keyword. Let's take an example:

```
let rec summation x = if x = 0 then 0 else x + summation(x-1)
printfn "The summation of first 10 integers is- %A" (summation 10)
```

In this code, we used the keyword `rec` for the recursion function and if the value passed is 0 , the sum would be 0; otherewise it will add `x + summation(x-1)`, like 1+0 then 2+1 and so on. We should take care with recursion because it can consume memory heavily.

Currying

This converts a function with multiple input parameter to a function which takes one parameter at a time, or we can say it breaks the function into multiple functions, each taking one parameter at a time. Here is an example:

```
int sum = (a,b) => a+b
int sumcurry = (a) =>(b) => a+b
sumcurry(5)(6) // 11
int sum8 = sumcurry(8) // b=> 8+b
sum8(5) // 13
```

Closure

Closure is a feature which allows us to access a variable which is not in the scope of the current module. It is a way of implementing lexically scoped named binding, for example:

```
int add = x=> y=> x+y
int addTen = add(10)
addTen(5) // this will return 15
```

In this example, the `add()` function is internally called by the `addTen()` function. In an ideal world, the variables x and y should not be accessible when the `add()` function finishes its execution, but when we are calling the function `addTen()`, it returns 15. So, the state of the function `add()` is saved though code execution is finished, otherwise there is no way of knowing the `add(10)` value, where x = 10. We are able to find the value of x because of lexical scoping and this is called closure.

Function composition

As we discussed earlier about HOF, function composition means getting two functions together to create a third new function where the output of a function is the input of another function.

There are *n* number of functional programming features. Functional programming is a technique to solve problems and write code in an efficient way. It is not language-specific, but many languages support functional programming. We can also use non-functional languages (such as C#) to write programs in a functional way. F# is a Microsoft programming language for concise and declarative syntax. We will learn more about F# in the next section.

Introduction to F#

In Chapter 1, *Getting Started*, we discussed the F# language and its functional programming features, basic keywords, operators, and variable declarations. We also looked at the difference between F# and C#, functions, and the basic input-output syntax. In this section, we will discuss F# in more detail.

Basics of classes

Classes are types of object which can contain functions, properties, and events. An F# class must have a parameter and a function attached like a member. Both properties and functions can use the `member` keyword. The following is the class definition syntax:

```
type [access-modifier] type-name [type-params] [access-modifier]
(parameter-list) [ as identifier ] =
[ class ]
[ inherit base-type-name(base-constructor-args) ]
[ let-bindings ]
[ do-bindings ]
member-list
 [ end ]

// Mutually recursive class definitions:

type [access-modifier] type-name1 ...
and [access-modifier] type-name2 ...
```

Let's discuss the preceding syntax for class declaration:

- `type`: In the F# language, class definition starts with a `type` keyword.
- `access-modifier`: The F# language supports three access modifiers—`public`, `private`, and `internal`. By default, it considers the `public` modifier if no other access modifier is provided. The `Protected` keyword is not used in the F# language, and the reason is that it will become object oriented rather than functional programming. For example, F# usually calls a member using a lambda expression and if we make a member type protected and call an object of a different instance, it will not work.
- `type-name`: It is any of the previously mentioned valid identifiers; the default access modifier is `public`.
- `type-params`: It defines optional generic type parameters.
- `parameter-list`: It defines constructor parameters; the default access modifier for the primary constructor is `public`.
- `identifier`: It is used with the optional `as` keyword, the `as` keyword gives a name to an instance variable which can be used in the type definition to refer to the instance of the type.
- `Inherit`: This keyword allows us to specify the base class for a class.
- `let-bindings`: This is used to declare fields or function values in the context of a class.
- `do-bindings`: This is useful for the execution of code to create an object
- `member-list`: The `member-list` comprises extra constructors, instance and static method declarations, abstract bindings, interface declarations, and event and property declarations.

Here is an example of a class:

```
type StudentName(firstName,lastName) =
member this.FirstName = firstName
member this.LastName = lastName
```

In the previous example, we have not defined the parameter type. By default, the program considers it as a string value but we can explicitly define a data type, as follows:

```
type StudentName(firstName:string,lastName:string) =
member this.FirstName = firstName
member this.LastName = lastName
```

Constructor of a class

In F#, the constructor works in a different way to any other .NET language. The constructor creates an instance of a class. A parameter list defines the arguments of the primary constructor and class. The constructor contains let and do bindings, which we will discuss next. We can add multiple constructors, apart from the primary constructor, using the new keyword and it must invoke the primary constructor, which is defined with the class declaration. The syntax of defining a new constructor is as shown:

```
new (argument-list) = constructor-body
```

Here is an example to explain the concept. In the following code, the StudentDetail class has two constructors: a primary constructor that takes two arguments and another constructor that takes no arguments:

```
type StudentDetail(x: int, y: int) =
do printfn "%d %d" x y
new() = StudentDetail(0, 0)
```

A let and do binding

A let and do binding creates the primary constructor of a class and runs when an instance of a class is created.

A function is compiled into a member if it has a let binding. If the let binding is a value which is not used in any function or member, then it is compiled into a local variable of a constructor; otherwise, it is compiled into a field of the class.

The do expression executes the initialized code. As any extra constructors always call the primary constructor, let and do bindings always execute, irrespective of which constructor is called.

Fields that are created by let bindings can be accessed through the methods and properties of the class, though they cannot be accessed from static methods, even if the static methods take an instance variable as a parameter:

```
type Student(name) as self =
    let data = name
    do
        self.PrintMessage()
        member this.PrintMessage() = printf " Student name is %s" data
```

Generic type parameters

F# also supports a generic parameter type. We can specify multiple generic type parameters separated by a comma. The syntax of a generic parameter declaration is as follows:

```
type MyGenericClassExample<'a> (x: 'a) =
    do printfn "%A" x
```

The type of the parameter infers where it is used. In the following code, we call the MyGenericClassExample method and pass a sequence of tuples, so here the parameter type became a sequence of tuples:

```
let g1 = MyGenericClassExample( seq { for i in 1 .. 10 -> (i, i*i) } )
```

Properties

Values related to an object are represented by properties. In object-oriented programming, properties represent data associated with an instance of an object. The following snippet shows two types of property syntax:

```
// Property that has both get and set defined.

[ attributes ]
[ static ] member [accessibility-modifier] [self-  identifier.]PropertyName
    with [accessibility-modifier] get() =
    get-function-body
    and [accessibility-modifier] set parameter =
    set-function-body

// Alternative syntax for a property that has get and set.

[ attributes-for-get ]
[ static ] member [accessibility-modifier-for-get] [self-
identifier.]PropertyName =
    get-function-body
    [ attributes-for-set ]
    [ static ] member [accessibility-modifier-for-set] [self-
    identifier.]PropertyName
    with set parameter =
    set-function-body
```

There are two kinds of property declaration:

- **Explicitly specify the value**: We should use the explicit way to implement the property if it has non-trivial implementation. We should use a member keyword for the explicit property declaration.
- **Automatically generate the value**: We should use this when the property is just a simple wrapper for a value.

There are many ways of implementing an explicit property syntax based on need:

- **Read-only**: Only the get() method
- **Write-only**: Only the set() method
- **Read/write**: Both get() and set() methods

An example is shown as follows:

```
// A read-only property.
member this.MyReadOnlyProperty = myInternalValue
// A write-only property.
member this.MyWriteOnlyProperty with set (value) = myInternalValue <- value
// A read-write property.
member this.MyReadWriteProperty
    with get () = myInternalValue
    and set (value) = myInternalValue <- value
```

Backing stores are private values that contain data for properties. The keyword, member val instructs the compiler to create backing stores automatically and then gives an expression to initialize the property. The F# language supports immutable types, but if we want to make a property mutable, we should use get and set. As shown in the following example, the MyClassExample class has two properties: propExample1 is read-only and is initialized to the argument provided to the primary constructor, and propExample2 is a settable property initialized with a string value ".Net Core 2.0":

```
type MyClassExample (propExample1 : int) =
member val propExample1 = property1
member val propExample2 = ".Net Core 2.0" with get, set
```

Automatically implemented properties don't work efficiently with some libraries, for example, Entity Framework. In these cases, we should use explicit properties.

Static and instance properties

There can be further categorization of properties as static or instance properties. Static, as the name suggests, can be invoked without any instance. The self-identifier is neglected by the `static` property while it is necessary for the instance property. The following is an example of the `static` property:

```
static member MyStaticProperty
    with get() = myStaticValue
    and set(value) = myStaticValue <- value
```

Abstract properties

Abstract properties have no implementation and are fully abstract. They can be virtual. It should not be `private` and if one accessor is `abstract` all others must be `abstract`. The following is an example of the `abstract` property and how to use it:

```
// Abstract property in abstract class.
// The property is an int type that has a get and
// set method
[<AbstractClass>]
type AbstractBase() =
    abstract Property1 : int with get, set

// Implementation of the abstract property
type Derived1() =
    inherit AbstractBase()
    let mutable value = 10
    override this.Property1 with get() = value and set(v : int) = value
    <- v

// A type with a "virtual" property.
type Base1() =
    let mutable value = 10
    abstract Property1 : int with get, set
    default this.Property1 with get() = value and set(v : int) = value
    <- v

// A derived type that overrides the virtual property
type Derived2() =
    inherit Base1()
    let mutable value2 = 11
    override this.Property1 with get() = value2 and set(v) = value2 <- v
```

Inheritance and casts

In F#, the inherit keyword is used while declaring a class. The following is the syntax:

```
type MyDerived(...) = inherit MyBase(...)
```

In a derived class, we can access all methods and members of the base class, but it should not be a private member. To refer to base class instances in the F# language, the base keyword is used.

Virtual methods and overrides

In F#, the `abstract` keyword is used to declare a virtual member. So, here we can write a complete definition of the `member` as we use `abstract` for virtual. F# is not similar to other .NET languages. Let's have a look at the following example:

```
type MyClassExampleBase() =
    let mutable x = 0
    abstract member virtualMethodExample : int -> int
    default u. virtualMethodExample (a : int) = x <- x + a; x

type MyClassExampleDerived() =
    inherit MyClassExampleBase ()
    override u. virtualMethodExample (a: int) = a + 1
```

In the previous example, we declared a virtual method, `virtualMethodExample`, in a base class, `MyClassExampleBase`, and overrode it in a derived class, `MyClassExampleDerived`.

Constructors and inheritance

An inherited class constructor must be called in a derived class. If a base class constructor contains some arguments, then it takes parameters of the derived class as input. In the following example, we will see how derived class arguments are passed in the base class constructor with inheritance:

```
type MyClassBase2(x: int) =
    let mutable z = x * x
    do for i in 1..z do printf "%d " i
```

```
type MyClassDerived2(y: int) =
    inherit MyClassBase2(y * 2)
    do for i in 1..y do printf "%d " i
```

If a class has multiple constructors, such as new(str) or new(), and this class is inherited in a derived class, we can use a base class constructor to assign values. For example, DerivedClass, which inherits BaseClass, has new(str1,str2), and in place of the first string, we pass inherit BaseClass(str1). Similarly for blank, we wrote inherit BaseClass(). Let's explore the following example for more detail:

```
type BaseClass =
    val string1 : string
    new (str) = { string1 = str }
    new () = { string1 = "" }

type DerivedClass =
    inherit BaseClass

    val string2 : string
    new (str1, str2) = { inherit BaseClass(str1); string2 = str2 }
    new (str2) = { inherit BaseClass(); string2 = str2 }

let obj1 = DerivedClass("A", "B")
let obj2 = DerivedClass("A")
```

Functions and lambda expressions

A lambda expression is one kind of anonymous function, which means it doesn't have a name attached to it. But if we want to create a function which can be called, we can use the fun keyword with a lambda expression. We can pass the input parameter in the lambda function, which is created using the fun keyword. This function is quite similar to a normal F# function. Let's see a normal F# function and a lambda function:

```
// Normal F# function
let addNumbers a b = a+b
// Evaluating values
let sumResult = addNumbers 5 6
// Lambda function and evaluating values
let sumResult = (fun (a:int) (b:int) -> a+b) 5 6
// Both the function will return value sumResult = 11
```

Handling data – tuples, lists, record types, and data manipulation

F# supports many data types, for example:

- **Primitive types**: `bool`, `int`, `float`, `string` values.
- **Aggregate type**: `class`, `struct`, `union`, `record`, and `enum`
- **Array**: `int[]`, `int[ , ]`, and `float[ , , ]`
- **Tuple**: `type1 * type2 *` like (a, 1, 2, true) type is—`char * int * int * bool`
- **Generic**: `list<'x>`, dictionary < 'key, 'value>

In an F# function, we can pass one tuple instead of multiple parameters of different types. Declaration of a `tuple` is very simple and we can assign values of a `tuple` to different variables, for example:

```
let tuple1 = 1,2,3

// assigning values to variables , v1=1, v2= 2, v3=3

let v1,v2,v3 = tuple1

// if we want to assign only two values out of three, use "_" to skip the
value. Assigned values: v1=1, //v3=3

let v1,_,v3 = tuple
```

In the preceding examples, we saw that `tuple` supports pattern matching. These are option types and an option type in F# supports the idea that the value may or not be present at runtime.

List

List is a generic type implementation. An F# list is similar to a linked list implementation in any other functional language. It has a special opening and closing bracket construct, a short form of the standard empty list ([ ]) syntax:

```
let empty = [] // This is an empty list of untyped type or we can say
//generic type. Here type is: 'a list
let intList = [10;20;30;40] // this is an integer type list
```

The `cons` operator is used to prepend an item to a list using a double colon `cons(prepend, ::)`. To append another list to one list, we use the append operator—`@`:

```
// prepend item x into a list
let addItem xs x = x :: xs
let newIntList = addItem intList 50 // add item 50 in above list
//"intlist", final result would be- [50;10;20;30;40]

// using @ to append two list
printfn "%A" (["hi"; "team"] @ ["how";"are";"you"])
// result - ["hi"; "team"; "how";"are";"you"]
```

Lists are decomposable using pattern matching into a head and a tail part, where the head is the first item in the list and the tail part is the remaining list, for example:

```
printfn "%A" newIntList.Head
printfn "%A" newIntList.Tail
printfn "%A" newIntList.Tail.Tail.Head
let rec listLength (l: 'a list) =
    if l.IsEmpty then 0
        else 1 + (listLength l.Tail)
printfn "%d" (listLength newIntList)
```

Record type

The `class`, `struct`, `union`, `record`, and `enum` types come under aggregate types. The record type is one of them, it can have *n* number of members of any individual type. Record type members are by default immutable but we can make them mutable. In general, a record type uses the members as an immutable data type. There is no way to execute logic during instantiation as a record type don't have constructors. A record type also supports match expression, depending on the values inside those records, and they can also again decompose those values for individual handling, for example:

```
type Box = {width: float ; height:int }
let giftbox = {width = 6.2 ; height = 3 }
```

In the previous example, we declared a `Box` with `float` a value `width` and an integer `height`. When we declare `giftbox`, the compiler automatically detects its type as `Box` by matching the value types. We can also specify type like this:

```
let giftbox = {Box.width = 6.2 ; Box.height = 3 }
```

or

```
let giftbox : Box = {width = 6.2 ; height = 3 }
```

This kind of type declaration is used when we have the same type of fields or field type declared in more than one type. This declaration is called a record expression.

Object-oriented programming in F#

F# also supports implementation inheritance, the creation of object, and interface instances. In F#, constructed types are fully compatible .NET classes which support one or more constructors. We can implement a `do` block with code logic, which can run at the time of class instance creation. The constructed type supports inheritance for class hierarchy creation. We use the `inherit` keyword to inherit a class. If the member doesn't have implementation, we can use the `abstract` keyword for declaration. We need to use the `abstractClass` attribute on the class to inform the compiler that it is abstract. If the `abstractClass` attribute is not used and `type` has all abstract members, the F# compiler automatically creates an `interface` type. Interface is automatically inferred by the compiler as shown in the following screenshot:

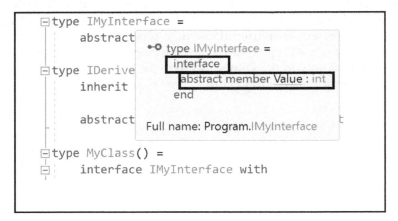

The `override` keyword is used to override the base class implementation; to use the base class implementation of the same member, we use the `base` keyword.

In F#, interfaces can be inherited from another interface. In a class, if we use the construct interface, we have to implement all the members in the interface in that class, as well. In general, it is not possible to use interface members from outside the class instance, unless we upcast the instance type to the required interface type.

To create an instance of a class or interface, the object expression syntax is used. We need to override virtual members if we are creating a class instance and need member implementation for interface instantiation:

```
type IExampleInterface =
    abstract member IntValue: int with get
    abstract member HelloString: unit -> string

type PrintValues() =
    interface IExampleInterface with
        member x.IntValue = 15
        member x.HelloString() = sprintf "Hello friends %d" (x :>
        IExampleInterface).IntValue

let example =
    let varValue = PrintValues() :> IExampleInterface
    { new IExampleInterface with
        member x.IntValue = varValue.IntValue
        member x.HelloString() = sprintf "<b>%s</b>"
        (varValue.HelloString()) }

printfn "%A" (example.HelloString())
```

Exception handling

The `exception` keyword is used to create a custom exception in F#; these exceptions adhere to Microsoft best practices, such as constructors supplied, serialization support, and so on. The keyword `raise` is used to throw an exception. Apart from this, F# has some helper functions, such as `failwith`, which throws a failure exception at F# runtime, and `invalidop`, `invalidarg`, which throw the .NET Framework standard type invalid operation and invalid argument exception, respectively.

try/with is used to catch an exception; if an exception occurred on an expression or while evaluating a value, then the try/with expression could be used on the right side of the value evaluation and to assign the value back to some other value. try/with also supports pattern matching to check an individual exception type and extract an item from it. try/finally expression handling depends on the actual code block. Let's take an example of declaring and using a custom exception:

```
exception MyCustomExceptionExample of int * string
    raise (MyCustomExceptionExample(10, "Error!"))
```

In the previous example, we created a custom exception called MyCustomExceptionExample, using the exception keyword, passing value fields which we want to pass. Then we used the raise keyword to raise exception passing values, which we want to display while running the application or throwing the exception. However, as shown here, while running this code, we don't get our custom message in the error value and the standard exception message is displayed:

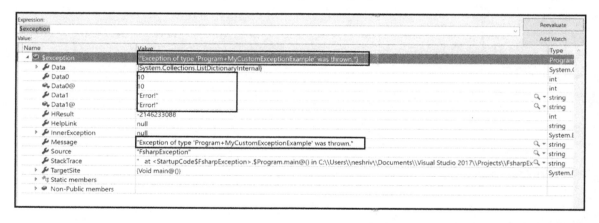

We can see in the previous screenshot that the exception message doesn't contain the message that we passed. In order to display our custom error message, we need to override the standard message property on the exception type. We will use pattern matching assignment to get two values and up-cast the actual type, due to the internal representation of the exception object.

If we run this program again, we will get the custom message in the exception:

```
exception MyCustomExceptionExample of int * string
  with
        override x.Message =
            let (MyCustomExceptionExample(i, s)) = upcast x
            sprintf "Int: %d Str: %s" i s
raise (MyCustomExceptionExample(20, "MyCustomErrorMessage!"))
```

Now, we will get the following error message:

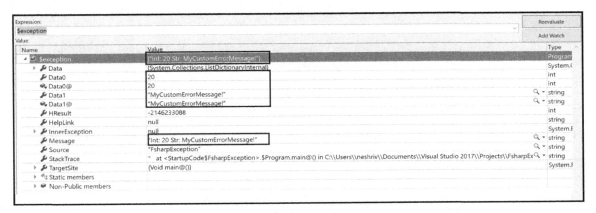

In the previous screenshot, we can see our custom message with integer and string values included in the output. We can also use the helper function, `failwith`, to raise a failure exception, as it includes our message as an error message, as follows:

```
failwith "An error has occurred"
```

The preceding error message can be seen in the following screenshot:

```
//exception MyCustomExceptionExample of int * string
//with
//        override x.Message =
//            let (MyCustomExceptionExample(i, s)) = upcast x
//            sprintf "Int: %d Str: %s" i s

//raise (MyCustomExceptionExample(20, "MyCustomErrorMessage!"))

failwith "An error has occurred"    ⊗

            Exception Unhandled                          ⊅ ✕

            System.Exception: 'An error has occurred'


            View Details | Copy Details
            ▷ Exception Settings
```

Here is a detailed exception screenshot:

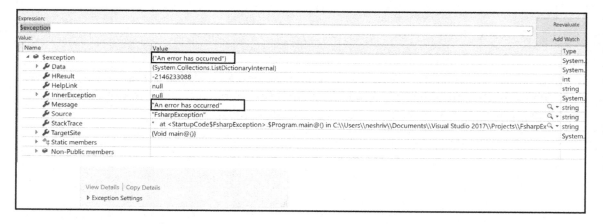

An example of the `invalidarg` helper function follows. In this factorial function, we are checking that the value of x is greater than zero. For cases where x is less than 0, we call `invalidarg`, pass x as the parameter name that is invalid, and then some error message saying the value should be greater than 0. The `invalidarg` helper function throws an invalid argument exception from the standard system namespace in .NET:

```
let rec factorial x =
    if x < 0 then invalidArg "x" "Value should be greater than zero"
    match x with
    | 0 -> 1
    | _ -> x * (factorial (x - 1))
```

Data access layer with F#

The F# type provider feature gives the flexibility to access different types of data, such as databases, structured types (that is, JSON, XML, CSV, HTML) and web-scale data.

First, let's look at data access resources.

CSV, HTML, JSON, and XML data

In F# applications and scripts, `FSharp.Data.dll` is used to implement the functionality to access data. It is also useful for structured file formats such as JSON, XML and for consuming freebase services. A sample document structure is used for type safe access to the document; it works as a type provider, like the CSV type provider takes a CSV sample as input and creates a column format data for that sample.

Providers

F# supports different types of provider, such as:

- `HtmlProvider<>`
- `JsonProvider<>`
- `XmlProvider<>`
- `WorldBankDataProvider<>`
- `CsvProvider<>`

Let's discuss one of them, for example, the CSV type provider. The `FSharp.Data` NuGet package contains `CsvProvider`. We can pass a `.csv` file and can read other `.csv` files; for example, we created a `.csv` file as follows:

```
ExampleCSV.csv - Notepad
File Edit Format View Help
Book name ,Date of publishing,price,Location
F#,27-01-2018,100,India
C#,27-01-2019,200,UK
.NET Core 2.0,27-01-2020,300,US
SQL Server,27-01-2021,400,Italy
```

Now, we have another `.csv` file which we want to read:

```
ExampleCSV-2.csv - Notepad
File Edit Format View Help
Item Name ,Date,price,Location
TV,27-01-2018,1000,India
remote,27-01-2019,2000,UK
Pen,27-01-2020,3000,US
Mobile,27-01-2021,4000,Italy
```

Here is a code snippet:

```
open FSharp.Data

type Books = CsvProvider<"..\ExampleCSV.csv">
let Saleitems = Books.Load("..\ExampleCSV-2.csv")
let firstRow = Saleitems.Rows |> Seq.head
```

Let's see what values are calculated by the F# compiler for `Salesitem`, as the `ExampleCSV` file is passed, for example:

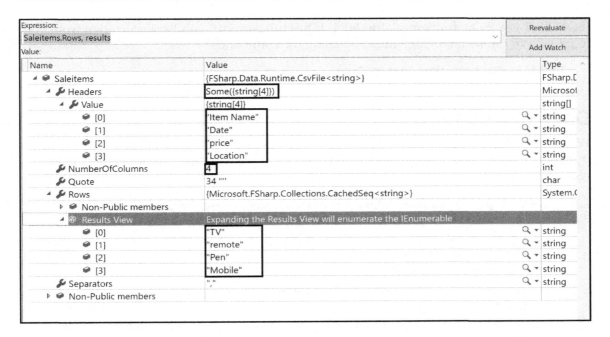

Here, we can see the compiler is able to detect the header name and took it from the second .csv file. We can control column types by customizing them using the `InferRows` static parameter of `CsvProvider`. To use the full file, we can pass 0. If the first row of a file is not a header, then we can pass the `HasHeaders` static parameter value to `false`, for example:

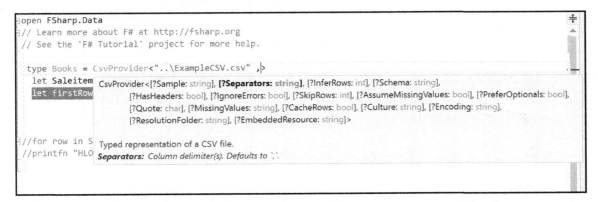

The `FSharp.Data` library also contains helpers for parsing JSON, HTML files, and helpers to send HTTP requests. It is available with the name `FSharp.Data` on NuGet.

JSON.NET is a JSON framework for .NET. It has full support with F# serialization from and to JSON. We can install using NuGet by using the command:

```
Install -Package Newtonsoft.Json
```

Data access tools

We discussed data type providers earlier. F# also has dynamic API support for faster and dynamic data retrieval. It contains CSV, HTML, JSON parsers, and also tools for HTTP request parsing. Let's briefly discuss each of them:

- **CSV parser**: To access data dynamically, we can use the CSV parser. The afore mentioned CSV provider is built on top of the F# CSV parser. The `FSharp.Data` namespace has the `CsvFile` type, which provides two methods for loading data: the `Parse` method for string data, and the `Load` method for reading data from a file or any web source (example: `CsvFIle.Load(<file path>)`).

- **HTML parser**: It parses HTML documents into the DOM. When it gets parsed into DOM, F# supports many extension functions for HTML DOM elements, to extract information from the web page. Let's see an example where we will search .NET Core in Google and parse the first search result page, getting all URLs and hyperlinks:

```
open FSharp.Data
let resultsDocument =
HtmlDocument.Load("http://www.google.co.in/search?q=.NET Core")
```

In the previous code, using `HtmlDocument.Load()`, we are parsing the web page into DOM. `resultsDocument` contains all data from the page, as this method will make a synchronous web call. We can also make an asynchronous call using the method, `HtmlDocument.AsyncLoad()`. To extract data from the result document, we first find all HTML anchor tags and then find all `href` tags to get the link and its text:

```
let x =
    resultsDocument.Descendants ["a"]
    |> Seq.choose (fun x ->
        x.TryGetAttribute("href")
        |> Option.map (fun a -> x.InnerText(), a.Value())
    )
let Z =
    x
    |> Seq.filter (fun (name, url) ->
                name <> "Cached" && name <> "Similar" &&
```

```
                        url.StartsWith("/url?"))
    |> Seq.map (fun (name, url) -> name, url.Substring(0,
    url.IndexOf("&sa=")).Replace("/url?q=", ""))
    |> Seq.toArray
```

The output will show all first page search results for `.NET Core` in Google. The result looks like this:

```
open FSharp.Data
open System

let resultsDocument = HtmlDocument.Load("http://www.google.co.in/search?q=.NET Core")

let x = resultsDocument.Descendants["a"] |> Seq.choose(fun x -> x.TryGetAttribute("href") |> Option.map(fun a -> x.InnerTe

let Z =
    x        ▲ ◉ Z {System.Tuple<string, string>[12]} ▣
    |> S  ▶ ◉ [0] {(NET Core - Microsoft, https://www.microsoft.com/net/learn/get-started)}
          ▶ ◉ [1] {(ASP.NET Core - Wikipedia, https://en.wikipedia.org/wiki/ASP.NET_Core)}
    |> S  ▶ ◉ [2] {(.NET Core - C# Corner, http://www.c-sharpcorner.com/technologies/dotnetcore)}
    |> S  ▶ ◉ [3] {(GitHub - dotnet/core: Home repository for .NET Core, https://github.com/dotnet/core)}
          ▶ ◉ [4] {(Welcome to .NET Core!, https://dotnet.github.io/)}
let y =   ▶ ◉ [5] {(.NET Core vs .NET Framework: Choosing a Runtime & How to Port, https://stackify.com/net-core-vs-net-framework/)}
  //let   ▶ ◉ [6] {(Company - Netcore, https://netcore.in/company/)}
  // re   ▶ ◉ [7] {(ASP.NET Core | The ASP.NET Site, https://www.asp.net/core/overview/aspnet-vnext)}
  // |>   ▶ ◉ [8] {(.Net Framework or .Net Core? When to use which | InfoWorld, https://www.infoworld.com/article/3180478/development-tool...
  //      ▶ ◉ [9] {(AWS Lambda Supports C# (.NET Core 2.0) - Amazon AWS, https://aws.amazon.com/about-aws/whats-new/2018/01/aws-laml...
  // )    ▶ ◉ [10] {(, https://dribbble.com/shots/3005807-Asp-Net-Core-Logo)}
          ▶ ◉ [11] {(Wikipedia, https://en.wikipedia.org/wiki/ASP.NET_Core)}
```

- **JSON Parser**: The same as the CSV provider, the JSON provider is built on top of the JSON parser. We need the same library for all the parsers: `FSharp.Data.dll`. It has the `JsonValue` type for parsing. Here is an example:

```
open FSharp.Data
let empInfo =
  JsonValue.Parse("""
    { "name": "Neha", "Company": "Microsoft","Projects": [ "Proj1",
    "Proj2" ] } """)
```

`FSharp.Data.Extensions` supports many extension methods such as `value.Properties()` and gives a list of properties of a record node.

- **HTTP Utilities**: In the `FSharp.Data` namespace, we have HTTP utilities, which are easy and quick for HTTP requests, post data or responses such as get status code. HTTP has a few overloaded methods, `requestString` and `AsyncRequest` or `AsyncRequestString` and `AsyncRequest`; these can create a simple request synchronously or asynchronously, respectively. Here is an example:

```
open FSharp.Data
Http.RequestString("http://rishabhverma.net ")

// Download web site asynchronously
async { let! html =
Http.AsyncRequestString("http://rishabhverma.net ")
        printfn "%d" html.Length }
        |> Async.Start

// Verifying the response:
let response =
Http.Request("http://rishabhverma.net/algorithmics-science-and-art/
", silentHttpErrors = true)

// Examine information about the response
response.Headers
response.Cookies
response.ResponseUrl
response.StatusCode
```

Here is the result:

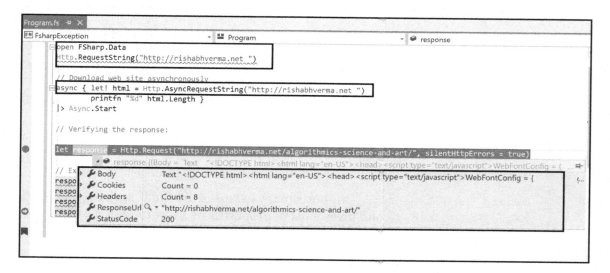

SQL data access

In F#, there are multiple libraries for SQL data access. We can browse them in NuGet; a few of them are discussed as follows:

- `FSharp.Data.SqlClient`: This library provides `SqlCommandProvider`, which gives type safe access to transactional SQL languages. `SqlProgrammabilityProvider` provides quick access to a SQL server **stored procedure (SP)**, tables, and functions, and `SqlEnumProvider` generates an enum type on the ground of static lookup data from an ADO.NET-compliant source. To install the `FSharp.Data.SqlClient` library from NuGet, use the following command:

      PM> Install-Package FSharp.Data.SqlClient

- `FSharp.Data.SQLProvider`: `SQLProvider` is a general .NET/Mono SQL database provider. This library supports automatic constraint navigation, CRUD operations with identity support, asynchronous operations, LINQ query, functions, SP support, record types mapping, .NET Core/.NET Standard, and so on. `SQLProvider` has explicit implementation for SQL Server, SQLite, Oracle, MySQL, MSAccess, Firebird, and so on. SQL Server and MS Access don't require third-party ADO.NET connector objects, the rest all require this. To install the `FSharp.Data.SqlProvider` library from NuGet, use the following command:

      PM> Install-Package SQLProvider

- The `SqlDataConnection`: `SqlDataConnection` type provider generates types, for data in SQL DB on live connections. It is for accessing SQL using LINQ queries. It requires a Microsoft SQL server. We need three references in a F# project—`FSharp.Data.TypeProviders`, `System.Data`, and `System.Data.Linq`. Here is an example:

```
type dbSchemaExample = SqlDataConnection<"Data
Source=SERVER\INSTANCENAME;Initial Catalog=MyDatabase;Integrated
Security=SSPI;">

let db = dbSchemaExample.GetDataContext()
```

- The `SqlEntityConnection`: `SqlEntityConnection` type provider is for accessing SQL through LINQ queries and Entity Framework. It works with many databases. We need `System.Data.Linq`, `System.Data.Entity`, and `Microsoft.FSharp.Data.TypeProviders` references. Here is an example:

```
type private EntityConnectionExample =
SqlEntityConnection<ConnectionString="Server=SERVER\InstanceName;In
itial Catalog=microsoft;Integrated
Security=SSPI;MultipleActiveResultSets=true",Pluralize = true>
```

- **ADO.NET**: It provides data access services and functionality for writing managed code and consistent data source access for SQL Server, and also data sources exposed through OLEDB or XML. Customers can use ADO.NET to connect with any data source to retrieve, manipulate, and update data. It can perform all CRUD operations. ADO.NET also supports frontend database creation, and middle-tier objects for application, tools, or browsers.

Web data access

The `FSharp.Data` library provides many type providers, and in F# it is very easy to integrate these data stores in programming. Additional web data stores can be accessed using JSON, XML, and CSV format support of F#.

Querying SQL vNext with F#

SQL vNext is Microsoft's major release for SQL open source and platform-independent DBs. It has introduced major features of the relational database to Linux: in-memory OLTP, in-memory columnstores, transparent data encryption, Always Encrypted, and row-level security, to make SQL Server the platform of choice across operating systems. It provides us with development language selection options, on-premise or cloud options, and operating system options such as Linux (Red Hat, SUSE, and Ubuntu), and Linux-based Docker containers or windows, adaptive query processing, SQL graphs, improvements to analysis services, reporting services, and integration services.

It has new features such as integration services; till now SQL Server 2016 SSIS package execution was limited to one machine, but now integration services give high-performance package execution by distributing execution on multiple machines like parallel execution on different servers. It involves:

- **SSIS Scale Out Master**: It is for scaling out management and receives package execution requests from the user
- **SSIS Scale Out Worker**: It pulls execution tasks from the scaled out master and works on package execution

In an F# program, we can read data using the LINQ query by writing in F# languages or by using ADO.NET classes, such as SqlCommand. Mostly ADO.NET classes are used when we need a simple query call but while calling SP, we must add multiple parameters using SqlParameter in this approach. We can use dynamic operators for dynamic invocations in F#. As we saw providers have helper functions, which are used but each has many drawbacks. Let's discuss how to define a query and create helper functions with parameters. Here is some example code for illustration:

```
open FSharp.Data
open System.Data.SqlClient

type SqlQueryExample =
    {
        Query : string
        Parameters : (string * obj) list
    }
```

To get Sqlconnection and other ADO.NET methods, install the NuGet package of System.Data.SqlClient. In the preceding code, we defined a type SqlQueryExample,where Query is a string and Parameters is a tuple type. We created a module, QueryHelpersForFsharp, where we defined param which takes two values, name and value, and a function, sqlFunction which takes two parameters, query and parameters; we are assigning these values:

```
module QueryHelpersForFsharp =

    let param name value =
        ( name, value )

    let sqlFunction query parameters =
        {
```

```
                    Query = query
                    Parameters = parameters
        }
```

We can use the preceding module and use `sqlFunction` and the `param` parameter to run a query. The `sqlFunction.query<type>` function will run the query and it will convert each data row into a specified type object. `Query` is not created in the same place where the `query` execution code is written. It is a separate piece of code:

```
open QueryHelpersForFsharp

let employeeDetail empId empName =
    sqlFunction
        """
        SELECT empId, empName
          FROM Employee
        OFFSET @EmpId ROWS
         FETCH
          NEXT @EmpName ROWS ONLY
        ;
        """
        [
            param "EmpId" empId
            param "EmpName" empName
type employeeDetail =
    {
        EmpId : int
        EmpName : string
    }

let query = employeeDetail request.EmpId request.EmpName
let EmployeeAsync = Sql.query<employeeDetail> connectString query
```

Let's see an example of data insertion using the ADO.NET function by `FsSql`. We will create an entity that is one row of a table and insert it into the DB:

```
open FSharp.Data
open System.Data.SqlClient
open System


type Employee() =
    member val Id = 0 with get,set

    member val EmpId = Guid.Empty with get,set
    member val JoiningDate = DateTimeOffset.MinValue with get,set
    member val LeftOrganizationOn = DateTimeOffset.MinValue with
```

```
    get,set
    member val Name = string with get,set
    member val ReportingTo = string with get,set
    member val Salary = 0.0m with get,set
```

To insert records, we created a type, changeQueryObject, which has query as string type
and parameters as the SqlParameter type list. We created a private insert
() method which takes Employee data as input, and here query has the insert sql
query string and parameter contains a list of SqlParameters:

```
type changeQueryObject =
{
    query : string;
    parameters : Sql.Parameter list;
}
let private insert (employee : Employee ) =
{
    query = "INSERT INTO \"intersect\".\"Employee\"(
                        empId, joiningDate, leftOrganizationOn, name,
                        reportingTo, salary)
            VALUES (@empId, @joiningDate, @leftOrganizationOn, @name,
            @reportingTo, @salary);
            RETURNING id;";
    parameters = [
                P("@empId", employee.EmpId);
                P("@joiningDate", employee.JoiningDate);
                P("@leftOrganizationOn", employee.LeftOrganizationOn);
                P("@name", employee.Name);
                P("@reportingTo", employee.ReportingTo);
                P("@salary", employee.Salary);
            ]
}
```

To execute this, code the following:

```
let executeScalar (queryObj : changeQueryObject) = sql.ExecScalar
queryObj.query queryObj.parameters
```

Summary

In this chapter, we discussed functional programming and its features, such as higher-order functions, purity, lazy evaluation, currying, and so on. We learned about F# basics such as classes, `let` and `do` bindings, generic type parameters, properties in F#, how to write functions and lambda expressions in F#, exception handling, and so on. Also, we saw different types of data provider in F# and how different types of data parser work. We also learned about querying SQL vNext with F#. This brings us towards the end of this book but our journey of learning has just got started.

Other Books You May Enjoy

If you enjoyed this book, you may be interested in these other books by Packt:

Mastering ASP.NET Core 2.0
Ricardo Peres

ISBN: 978-1-78728-368-8

- Get to know the new features of ASP.NET Core 2.0
- Find out how to configure ASP.NET Core
- Configure routes to access ASP.NET Core resources
- Create controllers and action methods and see how to maintain the state
- Create views to display contents
- Implement and validate forms and retrieve information from them
- Write reusable modules for ASP.NET Core
- Deploy ASP.NET Core to other environments

Learning ASP.NET Core 2.0
Jason De Oliveira, Michel Bruchet

ISBN: 978-1-78847-663-8

- Set up your development environment using Visual Studio 2017 and Visual Studio Code
- Create a fully automated continuous delivery pipeline using Visual Studio Team Services
- Get to know the basic and advanced concepts of ASP.NET Core 2.0 with detailed examples
- Build an MVC web application and use Entity Framework Core 2 to access data
- Add Web APIs to your web applications using RPC, REST, and HATEOAS
- Authenticate and authorize users with built-in ASP.NET Core 2.0 features
- Use Azure, Amazon Web Services, and Docker to deploy and monitor your applications

ASP.NET Core 2 High Performance - Second Edition
James Singleton

ISBN: 978-1-78839-976-0

- Understand ASP.NET Core 2 and how it differs from its predecessor
- Address performance issues at the early stages of development
- Set up development environments on Windows, Mac, and Linux
- Measure, profile and find the most significant problems
- Identify the differences between development workstations and production infrastructures, and how these can exacerbate problems
- Boost the performance of your application but with an eye to how it affects complexity and maintenance
- Explore a few cutting-edge techniques such as advanced hashing and custom transports

Leave a review - let other readers know what you think

Please share your thoughts on this book with others by leaving a review on the site that you bought it from. If you purchased the book from Amazon, please leave us an honest review on this book's Amazon page. This is vital so that other potential readers can see and use your unbiased opinion to make purchasing decisions, we can understand what our customers think about our products, and our authors can see your feedback on the title that they have worked with Packt to create. It will only take a few minutes of your time, but is valuable to other potential customers, our authors, and Packt. Thank you!

Index

Made in the USA
Columbia, SC
29 June 2020